The Spiritual Exercises
and
The Ignatian Mystical Horizon

This book is Number 5 in
Series IV: Study Aids on Jesuit Topics

Harvey D. Egan, S.J.

The Spiritual Exercises

and the

Ignatian Mystical Horizon

Foreword by Karl Rahner, S.J.

The Institute of Jesuit Sources
St. Louis, 1976

IMPRIMI POTEST: Very Reverend Richard T. Cleary, S.J.
Provincial of the New England Province
February 10, 1976

IMPRIMATUR: Most Reverend George J. Gottwald
Vicar General of St. Louis
March 12, 1976

©1976 The Institute of Jesuit Sources
Fusz Memorial, St. Louis University
3700 West Pine Blvd.
St. Louis, Missouri 63108

TO MY MOTHER AND FATHER

*Published through the aid of funds
donated by Mr. James L. Monaghan
of Milwaukee, Wisconsin,
1867–1963,
in memory of his brother,
Reverend Edward V. Monaghan, S.J.
1879–1922.*

Contents

 **Editor's Foreword**

On Series IV:
Study Aids on Jesuit Topics

The Institute of Jesuit Sources is privileged to offer the present book by Father Harvey D. Egan, S.J., of the theological faculty of Boston College, *The Spiritual Exercises and the Ignatian Mystical Horizon*, as Number 5 in its Series IV: Study Aids on Jesuit Topics. This book is a reworking and condensation of the more extensive doctoral dissertation which the author completed at the University of Münster under the direction of the renowned theologian, Father Karl Rahner. The worth of the book is amply attested by the observations which Rahner makes in his Foreword just below. But the present writer desires to point out an additional value of the work. Father Egan's book absorbs and transmits much of the valuable research and thought in the field of Ignatian study which have been done in Germany during the past few decades, and which have hitherto been relatively inaccessible in the English-speaking world. Hence Americans and others whose language is English who are interested in the proper interpretation of St. Ignatius' *Spiritual Exercises* will find this new work especially useful.

It seems advisable to state the rationale of Series IV in each volume published in it. The series is an effort to solve various aspects, different from book to book, of the following problem.

From its inception the Institute of Jesuit Sources has been oriented toward the publishing of books of quality in both scholarship and manufacture. Such books, carefully selected, obviously have advantages, especially the long-lasting values arising from their presence in libraries. But this orientation, if maintained exclusively, also entails two disadvantages which are especially hampering and costly in our present era of rapid developments and changes: the lengthy time required for the writing and editing, and the expense of typesetting, printing, and binding with cloth.

There are, however, many writings of genuine scholarly value which contain sound material truly helpful, especially if made available soon. Although an author or publisher might still desire, in more ideal circumstances, to add some improvements in the style of presentation, practical considerations make such procedure seem unfeasible now. Moreover, the delay entailed could all too easily turn out to be an instance in which the dreamed of best, which may never occur, is an enemy delaying or even defeating the good presently attainable.

This Series IV, Study Aids on Jesuit Topics, consists of studies in this category for one reason or another. Hopefully the series offers some solution of the problem sketched above. An effort will be made to keep the books or booklets inexpensive. Editorial time and cost, too, will be kept as low as possible, through omission of some stylistic practices insisted on by the Institute of Jesuit Sources in books in its other series. The responsibility for editorial and scholarly details, too, will be left to rest more fully on the authors than on the editors of the Institute of Jesuit Sources.

In the designing of this new series, many helpful ideas have been taken from the somewhat similar procedure in scholarly publishing which has been launched by the Council on the Study of Religion, for example, in the two "Dissertation Series" respectively of the American Academy of Religion and of the Society of Biblical Literature. The rationale of these series is well described by Robert W. Funk and Robert A. Spivey in the *Bulletin for the Council on the Study of Religion*, Volume IV, number 3 (June, 1973), pages 3-13, 28-29, and 36-37; and also at greater length, in the *Report of the Task Forces on Scholarly Communication and Publication*, edited by George W. MacRae, S.J. (1972, available from the Council on the Study of Religion Executive Office, Waterloo Lutheran University, Waterloo, Ontario, Canada). Indebtedness to this helpful information and example is gratefully acknowledged.

George E. Ganss, S.J.
Director and General Editor
The Institute of Jesuit Sources

 **Foreword**

Karl Rahner, S.J.

In the Foreword to a new German translation by Adolf Haas of the Spiritual Exercises of St. Ignatius of Loyola (Freiburg, 1975), I wrote:

> The theology hidden in the simple words of the Exercises belongs to the most important fundamentals of contemporary western Christianity. In fact, it has yet to be fully assimilated by the Church's academic theology and prevailing practice of piety; therefore, it still has an important future. Although it is obvious that the process sketched in Ignatius' Exercises for making a total life-decision arises from the basis of traditional Christianity and Roman Catholic conformity to the Church, the Spiritual Exercises intend to allow the person to experience a radical immediacy to God which, for Ignatius, ultimately supports and embraces everything Christian and ecclesial. Ignatius is convinced that such a "mystical" immediacy to God is really possible. For Ignatius, this immediacy to God is reciprocally conditioned by, related and united to the encounter with Jesus poor, crucified, and risen. For Ignatius, this immediacy to God occurs in the indifference given by God and concretely performed in "poverty." Biblically, this indifference means sovereign freedom over all principalities and powers. It consists in participating in the accomplishment of Jesus poor and His life of dying into God's incomprehensibility. This immediacy to God beyond all the particularities of human existence, however, certainly means for Ignatius not only a mystical losing of one's self in God's silent incomprehensibility. The Ignatian Exercises are rather a logic of concrete decision in which the person's individuality and the individuality of God's Will surpass the merely normative character of general principles. From his freedom in God and from God Himself, the person returns to a concrete decision, to the concrete duty and task in this world. He takes part in the creative and salvific descent of God's love to His world to find God not only in His transcendent incomprehensibility, but also in all created things.

From my conviction that the real theological (and not only the spiritual) significance of Ignatius' Spiritual Exercises to this day has not been exhausted by their commentators, and much less by the traditional theology, but presents a not-yet accomplished task to today's theology, it might be clear why I sincerely welcome the present book by my friend and former student, Father Harvey Egan, S.J. Thus, may I add a few introductory remarks about the contents and significance of his book.

Father Egan's book is of special importance because he attempts to narrow the gap between spirituality and systematic, dogmatic theology. Because he focuses upon the ultimate fundamental principles of spirituality, his book deals with the boundary area between mere spiritual doctrine and dogmatic theology. This book correctly seeks the ultimate principles of Ignatian spirituality—the principles of spirituality, therefore, not of mere dogmatic theology, not of a mere psychology of the Spiritual Exercises—but of a spirituality which, as a unity-in-accomplishment, precedes the difference between theoretical dogmatic theology as such and mere (secularized) psychology.

His entire book attempts to work out the fundamental individuality actually given in the Exercises. Because they present, at first glance, a bewildering array of individual instructions dealing with meditation matter and pious psychology, this attempt is neither superfluous nor easy. This ultimate, foundational individuality of the Spiritual Exercises cannot be unraveled either in dogmatic theology or in psychology because it is fixed on a point which lies *before* such a distinction. Father Egan sees the answer in the "anthropocentric-christocentric-mystagogical" character of the Exercises.

Despite past theological explanations, the question concerning the ultimate, fundamental structures of the Spiritual Exercises still remains open. In my opinion, Father Egan is well-read in this area and treats this important subject clearly and prudently so as to advance considerably the topic under discussion. Until now there has not been a book which critically synthesizes and completes past studies on the Exercises. Then too, there was no book which focused upon the Ignatian Exercises in their essence, treating this essence theologically and not only "piously." Father Egan's book has certainly progressed on this point. His book also offers a good, critical summary of old and contemporary commentaries on Ignatius and his spirituality.

"Mystagogy" means that the Exercises concern themselves not merely and not primarily with an extrinsic indoctrination stemming from dogmatic, moral, and ascetical insights, but rather evoke and actualize *the* humanity and *the* Christ-directedness, which through transcendentality and grace (in unity), are always given as an intrinsic, total thrust of the one, whole person into "loving Mystery." To be sure, this inner thrust anticipates, corresponds to, and is fulfilled by the history of salvation which encounters man from the outside.

This mystagogy is called "anthropocentric" because it intends to bring the person unconditionally and genuinely to radical self-acceptance in freedom. Father Egan clearly shows that the Spiritual Exercises ultimately deal, not with a moralistic manipulation of the person, but with his freedom to be himself and with the non-suppressed totality of his existential reality.

At the same time, this mystagogy is called "christocentric" because, and insofar as, it evokes the inner Christ-directedness of the person and leads it to an encounter with the historical Christ-event which comes from the outside. It is especially a question of the *inner* christocentric nature which is given in the essence of the graced person, and, by grace, is enabled to discover itself only through that personal encounter with the historical, and at the same time, "cosmic" Jesus Christ, as this encounter should, in fact, come about during the Exercises.

The christocentric and anthropocentric aspects of this mystagogy have an ultimate juncture. This means that the mystagogy into one's own humanity and the mystagogy into one's inner Christ-directedness really coincide. Interestingly, too, Father Egan develops the mystagogical dimension of the Spiritual Exercises by illuminating it from the trinitarian mystical perspective of Ignatius' *Spiritual Journal.* In the history of Christian piety and mysticism, trinitarian mysticism has almost been a mere marginal phenomenon.

Ignatius calls the highpoint and goal of such a mystagogy "consolation without previous cause." Father Egan fully explicates this very difficult and not easily understood Ignatian concept. This consolation is nothing other than the clear awareness of man's free, grace-elevated transcendentality which has not been distorted by any categorical object. This graced transcendentality always contains within itself a Christ-directed character. The discussion about this "consolation without previous cause" seems to me to be the most important part of the book.

If one really takes Father Egan's interpretation seriously, then one should certainly not evaluate this "consolation without previous cause" as a singular mystical phenomenon open only to a select few, but as the foundation and highpoint of "normal" Christian life. In other words, if there is such a thing as a mysticism and a mystagogy of Christian life, and this even in its everyday aspect in which concrete decisions arise out of the inner core of a theocentric and christocentric existence, and not as the mere result of religious indoctrination, and, if, on the other hand, the theological value of the Spiritual Exercises is correctly assessed by the official declarations of the Church and from her practice, then the results of Father Egan's book, if they are assimilated, could be of considerable significance for the religious, pedagogical and pastoral practices of the Church. It could mean both a positive evaluation and a critical stance with regard to today's enthusiastic movements which bring new life and, at the same time, new threats into the Church.

In addition to this fundamental assessment, we could also point out many individual results. Only a few of these will be given.

1. One should not take the writer of this Foreword amiss if he states with a certain satisfaction that Father Egan's interpretation of the "consolation without previous cause," in contrast to Fessard's based upon Hegel, Mendoza's based upon Heidegger, and Bakker's exegetical analysis, takes place with the help of a "transcendental theology."

2. Father Egan examines the "consolation without previous cause" as embedded in the context of the entire Ignatian Exercises, much more clearly than past commentaries.

3. The trinitarian dimension of Ignatian mysticism is presented from a broader basis than that, for example, of Przywara who proceeds almost exclusively from the "Contemplation to Obtain Divine Love."

4. When Father Egan understands consolation and desolation as a sign of the harmony or discord between the merely human (in its concrete, imperfect character) and the trinitarian-christocentric "existential," or when he understands the Ignatian *fuera* (*Ex* 32ff) not as a spatial dimension outside of the exercitant, but as something found outside of the deepest core of his freedom, then he has given a fine beginning and the initiative for today's somewhat necessary "demythologizing" of many expressions in the Exercises.

5. Also important is Father Egan's evidence that the "consolation without previous cause" in the Spiritual Exercises and other Ignatian writings is not as isolated a phenomenon as it may seem from other commentaries.

Finally, I agree, of course, with Father Egan when he emphasizes that in actual life the three different times for Election do not appear wholly separated from each other, but signify, rather, aspects of *one* Election in which all these three aspects appear, even if in very different intensities. In Ignatius' life these "times" were often fused.

One can ask oneself whether such a fusion does not precisely make the "ideal Election" possible.

I sincerely wish that Father Egan's book may be accorded the consideration it deserves.

Karl Rahner, S.J.

Munich, January 9, 1976

✤ Preface

We propose to examine the mystical horizon of St. Ignatius of Loyola. We intend, therefore, to examine the lived, internal unity, the fundamental, mystical matrix, the primordial mystical field, or the roots of all of Ignatius' experiences, knowledge and love. Because we wish to examine the *ultimate* structures of Ignatian mystical spirituality, this book goes beyond the usual ascetical, spiritual, mystical, psychological and pastoral concerns with St. Ignatius, as legitimate, necessary and fruitful as they may be. Not only what Ignatius explicitly experiences, knows and loves is at issue, but more importantly, his *implicit, non-verbal, non-conceptual* and *non-reflexive perspective.* We shall emphasize *how* Ignatius experiences, knows and loves, and what he *implicitly presupposes* in so doing. In short, we wish to explicate Ignatius' mystical horizon, that non-thematic, but real and ultimate matrix, against which and in which his individual experiences, actions, knowledge and love derive their ultimate meaning and find their core unity.

We also have a secondary purpose. We shall unfold Ignatius' mystical horizon by emphasizing how this horizon concretely shows itself in his Spiritual Exercises. The Exercises are basically a method of immersing the exercitant into the Mystery of God in Jesus Christ and into his own mystery as man to discover God's Will for him. Other Ignatian writings will be examined and used insofar as they illuminate Ignatius' primordial, mystical horizon as it is found in his Exercises.

The first chapter will focus upon the importance of the saints and their writings as a source of theological reflection. We shall also examine and relate Johannes B. Metz's *Christliche Anthropozentrik* to our own problematic. In the light of the Ignatian tradition, we shall then explicate nine excellent, twentieth-century commentators who are especially helpful for our own problematic. From these commentators, we shall indicate how our own problematic arises as a study of the Ignatian mystical horizon through the Exercises in terms of their anthropocentric ("mystically" plunging the exercitant into his own radical freedom), christocentric ("mystically" awakening the exercitant to his own total Christ-directedness), and mystagogical ("mystically" plunging the exercitant into the Mystery of the triune God) aspects.

The second chapter deals with the consolation without previous cause. This special Ignatian mystical experience is an excellent, experiential miniature of the Exercises and the Ignatian mystical horizon. We shall show that the elements found in the consolation without previous cause are the main elements, in a highly concentrated and experiential form, of the Ignatian mystical horizon and method.

The third chapter enucleates the anthropocentric moment of the Exercises in relation to Ignatius' mystical horizon. We shall see that Ignatius' various instructions have as their indirect goal the "return" of the exercitant to himself in unified, creative self-presence and radical freedom. In the same movement in which the exercitant surrenders to the Mystery of God in Jesus Christ, he is given to his own self-mystery.

The fourth chapter will center upon the christocentric moment of the Exercises in relation to Ignatius' mystical horizon. We shall unfold the implicit and explicit Christocentrism in the Exercises and the mystical horizon. The exercitant's transcendental openness to the Mystery of God in Jesus Christ made explicit in the election of Christ poor, suffering and humiliated, will be seen as the key to the Ignatian Election. We shall also point out that the success of the Exercises depends upon the quality of the exercitant's experience of Christ in His human, divine and cosmic dimensions.

The fifth chapter will enucleate the mystagogical moment of the Exercises in relation to Ignatius' mystical horizon. We shall explicate Ignatius' mystagogical experience of Jesus Christ as Mediator and as entrance into the Trinity. We shall also examine the Exercises as a method of awakening, deepening, strengthening and making more explicit the exercitant's trinitarian-directedness, his ever-present experience of the Trinity as Mystery, Revelation and Love-Given.

The sixth chapter will focus upon the Three Times of Election to illustrate the Ignatian mystical horizon. The totally God-initiated First Time underscores the mystagogical character of Ignatius' mystical horizon. The consolations and desolations resulting from the meditations on the life, death and resurrection of Jesus Christ during the Second Time highlight the christocentric character of Ignatius' mystical horizon. The use of the exercitant's natural powers during the Third Time brings out the anthropocentric character of Ignatius' mystical horizon. The interpenetration of the Three Times illustrates the unity-in-diversity of Ignatius' mystical horizon, the ultimate unity of a mystical horizon which is anthropocentric, christocentric and mystagogical.

I am deeply grateful to Father Karl Rahner, S.J. for his guidance during the writing of the original manuscript and for his fine Foreword. But I am especially grateful to him for pointing out through his example and life that theology must flow out of and back into prayer, that it must be worship with one's reason, as well as critical.

My very special thanks go to Mr. John Carmody of Pennsylvania State University and Bro. Thomas Lucas, N.S.J. of Montecito, California for reading the entire manuscript and making many valuable suggestions.

I sincerely thank Father Thomas A. Burke, S.J. of the Program to Adapt the Spiritual Exercises for encouraging me to rewrite the original manuscript. I am also grateful to Father George Ganss, S.J. of the Institute of Jesuit Sources for his gracious editing.

Finally, I wish to thank the Jesuit Communities of Santa Clara University and of Boston College for their extraordinary fraternal support.

Harvey D. Egan, S.J.

Boston College
February 2, 1976

The Spiritual Exercises
and
The Ignatian Mystical Horizon

 Chapter I

THE IGNATIAN
MYSTICAL HORIZON

INTRODUCTION

The Saints as Objects for Theological Reflection?

The saints are the creative prototypes in the history of holiness, because they make visible and livable new gifts of God's Spirit and create new modes of Christian existence. Just as there is a development of dogma resulting from the appropriation of truth, so too is there a development of holiness resulting from the historical appropriation of God's grace.[1] The saints are not simply models for Christian imitation; because they enflesh new modes of Christian existence, they should also be considered as sources for theological reflection.

The saints are sources for theological reflection because they *live* a theology born of prayer, adoration and service, a theology which explains and interprets the Gospels primarily through living and witnessing. The way the saints live and the actions they perform are the living questions put to God's revelation. But these same lives and these same actions are also the answers, the living answers, which God's revelation gives to man. There is a "metaphysics of the saints"[2] which has been too easily by-passed in theological reflection.

Although theologians readily grant the authority of the Bible, the Church Fathers, Papal pronouncements, the Councils, the Scholastics, etc. to be sources of theological reflection (and of course they should), they have failed to see that the saints should also have importance as a theological source. Could not today's theology of

For the ABBREVIATIONS used throughout this book, see below, p161.

[1] K. Rahner, "The Church of the Saints," *TI* 3, p99.
[2] H. Bremond, *La métaphysique des saints* (Paris, 1928), which constitutes volumes VII & VIII of his *Histoire du sentiment religieux en France*.

confession be deeply enriched by a profound study of the charism which the Curé of Ars demonstrated in his confessional? Could not a more profound theology of the role of women in the Church be derived from theological reflection on the lives of St. Teresa of Avila and St. Catherine of Sienna, to name but a few?[3]

The Ignatian Exercises as a
Theological Source

What we have said about the lives and actions of the saints, however, can also be said about their writings. Precisely because the Spiritual Exercises of St. Ignatius of Loyola blend his mystical experiences of the Trinity, Jesus Christ, man, the Church and the universe with profound pastoral experience, they belong to that type of pious literature which is more spontaneous, more experienced and more accurately called Christian wisdom than the explicit theology of the learned.[4] In fact, the absence from the Exercises of the school theology St. Ignatius learned at Alcala, Salamanca and Paris is most striking.[5] The Exercises, therefore, are a type of literature which precedes theological reflection and stimulates it. K. Rahner does not hesitate to call them a subject for tomorrow's theology.[6]

A careful reading of the early *Directories* to the Exercises and their classical commentaries, however, reveals very little in the way of comprehensive theological reflection. There is at least one major historical reason for this: serious attacks were made upon the Exercises very early in their history. Criticisms from such influential theologians as Melchior Cano[7] and others led to a flurry of written defenses of the Exercises.[8] The Ignatian commentators were forced

---

[3]P. Philipon, quoted by H. Urs von Balthasar, "Exerzitien und Theologie," *Orient* 12(1948), p230.

[4]K. Rahner, *The Dynamic Element in the Church* (=*Dynamic*), trans. by W.J. O'Hara, (Herder & Herder: New York, 1964), pp85ff. Abbreviated form of titles given in parentheses. The text of the Exercises we shall use is: *The Spiritual Exercises of St. Ignatius of Loyola* (=Ex, followed by the standard numbers), trans. by A. Mottola, (Doubleday: Garden City, NY, 1964).

[5]H. Urs von Balthasar, "Théologie et Sainteté," *DV* 12(1948), p22.

[6]K. Rahner, *Dynamic*, p87.

[7]Melchior Cano's critique of the Exercises can be found in: A. Astrain, *Historia de la Companïa de Jesús en la Asistencia de Espana* I (Madrid, 1902), pp369ff. See also: I. Iparraguirre, *Historia de la práctica de los Ejercicios Espirituales de San Ignacio de Loyola* (=*Historia*), II, pp402-12. See also: P. Dudon, *Saint Ignace de Loyola* (Paris, 1934), appendix, "Critiques et apologistes des Exercices."

[8]See *MI* II,1, pp573-7 & 649-701. Also see Nadal's classic defense of the Exercises in *M.Nad.* IV, pp820-6; *Chron* III, pp525-76; *M.Nad.* IV, pp827-73.

away from comprehensive theological reflection to the more mundane task of showing just how orthodox and traditional the Exercises actually were.

The great Jesuit theologian, Francisco Suarez, for example, noted the suspicion and calumny which had followed the Exercises, stressed their papal approbation and warned that certain terms in the Exercises, when ineptly understood, smacked of Illuminism.[9] In an attempt to stress Ignatius' orthodoxy, however, he and other Ignatian commentators overlooked the radically new elements in Ignatius, and, in some important instances, attempted to render this radicalism innocuous.[10]

The suspicion and attacks on the Exercises as being tainted with Alumbrado elements resulted, therefore, in an attempt on the part of the *Directories* and the Ignatian commentators to shift Ignatius' own emphases, to underplay the new in the Exercises, and to make Ignatius say only what the orthodox tradition, conservatively interpreted, allowed. Perhaps H. Bremond's remark that the Exercises were understood only by St. Ignatius and a few of his early companions and that their original spirit and depth were soon lost is not all that exaggerated.[11] Is it totally unreasonable to ask if the

---

[9] F. Suarez, *Tractatus de Religione Societas Jesu* (Paris, 1857). Liber IX, ccV-VII, pp494-524 deals specifically with the Exercises. See esp. pp493, 495, 506. See also: B. Llorca, *Die spanische Inquisition und die Alumbrados* (Berlin-Bonn, 1934), esp. pp35-40; B. Llorca, *San Ignacio y su relación con los alumbrados, en San Ignacio de Loyola ayer y hoy* (Barcelona, 1958); B. Llorca, "Sobre el espíritu de los alumbrados Francisco Hernández y fra Francisco Ortiz," *EstEc* 12(1933), pp383-404; J. Vincke, "Alumbrados," *LThK* I, p407; L. Koch, "Alumbrados," *Jesuiten Lexikon* (Paderborn, 1934), pp51-3.

[10] For example, J. Roi, "L'élection d'après Saint Ignace," *RAM* 38(1962), pp305-323 argues convincingly that the *Official Directory* of 1599 shifted the emphasis away from the Second Time of Election to the Third Time. P. Ferrusolae, *Commentaria in librum Exercitiorum B.P. Ignatii Loiolaei*, trans. by J. Nonell (Barcinone, 1885), p381 argues that the Second Time is more suited for "simple people or adolescents" whereas the Third Time is for "mature men." H. Urs von Balthasar, *Herrlichkeit* I (Einsiedeln, 1961), pp 360-5 and F. Marxer, *Die inneren geistlichen Sinne* (Freiburg i.B., 1963), pp29-38 have convincingly argued that the *Official Directory* of 1599 reduced the mystical significance of Ignatius' application of the senses teaching by presenting it as a lower form of prayer which is inferior to rational meditation. For commentaries which base themselves upon Suarez, the *Directory* of 1599 or Roothaan, see: A. Denis, *Commentarii in Exercitia Spiritualia* (Malines, 1891), 4 volumes; L. DuPont, *Méditations sur les mystères de notre sainte foi avec la pratique de l'oraison mentale* (Paris, 1933), 7 volumes; P. Vogt, *Exercitia Spiritualia Sancti Ignatii* (Bilbao, 1923), 3 volumes.

[11] H. Bremond, "Saint Ignace et les Exercises," *VSS* (1929), p103. For a part of Bremond's writings, see: J. C. Guy, "Henri Bremond et son commentaire des Exercices de saint Ignace," *RAM* 45(1969), pp191-223. For a response to

Church of Ignatius' day was not yet ready for his Catholic and orthodox presentation of what was good in the Illuminati movement in much the same way that the Church early in this century was not yet ready to accept what was orthodox and Catholic in the modernist movement?

JOHANNES B. METZ'S *CHRISTLICHE ANTHROPOZENTRIK* AND OUR PROBLEMATIC

The *Denkform* ("thought-form") of St. Thomas Aquinas

Johannes B. Metz's *Christliche Anthropozentrik*[12] is an attempt to study the thought-form of St. Thomas Aquinas. Metz intends to get beyond Aquinas' explicit philosophy and theology to the root, or all-embracing horizon, of his thought. As Metz says:

> That which most characterizes a way of thinking is not primarily what is explicit in it, but the dominating horizon presupposed in each expression, not what is thematically stated, but the dominating direction of the statement . . . not the statements themselves, but the way one looks upon them. (p34)

Metz is quite correct when he maintains that the decisive characteristic of an original thinker is not found primarily in what the thinker expressly thinks, but in the *way* he thinks, ". . . not in just any relation towards what is the object of thought, but rather in *the very act of thinking*" (p31). Metz, therefore, is not after Aquinas' explicit theology, nor even the logic of his philosophical-theological system. He will settle for nothing less than the inner principle of all of Aquinas' thought, the root of its unity, the formal principle behind the thinking which determines its direction and thrust, that through which he thinks, the all-embracing horizon in which all the explicit contents find their ultimate strength, meaning and unity, ". . . that oneness and totality which informs, the unique and unified *Arché*, from which all material multiplicity results" (p31).

Bremond's peppery charges, see: J. de Guibert, *The Jesuits. Their Spiritual Doctrine and Practice* (=*Jesuits*), trans. by W. Young (The Institute of Jesuit Sources: Chicago, 1964), p21, n1 and p561.

[12] Johannes B. Metz, *Christliche Anthropozentrik*, (München, 1962). Page numbers in parentheses in my text refer to this volume. Translations of this book and others are mine, unless otherwise noted.

The Mystical Horizon of
St. Ignatius of Loyola

Ignatius, of course, was neither a philosopher nor a theologian. His experiences during the early years of his conversion, especially those on the banks of the river Cardoner and at La Storta, drastically altered not only what he experienced, knew and loved, but especially *how* he experienced, knew and loved.[13] Ignatius' conversion experiences shifted the everyday horizon of his experience, knowledge and love so that the primordial horizon of his being became quasi-thematic, mystically active and played a decisive role in his life. He became a mystic *par excellence* whose main concern was to be with Christ to serve in his visible Church, the Roman Church.

Ignatius did not intend his Spiritual Exercises to be a theological treatise nor a summary of the spiritual life. They are a practical method to be used to seek and to find God's Will for the individual. They are a method of conversion, a means through which the exercitant's everyday focus of experience, knowledge and love is shifted by making his primordial horizon more mystically present and active. The Exercises are most important for tomorrow's theology because of the novelty and profundity of this method.

What Metz has attempted to do with St. Thomas Aquinas, we, to some extent, are attempting to do with St. Ignatius of Loyola. While Metz focused upon Aquinas' thought-form, we intend to focus upon Ignatius' *mystical horizon.* We wish, therefore, to go beyond Ignatius' explicit spirituality and theology to his all-embracing mystical horizon in which everything Ignatius experiences, knows and loves finds its ultimate meaning and unity. What are the ultimate structures of Ignatius' spirituality? What holds the Exercises together at their very roots? What is it that explains their entire perspective, their whole thrust and their inner dynamics? What, in short, is Ignatius' mystical horizon?

As indebted as we are to the classical commentaries on the Exercises, we soon found that they had little to say directly to our problematic. It was with special interest, however, that we read the works of Erich Przywara, Gaston Fessard, Karl Rahner, Hugo Rahner, Fridolin Marxer, Gilles Cusson, Daniel Gil, Leo Bakker and Ramón González de Mendoza. Because of their methodologies, the tools available to them and their particular problematics, we found

[13]See esp. J. de Guibert, *Jesuits*, chapters 1, 4; H. Rahner, "Die Vision des heiligen Ignatius in der Kapelle von La Storta" (="La Storta"), *ZAM* 10(1935), pp17-35, 124-39, 202-20, 265-82.

them most helpful for our own problematic, the Ignatian mystical horizon. A brief look at their problematics, the questions they raise, their answers, their links with the Ignatian tradition, and their new insights into Ignatius will be the eventual context of our questions and the basis upon which we intend to build our own problematic.

OUR PROBLEMATIC IN THE LIGHT OF RECENT IGNATIAN COMMENTATORS

Erich Przywara

Erich Przywara's three volume work, *Deus Semper Maior*, brings something new to the history of the Exercises, because it is the first major attempt to explore their rich, latent theology in an integrated, holistic way.[14] Because he focuses upon the inner rhythm and dynamics of the Exercises, Przywara's work is compelling, forceful and convincing.

Przywara regards the christological emphases of the Exercises as the key to their inner rhythm and dynamics. As he says, Christ "is the real *interiority* of all things: God in the 'outpouring' of His love" (III, 384) and the "essence of all things" (I, 231). For this reason, God's "Yes" is the deep center of creation (I, 227). Przywara strongly emphasizes the self-emptying aspects of Christ's life in order to highlight that the rhythm of Christ's life is God's rhythm, a rhythm strikingly captured in Ignatius' *Contemplation to Obtain Divine Love*. The self-giving and self-emptying of God to be all in all and draw all things to Himself (the basic descent-ascent theology of the *Contemplation to Obtain Divine Love*) is translated into radically historical and personal terms in the life, death and resurrection of Jesus Christ.[15]

[14] Erich Przywara, *Deus Semper Maior* (=*Deus*) (Freiburg i.B., 1938-9), 3 volumes. References in my text will simply state I, II or III, followed by the page number. CF. also: *Ignatianisch*, (Frankfurt a.M., 1956); *Majestas Divina. Ignatianische Frömmigkeit* (Augsburg, 1925). In marked contrast to Przywara's solidly theological and holistic approach, see the following commentators who are heavily pious and pastoral, but who pay little attention to the Ignatian texts: P. Ferrusolae, *op cit.*; Antonio Gaudier, *Introductio ad Solidam Perfectionem per Manuductionem ad S.P.N. Ignatii Exercitia Spiritualia* (Avenione, 1829); Johann B. Sailer, *Übungen des Geistes zur Gründung und Förderung eines heiligen Sinnes und Lebens* (Mannheim, 1804); Vincent Huby, *Oeuvres Spirituelles* (Rouen, 1786); *Retraite sur l'amour de Dieu et de Notre Seigneur Jesus Christ* (Bruxelles, 1887); Ambrose Matignon, *Exercices Spirituels de S. Ignace* (St. Germaine, 1920); P. J. Petitdidier, *Exercitia Spiritualia* (Parisiis, ⁹1880); J. P. Pinamonti, *Esercizi spirituali di S. Ignazio* (Padova, 1711).

[15] Przywara, *Deus* III, pp363ff. For a christological emphasis, cf. esp.: *Deus* III, p108; *Deus* II, p181. He maintains that in the one order of salvation, there is only one humility — that of the self-emptying Christ; Cf. also: *Deus* II, pp85ff; *Deus* III, p119.

Because Christ's rhythm is God's rhythm, and because this rhythm can be found in all things, Przywara views the Exercises as the way to develop an instinct for Christ and to have Christ as the instinct of our being (II, 354). Furthermore, the exercitant takes on Christ's rhythm through the basic rhythm of the consolations and desolations expected during the Exercises. These consolations and desolations are nothing other than Christ's rhythm in the exercitant (I, 232). By grasping this connection between God's rhythm, Christ's rhythm, and the exercitant's rhythm, Przywara has provided a major insight into the Ignatian mystical horizon in its mystagogical, christocentric and anthropocentric aspects.

Przywara considers the Election to be the heart of the Exercises and the Ignatian method. Because the Election calls the exercitant not only to this or that way of life but to the very life of Christ himself, it is the central element in the Exercises (II, 96). The Election arises out of the meditations on Christ's life, because the exercitant can find God's Will for him only if he flees from self-love and self-interest by making Christ's radical humility his own (II, 169ff).

Przywara's forceful focus upon the Election arising out of the meditations on Christ's life and his attempt to explain theologically why this is so has brought something new to Ignatian studies. The Election does not simply happen while meditating upon Christ's life. There is some major dynamic at work in the Exercises which unites the rhythm of the exercitant with the rhythm of Christ.[16]

Przywara locates the essence of the Exercises in the "consolation without previous cause" (=CSCP).[17] He notes that in the CSCP, the

[16]Przywara gives intrinsic as well as extrinsic reasons for linking the exercitant's rhythm with Christ's. Cf. esp. *Deus* I, pp232, 253ff; III, pp28ff for the intrinsic reasons. Cf. esp. *Deus* II, pp83-101 for the more extrinsic reasons. In spite of the unevenness of Przywara's analysis, he was the first one to force us to raise the question: Why does the Election occur in and through the meditations on Christ's life? Przywara's penetrating analysis contrasts sharply with many of the older commentaries, such as: L. DuPont, *op. cit.*; Franz de Hummelauer, *Meditationum et Contemplationum S. Ignatii de Loyola* (Freiburg i.B., 1896). Hummelauer's book is an excellent attempt to show why Ignatius selected the mysteries of Christ that he did. R. Silos, "Cardoner in the Life of St. Ignatius of Loyola," *AHSJ* 33(1964), pp3-43 has clearly shown that Ignatius chose the meditations he did because of the *consolation* he felt while meditating upon them. We disagree, therefore, with J. Sudbrack, "Fragestellung und Infragestellung der ignatianischen Exerzitien," *GuL* (1970), p219 who maintains that the exegesis of Ignatius' day is responsible. Przywara is also aware of the *consolation* element in the choice of mysteries, *Deus* I, p232, *Deus* II, p141.

[17]See *Ex* 330 and 336. CSCP=consolation without previous cause="consolación sin causa precedente." CCCP=consolation with previous cause="consolación 'con causa' " (*Ex* 331).

basic relationship which should exist between God and man becomes apparent: God as Creator holds sway over the soul in a non-manipulatable, free, ever-surprising manner and the soul responds with surrender and openness (II, 140). As he says, when "God, who comes freely, leaving freedom so that the soul may also grant Him freedom, leaving Him free to go when, how and where He will" (II, 147), finds the soul "objectively without grounds in itself (*sin causa precedente*) and subjectively anticipating nothing (*sin ningún previo sentimento o conoscimiento*), powerless both in reason and will" (II, 141), then that secret essence of the profound unity existing between God and the soul is manifested through a consolation which is "the only non-ambiguity in the life between God and the soul" (II, 141). The exercitant's basic disposition during the CSCP is precisely Christ's basic disposition: self-emptying (III, 119).

Przywara notes that for Ignatius, consolation is always more interior than desolation. Consolation is an "inner motion" (I, 251), whereas desolation is "a motion from the exterior to the interior" (I, 250).

In summary, Przywara has emphasized the integral and holistic nature of the Exercises. Through his insistence that the exercitant's rhythm corresponds to Christ's rhythm, especially during the CSCP, he has linked the anthropology of the Exercises with its Christology. This raises the possibility that the Exercises are not only anthropological and christological, but also anthropocentric and christocentric, a point to be discussed at length later on.[18]

Gaston Fessard

The next work in our study, Gaston Fessard's superb two volumes of *La Dialectique des Exercices Spirituels de Saint Ignace de Loyola*,[19] presents an unusually successful attempt to get at Ignatius'

---

[18] We found the strongly incarnational emphases in Przywara especially helpful. Cf. esp.: *Deus* I, p5; III, pp340ff and *passim*. He also called our attention to the trinitarian dimension of the Exercises, although this provides a good example of how Przywara sometimes imposes his theology upon the Ignatian texts. Cf. *Deus* III, pp386-405. His treatment of the Rules for the Discernment of Spirits and the three times of election are very weak. Some of the older commentaries are far superior. For example, see: A. Gagliardi, *Commentarii seu Explanationes in Ex. Spir. S.P. Ignatius de Loyola* (Brugge, 1882); M. Meschler, *Das Exerzitienbuch des heiligen Ignatius von Loyola* (Freiburg i.B., 1928), 3 volumes.

[19] G. Fessard, *La Dialectique des Exercices Spirituels de Saint Ignace de Loyola* (Paris, 1956 & 1966). 2 volumes. Page numbers in parentheses in my text refer to volume I.

mystical horizon. As Fessard himself says, what he wishes to do is:

> To stress the essentially intellectual and eminently *synthetic* character of the *act* by which Ignatius, through the conflict of 'spirits,' *discerns and at the same time* grasps in Christ and the Church the connection of all things, and of all truths, natural as well as revealed, with the Majesty of the Holy Trinity. (p13, n1)

Fessard intends, therefore, to stress Ignatius' mystically born architechtonic view,[20] a radically synthetic view which he unfolded and explicated in the Exercises.

Ignatius, according to Fessard, transformed this synthetic view into something eminently practical. Having grasped the profound unity which exists between human and divine freedom, an "Instant" (p244) which unites the temporal and the eternal, Ignatius posed his radical question: "How can one decide every time according to God's Will? "[21] Ignatius' equally radical answer is the Exercises, a method which offers through its codification of rules, regulations, directives and four weeks of meditations on Christ's life, death and resurrection, a way of finding out God's Will for the individual (p283).

Along with Przywara, Fessard emphasizes the Christ-initiated and Christ-seeking rhythm of the Exercises as the means by which the exercitant discovers God's Will for him. Because the Risen Christ is the "image of liberty" (p250), "the knot of all dogmatic predicates," "the Self of all the images wherein our ego objectifies itself purely," and the "essence of all the things wherein the soul seeks herself" (p142), the exercitant is a Christ-directed being.

The key christological meditations, therefore, evoke both the exercitant's true subjective liberty and the enemy of that liberty.[22]

[20] H. Rahner, *Ignatius von Loyola und das geschichtliche Werden seiner Frömmigkeit* (=*Werden*) (Salzburg, 1947), p97.

[21] G. Fessard, p236. Fessard I tends towards a more *Electionist*-centered treatment of the Exercises, whereas Fessard II is more *love-of-God* centered. See G. Fessard, II, p128. For the classic work representing the love-of-God school, see: L. Peeters, *Vers l'union divine par les Exercices de S. Ignace* (Louvain, 1931). For an excellent presentation of the Electionist school position, see: J. Roi, *op. cit.* For an excellent discussion of the entire problem and for an extraordinary solution, see: L. Bakker, *Freiheit und Erfahrung* (Würzburg, 1970), pp233ff.

[22] Fessard I, p60. Although it seems that Fessard realizes that grace and sin are not two realities of equal power conditioning man's freedom, he does seem to say that grace requires sin and that sin calls forth grace in much the same way that thesis calls forth antithesis in the Hegelian system. Cf. esp. pp53, 241 and chapters II-III. See: K. Rahner's, "The Immaculate Conception," *TI* 1, pp201-14; "The Dogma of the Immaculate Conception in our Spiritual Life," *TI* 3, pp129-40 for an excellent treatment of the primacy of grace in man's life. Rahner convincingly shows that redemption and damnation are *not* two equal possibilities. Cf. also: K. Rahner, "Eschatology," "Predestination" and "Original Sin," in *SM*.

The christological meditations set in motion the exercitant's Christ-directedness as well as his tendency to sin inherited from Adam. This results in various movements which must be discerned according to the Rules for the Discernment of Spirits (p64).

As with Przywara, Fessard sees the CSCP at the heart of the Ignatian method. This consolation *par excellence* measures and judges every other experience. As Fessard himself says:

> This consolation without previous cause, this Instant wherein the ego and God mingle immediately as the Eternal and the temporal, this is the immutable center of the Ignatian perspective. (pp299ff)

The CSCP, according to Fessard, is the immovable center of the Ignatian perspective for two reasons. First of all, it is "the Instant wherein Eternity becomes temporal and the temporal becomes eternal" (p258). Secondly, this moment in which eternity becomes temporal is initiated by the Father's entry into the soul. The *Father's* initiative is most significant here. He enters the soul by encouraging the exercitant's self-emptying and his taking on the sentiments of Christ. He then leaves the soul and draws it entirely into the love of the Father and the Son (p260). The Exercises, therefore, from their beginning to their end are an attempt to dispose the exercitant to receive this movement, to respond generously to it, and to prolong its effects as long as possible (pp299ff).

Fessard also highlights the role of the CSCP during the Three Times for Election.[23] Common to both the CSCP and the First Time is the "presence of this appeal from above, tangible to the soul to the point that she cannot doubt it nor wish to resist it" (p76). If the CSCP is the ideal and type of all consolations, even their measure and standard, the First Time is the "type and ideal of liberty" (p74). Fessard, however, locates the difference between the First Time and the CSCP in this:

> The difference between the two consists simply in the fact that the former, such as the vocation of Paul or Matthew, embraces and specifies the future of one's entire life which the latter leaves more or less indeterminate. (p76)

Just as the CSCP must be discerned from the consolations that follow in its wake, so too must the First Time be distinguished from

---

[23] Fessard's treatment of the Three Times (chap. IV, 3) and the Rules for the Discernment of Spirits (pp233ff) is one of the finest in the entire Ignatian tradition.

the Second Time. For Fessard, the Second Time is the First Time which has lost its unity, the Moment when eternity becomes temporal but refracted into moments (p77). The Second Time attempts to reach the one Moment by piecing together consolations and desolations, but remains a dissipated First Time.

The Third Time occurs when the First Time refracts itself to such a degree that the exercitant finds himself in a state of tranquillity. The refracted moments blend in with ordinary time, but can be put back together by the use of the exercitant's natural powers (p76). The Third Time, however, attempts "to surpass the purely rational of reflection alone and to find even within the calm period the 'motion and attraction' which comes from above" (p78).

Fessard shows very clearly that both the Second and the Third Time are shot through with components and images belonging to the First Time (pp78ff). He counters, therefore, that tendency in the Ignatian tradition which sees the Three Times of Election as three utterly distinct, discrete times.

Fessard also penetratingly reveals that Ignatius was profoundly aware of the interaction between reasoning and affectivity. The genius of Ignatian discernment appeals not only to reasoning, but also to the emotional echoes which this reasoning produces in the core of the person, and vice versa.[24] Ignatius recognized that at the critical stage of discerning true from false consolations, an insufficient intellectual criterion must link up with an affective criterion (p271). At this critical stage, after having recognized both the power and the limitations of the intellect as the criterion of perfection, Ignatius appeals to an affective criterion to decide the issue. He hardly wishes to abandon or suppress the intellectual criterion, but "to unite it so intimately with the affective that their interaction habitually and quasi-instinctively results in a superior and . . . connatural affectivity" (p295).

In summary, Fessard's strong Christocentrism, his profound analysis of the CSCP, the Three Times of Election and the Rules for the Discernment of Spirits, his linking of the affective and the intellectual criteria present the Ignatian dialectic in terms of a christocentric liberty, a penetration of the Three Times and a mystical connaturality. His analysis has been of considerable help for our consideration of Ignatius' mystical horizon.[25]

[24] Fessard I, p278. See also: J. Roi, p310; L. Peeters, p34.
[25] We call attention to three other areas of importance in Fessard's analysis. The first is the profound study in the second volume of the emotion *vergüenza* coupled with an intense awareness of the role of the other emotions in the

Karl Rahner

The next Ignatian commentator in our study is the profoundly original theologian, Karl Rahner.[26] For K. Rahner, the essence of the Exercises can be found in the Election, an Election, however, with a transcendental as well as a categorical aspect. K. Rahner emphasizes that the response to the ever-present, ever-loving immediacy of God through a personal conversion in faith, hope and love can never be separated from the concrete, historical realization of this conversion through specific action in one's daily life.[27] The one Ignatian Election, therefore, fuses a radically personal, transcendental conversion with a practical course of action.

K. Rahner praises the genius and originality of the Exercises, because they deal with more than some general Will of God or a syllogistically deductive ethics. As he says:

> They are rather an attempt, especially in the Rules for the Discernment of Spirits, to provide and give practice in a formal, systematical method of discovering this *individual* will of God . . . they are actually the first and so far the only detailed attempt at such a *systematic method* (p115). (Emphasis mine)

Exercises. The second is his insistence that the Exercises are not indoctrination, but evoke, strengthen, and intensify what all men in some way *already* know and live (cf. I, pp9ff, 135ff). The third is the providing of the hinge between the transcendental and the categorical Election through his analysis of the Passion and Eucharist as the embodiment and incarnation of Christ's decision to give himself to the world (cf. pp114ff). In the crucial Third Week the exercitant is also called upon to incarnate his decision in his everyday life. But we have a few questions for Fessard. In his treatment of the Second Time, is it enough to insist upon a convergence of consolations and desolations without asking what distinguishes true from false consolations? How do the emotions and the Election really interact? Although he has stressed an intellectual as well as an affective criterion for discernment, has he considered that the Third Time also contains elements which are important and present to the other two Times? For an excellent evaluation of Fessard, see: H. Rahner, *AHSJ* 27(1958), pp137-42; F. Roustang, *Orient* 24(1960), pp244-6.

[26] See esp.: Karl Rahner, *Dynamic*. Page numbers in parentheses in my text refer to this book. Important for our study is Rahner's response to A. Dulles, "Finding God's Will," *WL* 94(1965), pp139-52 and a brief sketch of what Rahner considers to be the heart of the Exercises. We shall refer to them as "Resp" and "Sketch." See also: "On the Question of a Formal Existential Ethics," *TI* 2, pp217-34; "Reflections on the Experience of Grace," *TI* 3, pp86-90; "The Ignatian Mysticism of Joy in the World," *TI* 3, pp277-93; "Being Open to God as Ever Greater," *TI* 7, pp25-46.

[27] K. Rahner, "Sketch." By setting up the problematic this way, Rahner avoids the overemphases of both the Electionists and the Love of God schools of interpretation.

For K. Rahner, Aristotle thematically, formally and systematically expressed the profane logic which every man uses daily, whether or not he specifically notices it. Every man thinks logically to some extent, and Aristotle systematized what every man does more or less spontaneously. Ignatius, moreover, thematically, formally and systematically expressed the *lived supernatural logic* which all men more or less implicitly use to decide the key issues of their lives. What Aristotle is to profane logic, Ignatius is to supernatural logic.

K. Rahner emphasizes that there are first principles not only of profane logic, but of supernatural logic as well. He points to the CSCP as the first principle, touchstone and utterly basic experience of Ignatian supernatural logic (p130). This central, core, touchstone experience cannot deceive and cannot in itself be measured; it is itself the measure and the standard of all other experiences, hence, the one movement among various movements of "spirits" which carries within itself its own indubitable evidence (p149). The CSCP carries within itself its own evidence and can serve as the Ignatian first principle in supernatural logic, because this CSCP is the becoming-thematic of supernaturally elevated transcendence, pure openness to God, and nothing else. It is essentially a consolation "without conceptual object in the actual concretely personal, radical love of God" (p134, n28).

During this consolation, the exercitant's deepest core is evoked, comes to itself in freedom and is led beyond every created object into the infinity of God's love (p135). The exercitant comes to himself, "returns" to himself before his departure from self into God's love. Because this experience is profoundly anthropocentric (return to self), it is also deeply mystagogical (into God's love). God's coming and going and His drawing the deepest core of the exercitant entirely to His love are the essentials of this experience (p143).

For K. Rahner, the CSCP does not merely accompany this becoming-thematic of supernatural transcendence, but *is* this becoming-thematic. The CSCP is radical freedom, spirit supernaturally present to itself, hence, a mystical, creative self-presence which leads the person into his own mysterious depths and into the Father's love (p150). This experience, moreover, allows Ignatius to judge an experience not only by its fruit, but also by its *origin*.[28]

[28] Although Rahner has certainly interpreted Ignatius correctly, much of the tradition would deny the possibility of tracing an experience to its origin. We suspect that the following statement by F. Roustang, *Growth in the Spirit*, trans. by K. Pond, (New York, 1966), p100 represents the majority opinion:

Essential to the Ignatian method in K. Rahner's view is the frequent bringing together of the exercitant's radical experience of God as the "Whither" of his supernaturally elevated transcendence and the particular object of Election. Does the exercitant experience a meshing, a synthesis or a congruence of his touchstone experience with the object of choice so that peace, joy, harmony, stillness, happiness and inner satisfaction result? Is his deepest, God-grounded and God-evoked basic religious stance deepened by the Election? If so, the Election is a good one, a good one for him. As K. Rahner says: "With Ignatius it is a question of recognizing the harmony between the object of choice and a person's precise individual mode of religious life" (p166).[29] By observing the subjective echoes and the resulting harmony or discord which arise from this confrontation, the exercitant can find the individual Will of God for him according to the principles of mystical connaturality.

Although K. Rahner, like Fessard, grants that the Three Times of Election interpenetrate and cannot be fully separated from each other and that each are aspects of a single choice and Election which appear in different intensities, he nevertheless regards the Second Time as the normal Ignatian Time (p95). K. Rahner considers the First Time as miraculous, prophetic and extraordinary (p127, n25). The Third Time, however, is only an expedient, an exception to "what is normal in a Christian life" (p127). In fact, the Third Time is actually a deficient form of the Second Time, strives to employ some of its elements, and can be understood only in terms of the Second Time (p105, n18). For K. Rahner, the Second Time holds the key to Ignatius' supernatural logic.[30]

In summary, therefore, K. Rahner highlights the Exercises as a method for making a supernatural, existential decision based upon an experienced concord or discord which occurs when a person's

---

"In the first place, no criterion enables us to recognize with certainty, at a given moment, the origin of a particular sentiment. To judge of the value of the tree we have to wait until the present consolation or desolation have born their fruit." Cf. also: F. Suarez, pp506-7 (impossible without a special revelation); A. Bellecius, *Medulla asceseos seu exercitia S.P. Ignatii accuratiori modo explanata* (Augsburg, 1757), p246; V. Mercier, *Manuel des Exercices de saint Ignace* (Poitiers, 1894); A. Matignon, p269.

[29] See also pp158ff. For Ignatius, finding God's Will is like offering a prince various foods and watching his reactions very closely to see which one he likes best. See: *MI* II, 2, pp67-79, esp. p77, § 21.

[30] For an excellent treatment of the Second Time, see: P. Sbandi, *Eine Untersuchung zur zweiten Wahlzeit in den geistlichen Übungen* (Innsbruck Dissertation, 1966); J. Nevado, "El segundo tiempo de elección en los Ejercicios," *Manr* 39(1967), pp41-54; J. Ayerra, "Función electiva de la consolación en el segundo tiempo," *MiCo* 26(1956), pp91-103.

concrete choice is savored in the presence of his central, God-evoked religious stance which becomes thematic as CSCP. K. Rahner's penetrating transcendental analysis of the Exercises has thrown considerable light on the anthropocentric and mystagogical character of Ignatius' mystical horizon.[31]

Hugo Rahner

The next Ignatian commentator in our study is Hugo Rahner.[32] H. Rahner focuses upon the strongly "from above" or mystagogical quality of Ignatius' mystical horizon (pp3ff). Mystagogical experiences "from above" result in a mystically communicated analogy of being and a "grasp of the interdependence of the mysteries" (p1). Ignatius, therefore, was able to find God in all things, because he had first found Him "from above." As H. Rahner says: "To rise from creatures upwards towards God is certainly one form of prayer; but the essential note of Ignatian theology is the way of descent" (p9). The Ignatian mystical horizon, then, begins with God and moves downward.

According to H. Rahner, however, Ignatius complemented his decidedly "from above" mystical horizon with an equally definite christocentric aspect, a christocentric aspect based upon a "mystically received *communicatio idiomatum*" (p15). Ignatius found in Christ the Mediator the only way to what is above and the definitive measure for what is creaturely (p18). As H. Rahner maintains: "It is, however, quite certain that the whole of Ignatian theology and mysticism was essentially christological" (p53).

---

[31] Rahner has been criticized by A. Dulles, *op. cit.*, p151 and J. Sudbrack, *op. cit.*, for his failure to bring out the christological and encounter-with-scripture dimension of the Exercises. Rahner admits as much in "Resp." Rahner, however, has done much to show why these meditations come alive during the Exercises. Furthermore, his other writings provide solid methodological tools for getting at the Ignatian mystical horizon. In fact, A. Dulles, "The Ignatian Experience as Reflected in the Spiritual Theology of Karl Rahner," *Philippine Studies* (1965), pp471-91 and J. Carmody, "Rahner's Spiritual Theology," *America* (Oct. 31, 1970), pp345-8 have shown how intrinsic Ignatian spirituality is to K. Rahner's own theology. Cf.: K. Rahner, *Schriften zur Theologie 12: Theologie aus Erfahrung des Geistes* (Benziger: Zurich--Einsiedeln-Köln, 1975), esp. pp7-13.

[32] A holistic presentation of H. Rahner's works is impossible, for he has done solid historical studies, bibliographical work, editorial work and theological reflection. Most important for our study, however, is: *Ignatius the Theologian* (=*Ignatius*), trans by M. Barry (Herder & Herder: New York, 1968). Page numbers in parentheses in my text refer to this book. CF. also: "Notes on the Spiritual Exercises," (="Notes"), *WL* (1956), pp281-336; "Die Liebe in den Exerzitien," *Orient* 12(1948), pp129-32; "Exerzitien," *LThK* III, pp1297-1300.

Ignatius experienced Christ not only as a Mediator, but also as his "Creator and Lord" (pp121ff). Because he experienced the man Jesus as his Creator and Lord, the Exercises exhibit a remarkable "hypostatic dialectic" (p16). H. Rahner stresses the sacramental structure of Christ's life in the Exercises, the " 'sacramental' polarity (as understood by the Council of Chalcedon) between the lowliness and wretchedness of Christ's historical human nature (*labor*) and the radiance of the Godhead (*gloria*) which this human nature at once revealed and concealed" (p100). The earthly life of this Ignatian "Creator and Lord" serves as the standard against which all experiences and decisions are measured. In fact, for H. Rahner, the Election takes place in and through the meditations on the life of Christ, because of the radically "incarnational or hypostatic structure" of the Election (p214). The Exercises, therefore, are both christological and christocentric.

For H. Rahner, however, the Ignatian Election possesses an incarnational structure for still another reason. The Election must take flesh and become visible. Because of the Incarnation, "all spirit tends towards flesh and all genuine movement of the Spirit tends towards the Church" (p214).[33] For H. Rahner:

> 'Church' embraces all visible things, from scripture to reason; 'Spirit' is the immediate interior contact of the soul with the power 'from above'. Mysticism and reason, Spirit and Church belong together, but always in such a way that the Spirit, however abundantly it may pour forth, will allow itself to be confined within the measure of the visible. (p217)

Ignatius' "hyper-papal" (p237), Roman-church orientation, therefore, is the classic case of where he allows "Spirit" and the "invisible" to be measured and controlled by "Body" and the "visible" (pp219ff).

For H. Rahner, Ignatius' instructions for the application of the senses also discloses an incarnational dimension to Ignatius' prayer (pp181-213). This Ignatian method of prayer involves a three-level movement of ever-greater interiority. First, the exercitant moves from the simple application of his outer senses to the meditation or mystery involved. Secondly, he proceeds to an inner understanding and tasting. Finally, he comes to that state of prayer wherein his "spiritual senses" are experiencing God's immediacy in a way

[33] We strongly recommend R. Schwager, *Das dramatische Kirchenverständnis bei Ignatius von Loyola* (Zürich, 1970), despite its many weaknesses. Cf. also J. Granero, "San Ignacio de Loyola ai servicio de la Iglesia," *CTom* 260(1956), pp529-72.

analogous to the bodily senses' experience of corporeal reality (p187). The exercitant, however, must focus his "spiritual senses" on Jesus Christ, God's incarnate Word. Utterly sensitive to Christ from the core of his spiritual senses, the exercitant discerns spirits almost instinctively (pp199ff).

H. Rahner agrees with those Ignatian commentators who stress the Election-centeredness of the Exercises. He describes the First Time Election as mystical and "from above," the Third as "theologico-discursive" and "from below," and the Second as ascetical and "in the middle" (p29, 214).[34] The Second time is the desired Time for finding God's Will and occurs "without ratiocination," but must be able to stand the test of reason (pp155ff).

In summary, H. Rahner emphasizes the mystagogical, christocentric, and, to some extent, the anthropocentric (reason, body, from below, etc.) dimensions of the Exercises. He has also shown to some degree how these three aspects are linked in the meditations on the life of Christ.[35]

Fridolin Marxer

The next Ignatian commentator in our study, Fridolin Marxer,[36] presents a profound analysis of the often unrecognized polydimensionality of Ignatian prayer by emphasizing its more mystical qualities. For our purposes, his analysis of the mystagogical, anthropocentric and christocentric character of Ignatian prayer in terms of the inner spiritual senses is extremely effective and important.

For Marxer, the emphatically mystagogical character of Ignatian prayer moves in two different, yet related, directions. The Exercises ask the exercitant to apply his senses to the Christian mystery before him in such a way that the deepest recesses of his being become saturated with the essence of that mystery. This concentration of the exercitant's various faculties upon the Christian mystery results in an effective unification and intuition. The affective intuition centers upon the mystery's inner core and causes this inner core to become part of the exercitant's interiority (p39). The movement here is *from outside to inside*, from the mystery to the exercitant's interiority.

---

[34] See also: "Notes," p297.

[35] *Ignatius*, pp32-52 presents an excellent treatment of the "metahistorical link and dependence" which exists among the saints in the mystical and ascetical traditions.

[36] Fridolin Marxer, *Die inneren geistlichen Sinne* (Freiburg i.B., 1963). Page numbers in parentheses in my text refer to this book.

This mystagogical movement from outside to inside, however, not only brings something in, but also evokes, awakens and sensitizes the exercitant's inner spiritual senses to a holistic realization and experience of God's immediacy already at work. Marxer emphasizes, however, that this intuitive, holistic experience is only evoked by the more exterior form of meditation. The inner spiritual senses achieve their goal through an inner perceiving of grace whose movement is *from inside to outside* (p117, 161).

Marxer also stresses the anthropocentric component of the Ignatian application of the senses. Ignatius' instructions for prayer center upon the involvement of the exercitant's entire body-spirit structure during prayer. The mystery being meditated upon must penetrate the exercitant's being at all levels (p43, 142). The exercitant's bodily, imaginative and spiritual senses are coordinated to produce a prayer of total experience involving all levels and every dimension of the exercitant's being (p22, 44). The exercitant's surface dimensions as well as his most intimate, personal center participate.

The anthropocentric dimension of Ignatian prayer centers upon Ignatius' concern for the exercitant's highly active, fully receptive and utterly reflective involvement in all the levels of his prayer (p124, 137). The exercitant must become holistically sensitive to what he is experiencing in his entire person, from the least stirrings of grace, to what can be called, strictly speaking, the mystical (pp157ff, 162).

Marxer takes note of the christocentric aspect of Ignatian prayer in two particular ways. First of all, because the proper object of the spiritual, imaginative and bodily senses is Jesus Christ, the anthropocentric element is solidly linked with the christocentric (p62). By walking, living, suffering, dying and rising with Christ throughout the Exercises, the bodily, imaginative and spiritual senses are awakened, deepened and transformed (p29). The exercitant comes to himself, experiences a fundamental reorientation of himself as a personal subject through Jesus Christ.

Secondly, Marxer attaches great value to the Ignatian formula, *sentir en nuestro Señor*. This Ignatian expression is no pious utterance, but a major factor in his spirituality. The origin, nature and goal of Ignatius' method of supernatural decision can be found therein (p132). Ignatian logic operates from Christ, in Christ and for Christ. A radically christocentric connaturality underpins the Ignatian method.

In summary, Marxer's analysis of the mystagogical, anthropocentric and christocentric character of the Ignatian application of the senses has proven most valuable for our study of the Ignatian mystical horizon.

Gilles Cusson

Gilles Cusson[37] attempts to present a fundamental interpretation of the Exercises which is both synthetic and comprehensive in scope. Like K. Rahner, he distinguishes two forms of the conversion in Ignatius' life which began at Loyola. Ignatius' first conversion, according to Cusson, involved his definitive consecration to the love and service of God in Jesus Christ. This was Ignatius' profoundly interior, primordial election (p24).

Ignatius' second conversion, however, resulted from his first. This second conversion attempted to actualize the first conversion through a clumsy and often crude form of spiritual life. Because it occupied itself all too much with exterior and false manifestations of piety, it demanded further purification (p38).

Cusson indirectly applies Ignatius' two-fold conversion to his understanding of the Exercises (p104, 108). For Cusson, the Exercises open the exercitant to an ever-greater service of Jesus Christ. They must free the person from inordinate attachments so that he can surrender to the call of grace to seek, to find and to accomplish God's Will for him.

The Scriptures, moreover, determine the objective content of the Exercises; they provide objective control over the evoked spiritual experience. In fact, the efficacy of the Exercises must be measured by the depth of the exercitant's experience of God's salvific action in Jesus Christ (p103, 60).

A deeply christological view directs Cusson's analysis of the Exercises. As he says: "It is always the experience basic to the Kingdom which we must have before us to guide our interpretation" (p340). The Ignatian Christ, for Cusson, is the foundation of salvation, the Word who reveals the Father, man's Creator, man's entry into God and the presence of God's action and mercy. Regardless of the meditations involved, Jesus Christ is always the Eternal Word and the Christ of Majesty (pp25ff, 166ff).

Although Cusson's explication of Ignatius' Christology does not measure up to his synthetic, comprehensive goal, he does bring into sharp relief that the mystagogical dimension in the Exercises results

---

[37] Gilles Cusson, *Pédagogie de l'expérience spirituelle personnelle* (=*Pédagogie*) (Paris, 1968). Page numbers in parentheses in my text refer to this book. Cf. G. Cusson: *Conduis moi sur le Chemin D'éternité* (Montréal, 1973); "S. Ignace de Loyola. III. Les Exercices Spirituels," (="Exercices"), *DSAM* VII, pp1306-18.

from their christological quality. The grace of "the intimate knowledge of our Lord" so ardently asked for passes into "a love of God in all things" during the *Contemplation to Obtain Divine Love* (pp375ff).

Cusson firmly insists upon the intellectual component in Ignatius' spirituality. The mystical graces of Manresa and Loyola radically energized and transformed Ignatius' understanding. Cusson explicates the intellect's role and the interplay of objective truth and evoked experience in Ignatius' life and Exercises. Although he hardly neglects the importance of the role of desire throughout the Exercises (p159), he does stress the experience of a purifying and challenging intellectual light (p126, 47). The Exercises derive much of their power from the objective truths of Scripture which evoke, clarify and control the desired subjective experience (p184). They communicate an experience of light which is primarily an interior, spiritual understanding of the mysteries of God which guides the will in its movement of love towards God (pp132ff). This experience of light or spiritual understanding always forms the origin of other graces which Ignatius refers to as "spiritual tasting" or spiritual "relish" (pp126ff). Essential to the Ignatian method, then, is a steely demand that one know the facts about any mystery being meditated upon, that one consider and reflect, and that one know in order to detest, be sorry, have shame, love, rejoice, etc. (pp128ff, 274ff, 35ff).[38]

As with many other Ignatian commentators, Cusson notes that the Election arises in and through the meditations on Christ's life (pp289ff). He insists, however, that the interrelation between the contemplations and the Election is so intense that "the ways of election and contemplation coincide exactly" (p299). "This mystery of contemplation-election where man's action and God's action meet and collaborate" (p325) becomes especially intense during the actual time of Election and allows the exercitant to discern which way God is moving him.

Ignatius' acceptance of the world is another important fact in his mystical horizon, according to Cusson. Ignatian mysticism is a mysticism of service in the Church and loves the world, because it

---

[38] See also: J. Roothaan, *Exercices spirituels de saint Ignace de Loyola,* Annotés par le R.P. Roothaan et traduit par le P.P. Jennesseaux (Paris, 1891), p26. The problem of religious knowledge in the Exercises, however, is much more complicated than Cusson indicates. In spite of its overly intellectual interpretation, see: H. Pinard de la Boullaye, "Sentir, sentimiento y sentido, dans le style de saint Ignace," (="Sentir"), *AHSJ* 25(1956), pp416-30.

loves God's Will. Ignatius discovered the deepest meaning and sense of human existence in service, for therein does man cooperate with God to bring about His tremendous plan (p89). Ignatius' service-mysticism and acceptance of the world, therefore, are one and the same thing.

Cusson's analysis of Ignatius' life and method in terms of his two conversions, his christological emphases, his respect for spiritual desire and knowledge, the election-contemplation unity, and his mysticism of service and world-acceptance have proved most useful for our study of Ignatius' mystical horizon.

Daniel Gil

Daniel Gil has done a penetrating analysis of one very important aspect of the Ignatian method, the CSCP.[39] Dissatisfied with the philosophical and theological emphases of past and present Ignatian commentaries, Gil prefers to explicate the empirically verifiable utility of the Exercises and to demonstrate their truth in terms of the way God normally deals with men. To underscore how he differs from the philosophical-theological commentaries, Gil gives the following example. Supposing a new sacristan were to ask Gil about the consecrated Hosts reserved in the tabernacle. He could either give the sacristan a theological explanation of transubstantiation, or he could point to the vigil light in the sanctuary. Gil believes that pointing to the sanctuary light would be the most helpful. For Gil, the Ignatian method is very much like pointing to the vigil light (R, 42).

Gil maintains that the Ignatian method centers upon the difficulty of distinguishing one form of consolation from another, especially true from false. Ignatius' solution can be traced to his criterion of "previous cause." Is the consolation in question with or without "previous cause" (C, 48)?

CSCP is the basis of the Ignatian method, for this way of consoling without a previous cause is proper to God *alone*. This consolation, for Gil, represents not only one way in which God may console, but the way most properly His. *Only God* can console in *this* precise way (R,121ff). The exercitant must see whether this

---

[39] Daniel Gil, *La Consolación sin causa precedente. Estudio hermeneutico-teológico sobre los nn. 330, 331 y 336 del libro de los Ejercicos de San Ignacio* (=C). Dissertatio ad Lauream (Pontificia Universitas Gregoriana, 1969-70, Rome). References in my text will be given as C, followed by page number. See also: "Algunas reflexiones sobra la Consolación sin causa," (=R), *Manr* 41(1969), pp39-64, 121-40. References in my text will be given as R, followed by the page number.

consolation is present or not, for it is the only type of consolation unequivocally and exclusively divine (C, 58, 60).

For Gil, when the exercitant discovers through a simple, non-scientific, non-philosophical reflection that there is no preceding cause for his consolation, he has found the empirical criterion for the CSCP (C, 169). When the spiritually sensitive exercitant, at this moment in his spiritual life and in the context of the Exercises, notices a disproportion, an interruption, something gratuitous, or a lack of correspondence between what he asked for in a particular meditation (the Ignatian "what I want") and what was actually given (hence, a concrete, subjective disproportion), and that he is entirely drawn into God's love, he has received the CSCP, a consolation exclusively divine in nature (C, 43; R, 125).[40]

Gil, however, focuses neither upon the origin nor the spiritual quality of the CSCP. He maintains that God *may* be the efficient cause. The unconscious, however, or some other factor *may* be the efficient cause. The CSCP may be a purely spiritual experience or merely an irruption from the unconscious (C,148,170).[41] The only criterion for Ignatius is the "without previous cause." The efficient cause, for Gil, however, is not really the issue.

The issue, for Gil, is the *religious significance* of the CSCP *for the exercitant*. The exercitant believes (and with some evidence) that the experience is without previous cause and exclusively divine because of its religious significance for him (C,169). According to Gil, the Ignatian method is open to all experiences regardless of their origin. Ignatius' method simply decodes the religious significance for the exercitant, the religious significance embedded in the experience. Ignatius' method proffers a profound understanding of the religious meaning and significance of an experience, but not a rational explanation of how this experience is produced. The Ignatian method pinpoints the religious meaning of an experience, but not its origin in terms of efficient causality.[42]

---

[40] Gil maintains the traditional position of Gagliardi and Suarez when he emphasizes the disproportion element in the CSCP. Gil's identification of the "preceding cause" with the exercitant's preparation to obtain a specific grace (the "what I want and desire") is excellent and novel.

[41] We find it difficult to reconcile Gil's assertion that the CSCP can be an irruption from the unconscious and still be one which *totally* draws the exercitant into God's love.

[42] K. Rahner in a seminar session one evening related how a young man on the brink of suicide pressed a gun to his head and said: "My life is as dark and as bleak as the weather." Suddenly the sun came through the clouds, and the young man put down the gun. The simple event of the sun shining through the clouds had had religious significance for him. Is Gil saying that the CSCP gives rise to religious significance in the same way that the sun did for the

Although we strongly disagree with the core of Gil's profound and very subtle analysis of the CSCP, his study represents a significant contribution to Ignatian studies and has been most stimulating for our own focus upon Ignatius' mystical horizon.

Leo Bakker

The next author in our study, Leo Bakker, has applied the methods of contemporary biblical criticism to the Exercises.[43] What occasions gave rise to the Exercises? What was behind the history of their formation? What was their place in the context of Ignatius' own spiritual life? These are some of Bakker's questions (p10).

Bakker has noted that the Exercises are not a carefully constructed logical whole, but actually an excellent patchwork construction best understood in the context of Ignatius' own spiritual experiences (pp226ff). Ignatius' own mystical life provides the hermeneutical key to the Exercises (p139).[44] Especially important was the ongoing process and genetic connection in Ignatius' spiritual life and pastoral experience (p141),

---

young man? We think that he is. Although we admit that the religious significance of the CSCP for the exercitant plays a major role in the Ignatian method, we do not believe that this is always the case. Fessard and others have pointed out that the CSCP functions not only as a source of religious meaning, but also as an intellectual *and affective* criterion for other experiences. In some cases, moreover, the exercitant merely presents one side of the Election one day and the other side the next to see which way he is *moved*.

Can Gil so easily avoid the problem of *causality* in religious signification? Can unconscious irruptions really be admitted as the source of CSCP when Gil himself seems to admit (cautiously) that the CSCP springs from the deepest depths of *liberty* (cf. R, pp132ff)? We think not. We maintain that the CSCP has religious significance for the exercitant because he *experiences* the religious *quality* of his own graced horizon in the CSCP. It is against this graced horizon that not only religious significance but also other consolations are grasped *precisely* as significant and valid. Cf. L. Bakker, pp88ff for a profound analysis of the Ignatian meat vision which explains our position in detail. We also maintain that Gil's analysis suffers from the weaknesses inherent in the religious epistemology of P. Ricoeur's, *The Conflict of Interpretations. Essays on Hermeneutics* (Northwestern University Press: Evanston, Ill., 1974), upon which Gil partially depends.

[43] Leo Bakker, *Freiheit und Erfahrung* (Würzburg, 1970). Page numbers in parentheses in my text refer to this book. In spite of the fine beginnings by H. Pinard de la Boullaye in *Les Étapes de Rédaction des Exercices de S. Ignace* (=*Étapes*) (Paris, 1945), Bakker's book is the first to apply to the Exercises the methods of contemporary biblical criticism. This masterful work ought to be translated into English as quickly as possible.

[44] See also: W. Peters, *The Spiritual Exercises of St. Ignatius-Exposition and Interpretation* (Program to Adapt the Spiritual Exercises: Jersey City, NJ, 1968).

Bakker cautions, however, that there are three significant differences to be constantly kept in mind: the difference between Ignatius and his own times; the difference between Ignatius and our own times; and, most important of all, the difference between Ignatius' own words in the Exercises and his own spiritual experiences (p12).

By means of a very careful analysis of Ignatius' letter to Sr. Teresa Rejadell and its biographical background, especially to the Rules for the Discernment of Spirits, Bakker concludes that the two rules dealing with the CSCP and the texts immediately connected with them are the mystical wisdom which Ignatius would impart only to the spiritually proficient (p62). For Bakker, these two rules dealing with the CSCP, and not the rules concerning "temptation under the appearance of good," form the core of the Rules for the Discernment of Spirits (p165).

Bakker notes, moreover, that the quality of the God experience during the CSCP, the passivity one experiences therein, most characterizes the CSCP (p98). For Bakker, the consolation which God gives here and now, a consolation which the exercitant himself cannot bring about, this experience of God and not the "without preceding cause," provides the best criterion for the correctness of the Election. It also provides the deepest reason for the experience of such unshakeable certitude (p98).

The heart of the Ignatian method, for Bakker, is the First Time of Election with CSCP linked to the basic Rules for Thinking with the Church (p64). Ignatius himself had experienced the First Time Election, and until 1539, this was the Time which he stressed and expected of his exercitants (pp281ff). According to Bakker, Ignatius had experienced an Election of the First Time at Cardoner. He knew that God wanted him to go to the Holy Land to labor and possibly die there (pp112ff). But when he was ordered out of the Holy Land by the Franciscan Provincial under threat of papal excommunication, not only did his view of Church authority crystallize, but *Ex* 336 also resulted, the rule concerned with the time following the CSCP when the exercitant is most inclined to add to or subtract from the God-given inspiration (pp116ff, 144ff).

Bakker also underscores the importance of the Second and Third Time of Election in Ignatius' life, explains their meaning, their special features, their place in the Exercises, and brings up difficulties associated with them, especially with the Third Time (pp281ff). Bakker notes, however, that the sharp division into three distinct times is artificial and introduced for methodological clarity. In the actual life of St. Ignatius, these Three Times were often fused together. Bakker considers this fusion of the Three Times in practice as the ideal Election (pp284ff).

For Bakker, Ignatius was the first in the Church's spiritual tradition to work out methodologically and explicitly the link between consolation and Election (p105). This is the original contribution of the Exercises to the tradition. Bakker emphasizes, moreover, that the Exercises center upon the choice of a way of life. For Ignatius, however, there are only two states or ways of life — one according to the commandments and the other according to the counsels. For Bakker, what Ignatius means primarily by counsels is *poverty* (p244, 247). The basic question for the exercitant is whether he is called to spiritual or to actual poverty.

Ignatius' Cardoner experience manifested a special Christ-centeredness which stamped the rest of his life and allowed him to actualize this Christ-centeredness in many different ways (pp263ff). For Bakker, this is the secret of the Ignatian method. Ignatius expects to bring about a fundamental conversion to Christ which leaves the exercitant's life open to many concrete realizations of this one conversion. Ignatius expects Christ to appear to the exercitant, to console him, and to place two alternatives before him — spiritual or literal imitation (p82, 255). Bakker views Election, consolation and the heart of the Exercises in radically christocentric terms.[45]

Bakker's study of the Exercises, employing the methods of contemporary biblical criticism, presents a profound and detailed exposition of many facets of Ignatian thought. His book ranks as one of the best among contemporary Ignatian studies.

Ramón González de Mendoza

The last author in our study, Ramón Gonzáles de Mendoza, has attempted to prove that Ignatius anticipated the existential-analytical problematic dealing with the existential-ontological significance of mood (*Stimmung*) which Martin Heidegger profoundly explicated.[46] Just as G. Fessard approached the Exercises armed with Hegelian methodology, Mendoza has analyzed the Exercises in terms of Heidegger's existential philosophy.[47]

---

[45]Cf. also: pp127-8, 253, 290, 299, 305ff.

[46]Ramón González de Mendoza, *Stimmung und Transzendenz. Die Antizipation der existential analytischen Stimmungsproblematik bei Ignatius von Loyola* (Berlin, 1970). Page numbers in parentheses in my text refer to this book.

[47]Mendoza, however, is far less successful. Fessard has *carefully* read Ignatius and Hegel. Mendoza imposes too much Heidegger onto Ignatius. His critique of Fessard, Suarez and K. Rahner, however, is excellent.

Mendoza stresses the Ignatian link between mood and Election as the basis of Ignatius' genius and originality. Ignatius was the first in a long line of Christian thinkers to have grasped so profoundly the existential significance of mood and to have made the link between mood and Election the centerpiece of his thinking (p205, 210). Mendoza, therefore, calls Ignatius "the mystic of moods" (p198).

According to Mendoza, although Ignatius hardly expected special revelations from God, he did seek and find God's Will for him. How was this possible? Ignatius, says Mendoza, had made the startling discovery that his moods were not always in conformity with his thoughts, that they often ran contrary to his thoughts, and that they were not the results of his thoughts. The sudden, non-manipulatable, non-calculable, variable, multi-faceted quality of his moods led Ignatius to see in them a sign of the divine approbation or disapproval (p214).

Mendoza emphasizes both the quality as well as the mode of arising of a mood. The CSCP, that very special Ignatian mood, is gentle and delicate, arises unexpectedly without any preparation on the exercitant's part, and is irresistible (p221).[48] Both the quality and the mode of arising of the CSCP render it an absolutely trustworthy criterion for judging the divine origin of a specific movement (p220).

Mendoza describes the CSCP as "the mood of theological difference" in which God is experienced precisely as God, as different from all else, including Being (p237). This utterly basic, mystical consolation comes suddenly, remains incalculable, and presents itself as a gentle, lofty mood of "loving reverence and respect" in which one experiences divine transcendence (p238).[49] Mendoza designates the discovery of the existential significance of this mood of loving respect and reverence, the CSCP, as the most important event in Ignatius' spiritual life (p239).

Mendoza's position, however, remains radically philosophical in the full Heideggerian sense. Ignatius' basic experience, when stripped of his own theological interpretations, expectations and attitudes which colored the experience, was a non-intentional mood of the experience of transcendence. This transcendence, however, is in no way supernatural and possesses no noetic content. It is the basic

[48] Mendoza emphasizes the *temporal* sense of "previous" in the CSCP as well as the element of disproportion. We agree with this.

[49] The Ignatian texts do not support the explicit identification of the CSCP with the experience of loving reverence and respect. For an excellent analysis of this experience, see: A. Haas and P. Knauer, *Ignatius von Loyola. Das geistliche Tagebuch* (=*Tagebuch*) (Freiburg i.B., 1961).

mood in which *Dasein* experiences his being-in-the-world as a basic openness to the world (p289). It is the utterly primordial mood which "dis-closes" and illuminates, but without any noetic content. The Ignatian method, for Mendoza, can be reduced to the listening for the harmony or disharmony which exists between an Election and the utterly basic, existential stance of *Dasein* (pp324ff).

In spite of the strong reservations and outright disagreement we have with Mendoza's basic thesis, we do find his problematic original, fascinating and provocative. His emphasis on mood in relation to transcendence has been especially fruitful for our own problematic, although we hardly accept his analysis and solution. His book, however, does remain a must for those interested in Ignatian research.

OUR PROBLEMATIC:
THE IGNATIAN MYSTICAL HORIZON

Let us now focus upon our problematic with clarity and precision. It centers upon Ignatius' mystical horizon as it reveals itself in and through the Exercises. We shall attempt, therefore, to explicate Ignatius' mystical horizon in which and through which everything explicit in Ignatius is anchored in its ultimate meaning and unity. We shall be searching for the implicit mystical thrust or movement which supports all explications.

Ignatius' mystical horizon resulted from an utterly basic experience which became ever more explicit and active throughout his life. Ignatius had lived and tasted in his core the intrinsic link between his own mystery as man and the mystery of God in Jesus Christ. Ignatius' mystical inner standpoint, his dominant, mystical spirituality, his mystical horizon is anthropocentric, christocentric and mystagogical.

This interpretation of Ignatius' mystical horizon arises from our study of the above nine authors in the light of the entire Ignatian tradition. Many of these authors stressed the importance and centrality of the CSCP. The CSCP is one, unified core experience with three aspects. It arises out of the meditations on the life of Christ, delivers the exercitant to his own deepest mystery as man and draws him entirely into the Mystery of God in Christ. The CSCP is an experience wherein the anthropocentric, christocentric and mystagogical dimensions of Ignatius' mystical horizon can best be seen.

These same authors led us to realize that Ignatius' mystical horizon can best be approached through the movement Ignatius sets in motion during the Exercises by means of their explicit Christology, theology and minute instructions. We shall examine the individual elements of the Exercises to explicate the *one basic movement with three moments* which result from them. We shall examine the anthropocentric, christocentric and mystagogical moments of the Exercises as aspects of one fundamental experience. The Exercises are an anthropocentric-christocentric Mystagogy which reveal the anthropocentric, christocentric and mystagogical aspects of Ignatius' mystical horizon.

Chapter II

The Consolation Without Previous Cause: A Concentrated, Experiential Example of the Ignatian Mystical Horizon

INTRODUCTION

Why begin with the Consolation Without Previous Cause (=CSCP)?

A study of the CSCP offers an excellent introduction to Ignatius' mystical horizon. As emphasized in the last chapter, the CSCP not only forms the basis of Ignatian discernment, but it also dominates his entire perspective. The CSCP presents itself as a key Ignatian experience which manifests in a highly concentrated way all of the facets of Ignatius' mystical horizon.

We also maintain that the CSCP recapitulates the basic mystical dynamic of Ignatius' own spiritual life which he translated so successfully into the Exercises "to help souls." Furthermore, the CSCP presents in a concentrated way not only Ignatius' mystical horizon, but also what is most characteristic of every man's life in the grace of Christ. The CSCP is essentially the becoming-thematic, the more explicit experience, of the mysticism of everyday life.

The Ignatian method, therefore, evokes, intensifies and strengthens for the exercitant what is actually every man's fundamental, yet most often anonymous, stance in the grace of Christ. The CSCP perhaps offers the best proof that the Exercises neither indoctrinate nor introduce some extrinsic value system for digestion. They bring to the fore what is most vital, dynamic and immanent in the depths of every human person. For these reasons, therefore, we know of no better way to take us so quickly to the heart of Ignatius' mystical horizon than a chapter immediately devoted to the CSCP.

Difficulties

Because both traditional and contemporary Ignatian commentators fail to present an intelligible, cohesive and unified presentation of the Ignatian CSCP, one can easily understand and appreciate Suarez's candid admission relative to the CSCP: "I do not find it easy to understand these words."[1] The fault, however, hardly rests with the commentators alone. J. H. T. van den Berg has noted that the explicit Ignatian formulation, "without previous cause," appears only in *Ex* 330 and 336, but not in Ignatius' *Autobiography*, *Spiritual Journal*, personal letters, nor even in his famous letter on discernment to Sr. Teresa Rejadell.[2] We are forced to agree with K. Rahner that Ignatius "has here accomplished a masterpiece of brevity but not of clarity" (p131). It is with these difficulties in mind that we begin our own study of the Ignatian CSCP.

The Importance of the Context of the CSCP

We insist at the outset of our study that the CSCP must be studied within its natural Ignatian context, the Exercises. The CSCP must not be analyzed as an isolated element; it properly belongs to the Rules for the Discernment of Spirits most suited for the Second Week of the Exercises. Moreover, it maintains an intrinsic link with the Rules for Thinking with the Church.

The CSCP, therefore, belongs to that part of the Exercises wherein some of the deepest experiences and dynamics of the spiritual life are called into play. This means that the CSCP directly

---

[1] F. Suarez, p510. Note the following: A. Gagliardi, p155 and J. Nonell, *Mélanges Watrigant*, *CBE* 73-4(1922), p171 merely treat the CSCP in passing. F. Hettinger, *Die Idee der geistlichen Übungen nach dem Plane des hl. Ignatius von Loyola* (Regensburg, [2] 1908) does not even mention it. J. Pegon, "Discernement des esprits. Période modern," *DSAM* III, p1269 and A. Ambruzzi, *The Spiritual Exercises* (Bangalore, 1939) merely paraphrase the Ignatian formulation. I. Diertins, *Exercitia Spiritualia S.P. Ignatii Loyolae cum sensu eorumdem explanato* (Rome, 1836), pp314ff and W. Sierp, *Hochschule der Gottesliebe* (=*Hochschule*) (Warendorf, 1935-9), 4 volumes, II, pp469ff follow Suarez very closely.

[2] J.H.T. van den Berg, *De onderscheiding der geesten in de correspondentie van Sint Ignatius van Loyola* (Canisianum, Maastricht, 1958). The beginnings of the explicit formulation of the CSCP can be found in the rather early Helyar text (c.1535), *MI* II, 3, p450-1.

concerns not just any exercitant, but someone elite.[3] He must be someone from whom great things in God's service can be expected. He must possess the requisite natural and supernatural endowments. He must also be someone who has shown fervor and generosity during the First Week. It is likely that he has reached the Second Degree of Humility and is involved with an Election of the Second Time. He can cope with the "subtle" and "advanced" knowledge (*Ex* 9) required for discernment when tempted under the appearance of good.

THE CSCP IN *EX* 330 AND 336

Exclusively Divine Nature

Ignatius tersely describes the CSCP in *Ex* 330 as follows:

> It belongs to God alone to give consolation without previous cause, for it belongs to the Creator to enter into the soul, to leave it, and to act upon it, drawing it wholly to the love of his Divine Majesty. I say without previous cause, that is, without any previous perception or knowledge of any object from which such consolation might come to the soul through its own acts of intellect and will.

The first few words of *Ex* 330 clearly indicate the unequivocally and exclusively divine nature of this consolation. When God *alone* consoles, He consoles in precisely *this way*. Although *Ex* 329 shows that Ignatius knew of other ways in which both God and His angels could console, the exclusively divine prerogative during the CSCP is unquestionable. The CSCP, therefore, is not simply one consolation among many, but *the* God-given consolation. Only God, and He alone, can and does console in this precise way.

The CSCP is the apex of the Ignatian expectation that "our Lord and Savior should communicate Himself to the devout soul, inflaming it with His love and praise" (*Ex* 15). Ignatius had nothing less in mind for the exercitant than God working directly in his soul to unite him with his Creator and Lord (*Ex* 16, 20). We fully agree with Przywara that the CSCP dramatically expresses God's immediacy to the exercitant (II, 141ff).

---

[3] For the exercitant's necessary qualities, see: *MI* II, 2, pp73, 76-7, 87, 90-1, 111-371, 578-81. See also *Ex* 1-20. A. Haas, *Ignatius von Loyola. Geistliche Übungen* (=*GÜ*) (Freiburg, i.B., 1967), pp121-85 offers an excellent commentary on *Ex* 1-20.

The Meaning of "without previous cause"

In the last part of *Ex* 330, Ignatius himself tells us what he means by "without previous cause":

> Without any previous perception or knowledge of any object from which such consolation might come to the soul through its own acts of intellect and will.

What does this really mean, however?

K. Rahner interprets this to mean "without conceptual object" (pp133-4, n28). L. Peeters asserts that it is "impossible to admit the least created operation, be it unconscious or subconscious."[4] J. de Tonquedec reduces "without previous cause" to "without created cause."[5] J. Clémence sees an insurmountable difficulty here, because "a psychological phenomenon in no way consciously, subconsciously or unconsciously motivated . . . seems unthinkable to us, because contradictory."[6] Some of the traditional commentators remain safe by merely restating Ignatius' own words.[7]

The key to the meaning of this Ignatian phrase, however, comes from what we said above about analyzing the CSCP in its natural context of the Exercises. Ignatius expects the exercitant throughout the Exercises to apply his intellect, will, memory, imagination, senses, reflective ability, etc. actively, courageously and generously to specific meditations and contemplations.[8] In *Ex* 48, for example, we are told:

> To ask God our Lord for *what I want and desire.* The request must be made according to the subject matter. Therefore, if the contemplation is on the Resurrection, I shall ask for joy with Christ rejoicing; if it is on the passion, I shall ask for pain, tears, and suffering with Christ suffering. (Emphasis mine)

The "without previous cause," therefore, makes sense only in the context of the direct application of the exercitant's intellect, will,

---

[4] L. Peeters, p158.

[5] J. de Tonquedec, "De la certitude dans les états mystiques. A propos d'une règle ignatienne du discernement des esprits," *NRTh* 75(1953), p399.

[6] J. Clémence, "Le discernement des espirits dans les Exercices spirituels de S. Ignace de Loyola," *RAM* 28(1952), p66. J. Roothaan, p316, n2 insists that the faculties need an object to be consoled, but this object does not have to be recognized as such. P. Ferrusolae, pp420ff states that the CSCP proves that God can operate secretly. If so, why *Ex* 336?

[7] See: A. Denis, IV, p301; W. Sierp, *Hochschule*, I, pp25ff.

[8] *Ex* 3, 77, 78, 130, 206, 229, etc.

memory, imagination, senses, etc. to the particular meditation or contemplation at hand. The "without previous cause" is intimately tied to the specific "what I want and desire" requested and expected from each meditation or contemplation. This request and expectation of *specific* graces of consolation, knowledge, sorrow, joy, etc. in reference to these specific meditations and contemplations is constantly found throughout the Exercises.[9] It is one of the basic pillars of the Exercises and the key to the "without previous cause."

We maintain, therefore, that if a consolation is given in such a way that it was *not previously* asked for, that it is out of proportion to "what I want and desire," that it transcends the grace *expected* from the meditation at hand and draws the exercitant wholly into God's love, then we have the consolation without previous cause. We agree, therefore, with J. Clémence that the consolation cannot be causeless, with J. de Tonquedec that it is an uncreated cause, and with K. Rahner that it is "without conceptual object." God alone enters, renders the specific meditation at hand transparent (hence, "without conceptual object") and draws the exercitant beyond what he wants and desires, entirely into His love. We understand the Ignatian "without previous cause," therefore, to mean a consolation which totally transcends the "what I want and desire" of a particular meditation, a disproportionate consolation which God alone can cause.

L. Bakker is correct, therefore, when he emphasizes that the CSCP is simply "the consolation caused here and now by God Himself" (p98). He is also correct when he stresses "the passivity in the experience in which one experiences that something new comes about for which one was not prepared" (p98). But he incorrectly maintains that Ignatius used the "without previous cause" as an explicit criterion only because it was a known phrase acceptable to Church authorities who suspected him of heresy (p97).

The word "previous" in the context of the Exercises clearly refers to a specific meditation from which specific graces are expected. *Ex* 113, 117, 132, 156, 305 link "previous" with "contemplation," "day," or "apparition." D. Gil, moreover, has proven beyond all doubt that the word "previous" with its *temporal* meaning cannot be eliminated from the Ignatian formulation (C, 134ff, 39ff). Ignatius definitely expected the exercitant to notice changes in his experiences with the passage of time. The tides of consolation and desolation are most important. The Exercises are an

[9]*Ex* 48, 55, 65, 193, 203, 221, 76, 78, 79, 80, 229, 63, 258, 106-8, 114-6, 194, etc.

apprenticeship in observing quantitative and qualitative changes in the exercitant's experiences with respect to time.[10] The exercitant, therefore, must note any disproportion between the "what I want and desire" consolation of a specific meditation and a God-initiated consolation here and now.

Mystagogical, Christocentric, and Anthropocentric

Not every disproportion between the expected "what I want and desire" grace and the grace actually received however, fulfills the Ignatian requirements for the CSCP. The disproportionate grace received, as *Ex* 330 says, must be one in which the *Creator* enters the soul, acts upon it, leaves it, and draws it totally into His love. Not just any disproportion, not just any sort of movement in the soul, and not even any sort of entering and leaving decides the issue. Only that coming and going in which God Himself is given and in which the person is totally drawn to His love captures the essence of the CSCP.[11] The Father Himself enters the soul and initiates an action in which the exercitant begins to die to himself by taking on the sentiments of Christ. The Father then leaves the soul, but in such a way that He draws the exercitant entirely into His love.[12] The CSCP is emphatically *mystagogical*.

The exercitant's self-emptying through the Father's initiative must be understood in relation to God's Self-emptying through the Incarnation and Christ's death on the Cross, which underpins all self-emptying to be filled with love. For reasons to be specifically taken up later on, the exercitant is a Christ-directed being whose structure, rhythm and dynamics correspond to Christ's. Christ is God's Self-emptying to the point of death on the Cross. He is also the fontal fulness of Love-Given. For this reason, the Father's entry into the exercitant to initiate a self-emptying which draws him entirely to His love corresponds intrinsically to the deepest "demands" of the exercitant's being. Man fulfills himself and finds his deepest meaning when he is entirely taken up into the Father's loving Mystery.

The CSCP, therefore, sums up that Father-initiated "flight from self-love, self-will, and self-interest" (*Ex* 189) and that desire to imitate Christ "in bearing all injuries, all evils, and all poverty both physical and spiritual" (*Ex* 98). This is central to the Exercises and corresponds to the exercitant's basic dynamic for fulfillment, a

---

[10] *Ex* 24-6, 33-7, 43, 62, 76, 118, 227, 239, 252-4, 332-3, 336.
[11] K. Rahner, *Dynamic*, p143.
[12] G. Fessard, I, p261.

fulfillment arising from a gratuitous and purely disinterested love which profoundly tastes the Mystery of the Cross as its deepest calling.[13] The CSCP is emphatically *christocentric*.

Again for reasons to be dealt with specifically later, the CSCP summarizes and concentrates within itself the essential anthropocentric-christocentric rhythm basic to the Exercises. This rhythm is nothing other than the basic anthropocentric-christocentric rhythm of every man's (although most often anonymous) life in the grace of Christ explicitly amplified. The CSCP, therefore, is an experience involving the exercitant's inmost depth and freedom.[14] In contrast to movements of the soul initiated and coming "from without" (*Ex 32, 347*), the CSCP is initiated and arises *from within* the very core, the exercitant's fine point of the spirit, his deepest freedom and mystery, his sacred center. Exercising His rights as Creator, God enters the soul *from the inside*, without violence, and without being a stranger to this most intimate sphere. He takes full possession of the exercitant by opening up his spiritual core in such a way that its deepest center comes expressly and thematically into play.[15] Not only is the exercitant led into the Mystery of God, but he is also led into his own deepest mystery as man. He finds therein "an interior understanding and savoring" (*Ex 2*) of the meaning of his anthropocentric-christocentric structure: surrender to loving Mystery as the most intimate and most interior fulfillment of his being. The CSCP is emphatically *anthropocentric*.

The CSCP as a non-conceptual Experience of God

According to good Thomistic epistemology, whenever a person knows anything by means of a *species*, he also has a *concomitant* self-knowledge.[16] The human spirit imperfectly knows itself and is imperfectly present to itself, because the *species* is the *sine qua non* for this intelligent, intelligible, non-conceptual self-presence containing positive content. The "other" remains the necessary condition for spirit's "return to self" in radical self-awareness. Moreover, as K. Rahner says:

> There is at least one awareness which is not consciousness of an *object*: the concomitant self-awareness in every act of the mind when it is

[13] J. Clémence, p67.
[14] L. Bakker, p21, n18.
[15] K. Rahner, *Dynamic*, pp153ff; A. Brunner, "Die Erkenntnis des Willen Gottes nach dem geistlichen Übungen des hl. Ignatius," *GuL* 30(1957), p209.
[16] P. Scheuer, *An Interior Metaphysics*. Ed. and trans. by D. Shine, (Weston College Press: Weston, Mass., 1966), esp. "Human Consciousness," pp123-40.

directed to any object. This self-awareness is something different in kind, too, from cognition wherein one's own "I" can be conceptually made the focus of a mental act, that is, when I reflect upon the first kind of awareness and express it in concepts and propositions. (p134, n28)

We agree with K. Rahner that there is at least one awareness which is not awareness of an object. Full consciousness cannot be reduced to conceptual consciousness. This non-conceptual awareness takes place in the intuitive function of consciousness which accompanies every act of the human spirit, giving it a non-conceptual, imperfectly intuitive, intelligent and intelligible consciousness of itself.

For this reason, P. Scheuer describes human knowledge and love as *identity with opposition*, because in knowing or loving, one necessarily and simultaneously knows or loves oneself and the other [17] In this deepest identity of spirit present to itself, however, there is another opposition which presents itself as the very ground for spirit's knowledge and love of self, or radical presence to itself, namely, God. In the most fundamental experience of self, when the person experiences his most radical active self-identity, he also mysteriously experiences himself as somehow greater or more than himself. Somehow more than himself, he becomes most himself when he surrenders to the greater in himself which opposes as it unites.[18] This surplus or opposition which unites is God as the activation and drawing force of the person's subjective transcendence.

It is theologically sound, as K. Rahner has shown (pp142ff), that the human spirit's natural dynamism as intellect and will has been supernaturally elevated by grace. The direction and thrust of this supernaturally elevated transcendence, therefore, is towards God as the "Whither" of this transcendence. This supernatural formal object is always present as the horizon of any explicit consciousness, although what is natural and what is graced cannot be separated out and made explicit through reflection.

This implicit, non-conceptual horizon whose "Whither" is God is always concomitantly and *indirectly* known whenever anything is directly and conceptually grasped. Contained in every conscious act, therefore, is at least a vague awareness of God as the Whither of transcendental subjectivity. When the human spirit knows anything,

[17] *Ibid.*, p79, n1.
[18] *Ibid.*, pp162-72.

it concomitantly "returns to itself" in active self-identity and therein grasps God as the pure and unlimited term of its dynamism. The fundamental experience of spirit in knowing the other is a simple presence to itself of an intrinsically intelligible subject which also contains a non-conceptual, concomitant "sense" of God.

Because this horizon usually remains horizon, it is not one object among the many objects of our consciousness. Overlooked, denied or often confused with the unconscious, this supernaturally elevated horizon does not ordinarily emerge into express, thematic consciousness. Implicit, however, to the experience of self always concomitantly present to all conceptual knowing is a simple grasp of God as the Whither of transcendental subjectivity and as the Ground of the active self-identity of one's own spirit.

Because man's transcendence is supernaturally elevated and has God as the pure and unlimited term of its dynamism, a term which also gives itself, man's "supernatural existential" situation is such that:

> Antecedently to justification by grace, received sacramentally or extra-sacramentally, man is already subject to the universal will of God, he *is* already redeemed and absolutely obliged to tend to his supernatural end.[19]

This objective, metaphysical alteration of man shows up in his conscious horizon, as we have seen above.

Although we intend to leave the details to another chapter, we must stress here another objective, metaphysical modification of man which also shows up in his conscious horizon. Because the Word became flesh, lived, died and rose, He became in his very humanity what He had always been in His divinity, the very heart of the universe, the innermost center of creation. We, therefore, experience ourselves and our world differently than if God had not become man to live, die and rise.[20] Both the supernatural existential and this "christic" existential are objective, metaphysical modifications of man which have affected his consciousness. The CSCP cannot be properly understood unless these two existentials are understood.

---

[19] K. Rahner, "Existential, Supernatural," *TD*, p161.
[20] K. Rahner, "Hidden Victory," *TI* 7, pp151-8; "Thoughts on the Theology of Christmas," *TI* 3, p33.

CSCP, Consolation With Previous Cause (=CCCP)
and a Shift of Horizon

The supernaturally elevated and Christ-affected horizon of consciousness supports conceptual consciousness, but does not ordinarily move into the focal point of consciousness. But what if the conceptual object which in the normal act of consciousness is the required *sine qua non* for consciousness of this supernaturally and Christ-affected transcendence becomes more transparent, almost disappears, so that the pure christic movement of supernatural transcendence with God as its Whither becomes more directly present and dominates the focal point of consciousness? In much the same way, a poet or a metaphysician can have a quasi-intuitive glance at his own spiritual dynamism.[21] If this occurs, we have non-conceptual consolation, the CSCP. We basically agree, therefore, with K. Rahner that the CSCP is an experience in which the exercitant becomes more directly aware of his supernaturally elevated transcendence, and nothing else (pp145ff).

Let us state this another way by once again emphasizing the context of the CSCP, the Exercises. Let us consider an exercitant directing his intellect, will, imagination, memory and emotions to the particular meditation at hand. Let us assume that he is receiving the "what I want and desire" consolation of that meditation, the consolation *with* previous cause (=CCCP). Gradually the mystery before him becomes more and more transparent, although this does not necessarily mean that all conceptual awareness must vanish. The exercitant in his inmost center feels himself totally drawn beyond anything conceptual or individual into God's love. He becomes, as it were, pure openness and receptivity. He experiences everything he is as drawn to and united with God's love.

The exercitant now has an inexpressible, non-conceptual experience of his Christ-affected and supernaturally elevated transcendence. What had been experienced indirectly and at the "fringe" of his consciousness, has now moved into more direct awareness. There is a qualitative shift in the exercitant's horizon. What was previously central to his consciousness, becomes almost transparent; what was previously marginal, moves into center stage. Just as a person looking at a psychological illustration of Figure/Ground experiences a changing Figure/Ground before his eyes, we maintain that during the CSCP, what was Figure (the conceptual mystery, CCCP, etc.) becomes Ground or horizon, and what was Ground or horizon

---

[21]P. Scheuer, p127.

(Christ-affected, supernatural transcendence) becomes Figure and directly dominates consciousness, but in a quasi-intuitive way.[22]

The CSCP begins, therefore, as the CCCP, or the specific grace requested during a particular meditation. The CCCP, however, diminishes in importance so that the exercitant's Christ-affected, supernaturally elevated subjective transcendence gradually, yet always non-conceptually, moves into the focal point of consciousness and draws the exercitant wholly into God's love. The CCCP, however, is not necessarily eliminated. Although the CSCP can grow in depth, intensity and purity, it always arises from and is dialectically linked with the CCCP. The CCCP remains the *sine qua non* and a basic dialectical moment of the CSCP.

The CSCP, the non-conceptual experience of Christ-affected and Whither-directed subjective transcendence, arises in and through the meditations on the life of Christ. Arising in and through these meditations, the CSCP reaches the goal "demanded" of supernaturally elevated transcendence: to be taken up and to surrender to the Father's loving Mystery. As we shall see later on, Christ is the supreme case of the success of created self-transcendence to give itself totally to the loving Mystery which calls it out of and beyond itself. Because our subjective transcendence has been supernaturally elevated and also touched by the historical Christ, the basic dynamism of our transcendence corresponds to Christ's. When this Christ-affected, supernaturally elevated transcendence completes itself by being entirely drawn into the Father's Mystery, just as Christ himself was, the exercitant experiences CSCP. The CSCP sums up, concentrates and then fulfills the mystagogical movement of the CCCP, just as Christ himself is the fulfillment of all created transcendence's dynamism to surrender itself totally to the loving Mystery which haunts it.

The CSCP — a Consolation without Christ?

How can an interpretation of the CSCP as a non-conceptual awareness of transcendence be reconciled with Ignatius' strongly Christ-centered mysticism, asks R. González de Mendoza (pp233ff)? If the CSCP is non-conceptual, does that not necessitate putting aside the Gospels, which are clearly conceptual, and eventually Jesus Christ himself, asks D. Gil (R,138ff)? Are the Gospels and Christ

---

[22] D. Gil, C, p81 argues that if the CSCP were non-conceptual, it would be rather easy to distinguish it from the consolations in "the time that follow" the CSCP. A phenomenology of human consciousness indicates, however, that the boundaries between figure and ground are not that distinct at times.

merely obstacles which must pass away if a truly non-conceptual consolation is to arise?

D. Gil attempts to save the Christ-related quality of the CSCP by emphasizing that this non-conceptual consolation happened first and foremost to Christ in his obscurity and abandonment on the Cross. On the other hand, Gil stresses Suarez's example of the pagan who suddenly and without reasoning comes to the idea of a Creator as the best case of CSCP. For Gil, non-conceptual consolation best befits the anonymous, but not the professing, Christian.

We maintain, however, that the CSCP as a non-conceptual consolation roots itself directly in the Gospels and Jesus Christ for two reasons we have already partially indicated. First of all, the CSCP remains forever linked to the Gospels and Jesus Christ because the CSCP arises in and through the meditations on the life of Jesus Christ. The Christ-centered context of the CSCP is, therefore, obvious.

The second reason flows from the Christ-affected, supernaturally elevated structure of human consciousness itself. What Christ was and is by nature, man is by grace: created self-transcendence, activated and called forth by Mystery to surrender itself. What Christ did by nature, man can do through the grace of Christ. The CSCP, therefore, is solidly linked with the Gospels and Jesus Christ, because Christ's success in surrendering to the Father's loving Mystery grounds the exercitant's surrender.

Because man's transcendence is supernaturally elevated, God is the Whither of, the Truth of and the Love-Given to this transcendence. Because Christ is the Way to this Whither, Truth incarnate and the bearer and giver of Love-Given, the CSCP is radically Christ-centered. If Christ himself is to be grasped in all his depths, he must lead the exercitant into the Father's Mystery, the depths of his own Truth as Son, and into the Holy Spirit's Love.

During the meditations on the life of Christ, therefore, Christ and the specific meditation at hand should become transparent, but not disappear. They become transparent, not because the CSCP mirrors the desolation of Christ on the Cross, but because they must become transparent if the Father's Mystery, the Son's Truth and the Holy Spirit's Love are to dominate the exercitant's awareness.

Through Christ's transparency,[23] the CCCP becomes CSCP. This CSCP, mediated by Christ's transparency, is an experience which

---

[23] Ignatius' Spanish Autograph rendition of the Exercises indicates that it belongs to *Christ* ("solo es de Dios *nuestro Señor*") (emphasis mine) to bring the exercitant wholly into the *Father's* ("divina majestad") love.

leads the exercitant to the Father, to the depths of Christ's Sonship and to the Holy Spirit. The most deeply christocentric moment of the Exercises occurs when there is a non-conceptual transformation of Christ, a gradual transparency of his person, his words, his actions and his consolation which plunges the exercitant into the Father's Mystery, Truth and Gift of Love. The Exercises most radical christocentric moment occurs when their *trinitarian* dimension appears.

The CSCP as the First Principle of Ignatian Supernatural Logic

Ignatius says in *Ex* 336 that: "When consolation is without preceding cause, . . . there is no deception in it, since it proceeds only from God our Lord." Because of the exclusively divine nature of the CSCP, therefore, "there is no deception in it." Because this experience comes from God and from Him alone, it is the touchstone experience, the consolation *par excellence* against which all other experiences can be measured. Because the CSCP is the pure openness of subjective transcendence which draws the exercitant wholly into God's love, it contains *within itself* the evidence of its divine origin. As K. Rahner says, "this consolation shows itself to be divine in origin itself" (p153). "It has to do with God himself, not with a concept of him" (p149).

Because the CSCP has to do with God alone and draws the person entirely into God's love, it "possesses an irreducibly self-evident self-sufficient character."[24] The CSCP, therefore, provides the exercitant with a basic, irrefutable evidence offered in the very experience of the CSCP itself. This experience, as pure divine consolation, "lays hold of the soul completely, opens the soul in a way in which it is clearly not generally open."[25] As K. Rahner says further, we are "dealing with an experience in which the very centre of the spiritual person as such comes into action and expressly so, experienced as such" (p154).

The CSCP, therefore, cannot in itself be measured or tested, but provides in itself the basic measure against which all other consolations are to be measured. We agree with K. Rahner that the CSCP is a supernatural first principle which plays the same role in the area of supernatural logic and decision as the first principles of logic and metaphysics play for the other sciences (p130, 142).

---

[24] K. Rahner, *Dynamic*, p143.
[25] *Ibid.*, p153.

If Ignatius says in *Ex* 336 that "there is no deception in it," it seems clear that Ignatius considered the CSCP at least objectively certain. Ignatius, moreover, considered the CSCP to be also subjectively certain, and this in a reflexive way, because he expressly says:

> The spiritual person to whom God gives such consolation ought still to consider it with great vigilance and attention. *He should carefully distinguish the exact time of such consolation from the time that follows it,* during which time the soul continues in fervor and feels the divine favor and the after effects of the consolation which has passed. (*Ex* 336) (Emphasis mine)

Ignatius definitely states that the exercitant can distinguish the CSCP from the human echoes it will produce in the exercitant as time progresses. Ignatius considered the CSCP an objectively as well as a subjectively certain criterion.[26]

Suarez has argued, however, that the evidence resulting from the CSCP is at best a moral certitude, a certitude which is "almost evident."[27] Gil seems to uphold the objective certainty of the CSCP, but sides with Suarez. Because the CSCP and the time after are so difficult to distinguish in practice, the best one can hope for, says Gil, is moral certitude (R,132ff, C,267ff).

We tend to agree with Gil. We saw above that the CSCP always maintains itself in a dialectical relationship with the specific "what I want and desire" consolation of a specific meditation. Furthermore, as L. Bakker has shown, the CSCP always contains within itself "the time that follows it" as a dialectical moment of its existence (p118). The CSCP, therefore, is very difficult to distinguish at times from the CCCP and the "time after" consolations.

A glance at Ignatius' *Spiritual Journal* makes this clear. Ignatius' Election regarding the question of poverty in the Society of Jesus took some 40 intensive days of prayer to complete. During this time, although Ignatius experienced profound christocentric and trinitarian mystical favors, he was also plagued with doubts, hesitations, false stops and starts. It is also unclear whether Ignatius finally decided according to the First, Second or Third Times of Election or a combination of all three.[28]

---

[26] L. Gonzalez Hernandez, *El primer tiempo de de elección según San Ignacio* (Madrid, 1956).

[27] F. Suarez, pp501ff.

[28] See: *The Spiritual Journal of Saint Ignatius* (=*SJ*, followed by date), trans. with an introduction by W.J. Young, *WL* 87(1958), pp195-267. W. Young (p238, n49) maintains that Ignatius concluded his Election on poverty with methods of the Third Time. This is highly doubtful.

L. Bakker has shown, moreover, that Ignatius' decision to go to work in the Holy Land was made with all the certainty of the First Time Election. This decision, however, had to be modified. For Bakker, Ignatius' warning about "the time that follows" the CSCP in *Ex* 336 resulted from a certainty which had proven false (pp99ff, 142ff).

If the highly experienced Ignatius, in the midst of so many mystical favors, and after devoting almost all of his time and energies to the question of poverty in the Society of Jesus, had such a difficult time making his decision, and, if at least in one case of extraordinary certainty he had discovered that he was mistaken, what can be said about the average exercitant who must decide according to the degree of purity of the CSCP he has received?

We maintain, therefore, that the CSCP offers the exercitant a supernatural first principle for the application of a supernatural logic to find God's Will. This first principle, moreover, is *objectively* certain, because this consolation flows from God alone. Because the CSCP, however, is rarely given in an absolutely pure state and always maintains itself in a dialectical relationship with the CCCP and the time-after consolations, it renders only a *greater or lesser subjective* evidence, depending upon the exercitant's maturity, the depth and quality of the CSCP, and the exercitant's own gifts for discernment.

We agree, nevertheless, that the CSCP is the basic self-evident principle in Ignatius' method of supernatural logic. It is also the fundamental principle and dynamic according to which every man decides, whether or not he explicitly notices it. To some extent, every person thinks logically and uses the first principles of logic. In the same way, every person to some extent instinctively uses the first principles of supernatural logic for many of the decisions of his life.

Although self-evident principles are intrinsically free of error, they present subjective difficulties, for extrinsic reasons. The first principles of metaphysics and logic provide psychological certitude to few of their users. Some philosophers deny them altogether, although the dynamic through which they deny them is already their implicit affirmation.

The same seems true in the even more difficult area of supernatural logic. Because the first principles of metaphysics and logic are lived, incarnate principles, they render difficulties in their application. So, too, with the CSCP as the first principle of supernatural logic. The CSCP is a lived, incarnate first principle. It belongs to the basic dynamism of consciousness, just as the first principles of metaphysics and logic do. These incarnate first principles belong to the very structure and dynamism of human consciousness itself. They are this dynamism.

We maintain, therefore, that the CSCP is hardly a foreign element dragged into human consciousness, nor a psychological burp. It belongs in a special way to the very roots of the transcendental dynamism of human consciousness.[29] Because first principles belong to the horizon of consciousness and are always pre-conceptual, they can never appear in explicit consciousness in pure form. Explicit consciousness of first principles can at times be very intense, but it always remains a non-conceptual, intuitive type of awareness. For this reason, the CSCP possesses all of the clarity and darkness[30] of any first principle, be it mystical or not: clarity, because it belongs to the very horizon of consciousness; darkness, because non-conceptual awareness is often overlooked by persons most at home with conceptual thinking.

THE CSCP IN OTHER IGNATIAN WRITINGS?

Our analysis of the CSCP thus far has centered upon *Ex* 330 and 336, because these are the only two places in the entire Ignatian corpus which use the explicit words, "consolation without previous cause." Are there other places in the Ignatian corpus, however, which describe the CSCP at least implicitly and which prove helpful in an analysis of *Ex* 330 and 336?

Ignatius' Letter to Sr. Teresa Rejadell
In Ignatius' famous letter to Sr. Teresa Rejadell, we read:

> For a clearer understanding of this fear and its origins I will call your attention to two lessons which our Lord usually gives or permits. The one of them He gives, the other He permits. The first is an interior consolation which casts out all uneasiness and draws one to a complete love of our Lord. In this consolation He enlightens some, and to others He reveals many secrets as a preparation for later visits. In a word, when this divine consolation is present all trials are pleasant and all weariness rest ... This consolation points out and opens up the way we are to follow and points out the way we are to avoid. It does not remain with us always, but it will always accompany us on the way at the times that God designates. All this is for our progress ...

---

[29] This is basically the position of K. Rahner's *Dynamic*.
[30] H. Rahner, "La Storta," pp273ff.

For it frequently happens that our Lord moves and urges the soul to this or that activity. He begins by enlightening the soul; that is to say, by speaking interiorly to it without the din of words, lifting it up wholly to His divine love and ourselves to His meaning (*a su sentido*) without any possibility of resistance on our part, even should we wish to resist. This thought of His (*el sentido suyo*) which we take is of necessity in conformity with the commandments, the precepts of the Church, and obedience to our superiors ... But we can frequently be deceived, however, because after such consolation or inspiration, when the soul is still abiding in its joy, the enemy tries under the impetus of this joy to make us innocently add to what we have received from God our Lord ...

At other times he makes us lessen the import of the message (*la lección*) we have received and confronts us with obstacles and difficulties, so as to prevent us from carrying out completely what had been made known to us. Right here there is more need of attention than anywhere else. We may often have to control the desire we feel and speak less of the things of God our Lord; at other times we may speak more than the satisfaction or movement we feel prompts us to ... When the enemy thus tries to magnify or diminish the communication received, we must proceed for the purpose of helping others, like a man who is crossing a ford ... Even then there could be matters that could better be felt than put into words, let alone written down in a letter.[31]

A careful reading of Ignatius' letter discloses many of the elements of the CSCP already described in *Ex* 330 and 336. Ignatius' letter definitely stresses a consolation ("interior consolation," "this consolation," "this divine consolation," "such consolation") which is exclusively divine, a consolation which God alone can give ("our Lord gives," "He enlightens," "He reveals," "divine consolation," "God designates," "our Lord moves and urges," "He begins," "from God our Lord"). This divine consolation, moreover, serves as a touchstone experience, a first principle in supernatural logic, for "this consolation points out and opens the way we are to follow and points out the way we are to avoid." This deeply interior experience ("interior consolation," "speaking interiorly") contains within itself both subjective and objective certitude, for this exclusively divine consolation acts "without any possibility of resistance on our part, even though we should wish to resist."

---

[31] *Letters of St. Ignatius of Loyola* (=*Letters*), trans. by W.J. Young, (Chicago, 1959), pp21-3.

Ex 330 speaks of the Creator entering, leaving, acting and drawing the person wholly to His love. From what we have already said, it is clear that the letter also speaks of the Creator entering. The letter indicates, too, that God may leave, for this consolation "does not always remain with us." The letter describes God's acting "by enlightening . . . by speaking interiorly . . . by lifting it up." God also "moves and urges the soul." His consolation, moreover, "draws one to a complete love of our Lord . . . lifting it up wholly to His divine love."

From *Ex* 336, we noted that Ignatius cautions the exercitant about the consolations which follow the CSCP. The consolations during "the time that follows" the CSCP are not exclusively divine; they may be human echoes of the CSCP, or simply CCCP, given by both the good and the bad angel. Ignatius' letter takes up this same teaching, "because after such consolation or inspirations . . . the enemy tries under the impetus of this joy to make us innocently add . . . [or to] lessen the import; . . . the enemy tries to magnify or diminish the communication received." Just as *Ex* 336 counsels the exercitant to examine everything "very carefully," the letter stresses that "right here there is more need of attention than anywhere else." Both the letter and *Ex* 336 stress the "time that follows" as a dialectical moment of the CSCP.

K. Rahner finds in Ignatius' letter to Sr. Rejadell a confirmation of his interpretation of the CSCP as a consolation without conceptual object which draws the person wholly into God's love. He notes that the letter's wordless experience ("without the din of words") means "without concepts," "without particular objects of thought" (p153).

Both D. Gil (C, 132ff) and L. Bakker (pp51ff), however, strongly disagree with K. Rahner. They stress against K. Rahner that the letter does not describe a non-conceptual consolation, because the letter expressly says that God communicates *something* which the exercitant must not add to nor subtract from. A consolation in which something is communicated cannot be only a consolation of the pure, non-conceptual experience of God.

There can be no doubt from Ignatius' letter, however, that when the person is totally drawn into God's love that something is communicated. It clearly states that God moves "to *this* or *that* activity . . . lifting ourselves to *His meaning*" (emphasis mine). Moreover, "this thought of His" must be "in conformity with the commandments, the precepts of the Church, and obedience to our superiors." God communicates a "message" to which or from which the devil encourages the exercitant to add or subtract ("When the enemy thus tries to magnify or diminish the communication received"). And this is also true of the CSCP, as described in *Ex* 336, for "often in this latter period the soul makes various *plans* and *resolutions* which are not *inspired directly* by God our Lord" (emphasis mine).

We must be extremely cautious here. First of all, the Rejadell letter clearly describes not one experience, but many, or at least one experience with many facets, not all of which have to be present at any given time. Ignatius says that "this consolation enlightens *some*, and to *others* He reveals many secrets" (emphasis mine). We are inclined, therefore, to see in Ignatius' letter a description of *various kinds* of CSCP.

Secondly, as F. Marxer notes (p148), although the "activity" (*operación*) to which God moves the person could possibly be a specific apostolic activity, it could also be a remarkably strong experience of being drawn into God's love. This *operación* could just as easily mean internal, mystical experience as external, apostolic activity.

Thirdly, does "His meaning" (*a su sentido*), "this Thought of His" (*el sentido suyo*), "the message" (*la lección*) and "the communication" (*sentido*) necessarily imply *conceptual* or *verbal* meaning, thought, message and communication? Although K. Rahner seems to overlook the importance of conceptual thoughts in Ignatian discernment,[32] D. Gil and L. Bakker seem too eager to reduce the Ignatian *sentido* to conceptual thoughts and ideas. F. Marxer, correctly, we believe, stresses the multi-faceted meanings of the Ignatian *sentir, sentido, sentimiento* (pp119ff). Although *sentido* can mean rational, conceptual, explicit knowledge, it seldom does so. For Ignatius, *sentido* almost always means felt-knowledge, personal knowledge, connatural knowledge, a knowledge flowing from love and the heart, a non-conceptual, non-verbal, mystical knowledge often described as a "tasting" or a "savoring." Ignatius himself admits in the letter that "there could be matters that could be better felt than put into words."

Fourthly, although the sentence, "This thought of His (*el sentido suyo*) which we take is of necessity in conformity with the commandments, the precepts of the Church, and obedience to our superiors," seems to mean primarily (but not exclusively) a verbal,

---

[32]*Ex* 32-7, 78, 315, 317-8, 322, 322-4, 336 definitely deal with "thoughts" and reasoning.

conceptual, explicit communication, the phrases, "lifting it up wholly to His divine love and ourselves to His meaning (*a su sentido*) and "to magnify or diminish the communication (*sentido*) received," seem to mean primarily the non-conceptual, felt-knowledge resulting from love.

To illustrate what we mean, consider a happily married couple. From time to time, they will experience explicitly and directly the total openness in love which they have for each other. This is analogous to the CSCP as the pure openness and receptivity to God. At other times, however, one of the spouses will formally communicate, but not formally say, what she or he expects from this love. A husband returning home from work, after a few moments with his wife, may *instinctively* know, without her having said so, that she wants to go out that evening. This is analogous to the CSCP which formally communicates God's *sentido* in a non-verbal, connatural way. There will be times, however, when the wife simply says: "Take me out to dinner this evening." This is analogous to the CSCP which formally communicates God's *sentido* expressly, conceptually and verbally.

Ignatius' letter brings out this knowledge midway between the pure, transcendental experience of God and explicit, verbal, conceptual knowledge in still another way. Ignatius warns Sr. Rejadell against the devil's weapons of pride and false humility. For Ignatius, pride is dangerous because "the enemy tries to magnify . . . the communication received." False humility is dangerous because "in this way he [devil] tries to prevent him [person] from speaking of any of the blessings he has received."

Ignatius, therefore, expects the person who receives God's favors to speak about these gifts without pride to produce "fruit in others" and "for the purpose of helping others." It is especially in speaking of these gifts to others than one must be careful. As he says:

> When the enemy thus tries to magnify or diminish the communication received, we must proceed for the purpose of helping others, like a man who is crossing a ford. If I find a good footing — that is, some way or hope of profiting the neighbor — I will pass right on. But if the ford is muddied or disturbed and there is danger that scandal may be taken from what I say, I will rein in and seek an occasion more favorable to what I have to say.[33]

---

[33]*Letters*, p23.

We maintain, however, that Ignatius does not have only verbal inspiration in mind. Just as a young man in love knows much more about the woman than what she explicitly tells him, and feels compelled to talk about his love in a way that makes him more than a recording of her express words, Ignatius, too, expects the person who has received God's communication of love and felt-knowledge to speak of and from this communication transcending words. What God formally communicates through His Self-communication in love is much deeper than what He expressly communicates in words from time to time.

We see in Ignatius' letter, therefore, a description of several kinds of CSCP. The CSCP can be a pure, transcendental experience of God in utter receptivity and openness, and nothing more. But the CSCP may also be a pure openness to God which contains as a moment of its realization a specific, non-conceptual, felt-knowledge guaranteed by God Himself. Or, the CSCP may also support within its pure openness to God a specific, conceptual, verbal knowledge guaranteed by God Himself. As this *God-guaranteed* specification and conceptualization becomes more dominant and clear, the CSCP approaches what Ignatius calls the First Time Election. As the CSCP approaches the First Time Election, therefore, God guarantees the outcome of the explicit, conceptual knowledge.

As the CSCP approaches the "time that follows," however, it loses its God-guaranteed specification and explicitness. Human echoes, the good spirit or the evil spirit may be responsible for the non-conceptual, felt-knowledge or the explicit conceptual knowledge accompanying the exercitant's pure openness to God, as *Ex* 336 and Ignatius' letter note.

We maintain, therefore that the CSCP as the pure openness and receptivity to God grounds every kind of CSCP. This pure openness, however, is always dialectically related to an upward (God-alone) and downward (human, good spirit, evil spirit) specification and conceptualization. The CSCP as the pure openness and receptivity to God, the primordial "sense" of God, and nothing else, always tends to complete itself upwards or downwards.

The Spiritual Journal

This matter becomes somewhat clearer when we examine the "interior words" (*loqüela interna*) described in Ignatius' *Spiritual Journal*:

> Tears before Mass ... and continued, together with the interior 'loqüela' during the Mass. It seems to me that it was given miraculously

> ... I sometimes found the external 'loqüela' ... and the interior less ... Those of today seemed to be much, much different from those of former days, as they came more slowly, more interiorly, gently without noise or notable movements, coming apparently from within without my knowing how to explain them. In the interior and exterior 'loqüela' everything moved me to divine love and to the gifts of the 'loqüela' divinely bestowed, with so much interior harmony in the interior 'loqüela' that I cannot explain it. (*SJ*, May 11)

> I thought that I took too much delight in the tone of the 'loqüela', attending to the sound, without paying so much attention to the meaning of the words and of the 'loqüela.' (*SJ*, May 22)

Let us immediately note that these rather mysterious Ignatian *loqüela* are of varying quality and exhibit different characteristics. Some are external; some are internal. Some come more quickly, others more slowly, and still others more gently and "without noise." They bring with them a certain interior relish and sweetness. Some are accompanied by tones (*tono*), words (*palabras*) and may have a meaning (*sinificación*).

Moreover, *Ex* 32-33 suggests that for Ignatius the more an experience arises "solely from my own liberty and will," the more interior it is. Internal experiences whose origins are other than this "will and liberty" arise "from without." It would seem, therefore, that the Ignatian interior *loqüela* arise from the soul's fine point, whereas the exterior *loqüela* arise from a dimension of the person not as profound as his fine point.

We mentioned above that the CSCP begins at the exercitant's deepest core and center, that point of the human spirit prior to its division into intellect and will. The interior *loqüela* seem to be the CSCP, or that moment thereof, as the CSCP makes its way through the fine point of the soul and begins to affect the intellect as intellect and the will as will, but still in a non-conceptual way. The CSCP as it affects the intellect and will is not as concentrated as it was at the core, but still not diffuse enough to be conceptual. It is at this juncture of intellect and will that connatural, felt-knowledge in the Thomistic sense occurs.[34] Although Ignatius notes that during an experience of either interior or exterior *loqüela*, "everything moved me to divine love," he prefers the interior *loqüela*. These come "more slowly, more interiorly, gently without noise ... with so much interior harmony."

---

[34]*STh* II-II, q45, a2; q24, a11; q162, a3, ad1; q1, a4, ad3.

The Rejadell letter says that God speaks interiorly to the soul "without the din of words" (*sin ruido alguna de voces*). These brusque (*ruido*) *voces*, however, seem to be similar to the exterior *loqüela* and *palabras* described in the *Spiritual Journal*. The *voces*, the external *loqüela*, the tone, and the words found with the *loqüela* are the "exteriorized-interiority" of the more internal *loqüela*. Perhaps the internal *loqüela* are the *meaning* (*sinificación*) of the external *loqüela* which Ignatius overlooked because of the tone.

Although these *loqüela* seem to arise before the CSCP (the movement to divine love comes *after*), it seems better to say that they are the echoes *first* noticed, before one becomes explicitly aware of a movement to divine love. One first notices the echoes and is led to the source.

The exterior *loqüela*, moreover, appear to be the CSCP as the human faculties by their very nature respond to it, or as the angelic-initiated echoes in the "time that follows" the CSCP. They are the human or angelic-initiated reverberations, or *redundantia*, as St. Thomas says,[35] to this profound, God-initiated consolation. These exterior *loqüela* must be carefully distinguished from the CSCP, as well as from the interior *loqüela*.

We maintain, therefore, that the interior *loqüela* can be the God-guaranteed, non-conceptual, intuitive felt-knowledge we discussed above. God communicates Himself and His *sentido*. If these become more lucid and conceptual, they approach divine, verbal inspiration and the First Time Election. The exterior *loqüela*, however, are the human or angelic-initiated, subjective echoes of the CSCP found in "the time that follows" the exclusively God-initiated consolation.

The *Spiritual Journal* (Mar. 13 - Apr. 4, 1544) also recounts Ignatius' experience of loving reverence, respect and humility. This experience was so profound that "a higher value was placed on this grace and knowledge for the spiritual advantage of my soul, than on all those that went before" (*SJ*, Mar. 14). As we saw in the first chapter, R. González de Mendoza identifies this experience with the CSCP. Is this so?

Although the wording of *Ex* 330 and 336 does not explicitly support the identification of the CSCP with loving reverence, respect and humility, there does, however, seem to be an implicit connection. This experience of loving reverence, respect and humility seems to come from God alone, as does the CSCP. The pronouncing of the names, the calling upon or the experiencing of God, the Trinity,

[35]St. Thomas Aquinas, *De Veritate*, q10, a11, ad3; q13, a3, ad3; q26, a10; III *Sent*, d23, q1, a2, ad3.

Christ, or any of the Divine Persons may initiate the experience (*SJ*, Mar. 13, 16, 17, 22, 27).

Although loving reverence, respect and humility may terminate in something other than God (*SJ*, Mar. 16: the altar, things connected with Mass; Mar. 30: creatures; *Ex* 3: the saints), *Ex* 38-9 stress that the "Creator and Lord" grounds this experience. Only the disproportion existing between the Creator and the creature can provide the basis for such an experience. Because he found God in all things (*Ex* 230-7), Ignatius experienced loving reverence, respect and humility in the face of all creation (*Ex* 58). The person experiences humility because of God alone, and nothing else (*Ex* 125, 165-8, 258).

Ignatius also realized that this experience was not at his disposal (*SJ*, Mar. 15, 21, 31, Apr. 4). Perhaps this is similar to God's coming and going in the CSCP. The experience of *loving* reverence, respect and humility seems analogous to being drawn entirely into God's love in the CSCP.

Although a strong case can be made that the CSCP as the pure experience of supernaturally elevated transcendence implicitly underpins all mystical experience, the *Spiritual Journal* describes some experiences which seem to contain explicit components of the CSCP. Perhaps all of the "on high" experiences are a form of CSCP (*SJ*, Feb. 15, etc). Ignatius says: "I seemed thus to understand that there was nothing more to learn from the Most Holy Trinity in this matter" (*SJ*, Feb. 21); "I felt or rather saw beyond my natural strength the Most Holy Trinity and Jesus, presenting me, or placing me, or simply being the means of union in the midst of the Most Holy Trinity" (*SJ*, Feb. 27). Could this possibly be an intellectual form of the CSCP? Ignatius also says: ". . . perceiving in one luminous clarity a single Essence, I was drawn entirely to Its [Trinity's] love . . . I felt the same, directed to Jesus, as though finding myself in His shadow . . . I thought I was more closely joined to their Divine Majesty" (*SJ*, Mar. 3); "I was overcome with . . . most intense love for the Most Holy Trinity . . . I felt very great touches and intense devotion to the Most Holy Trinity . . . all ending in the love of the Most Holy Trinity" (*SJ*, Mar. 4); "I felt the consolation and visions of the Divine Persons and mediators, I had every firmness and confirmation of the matter" (*SJ*, Mar. 12). The resemblance to the CSCP seems evident. Perhaps any experience which terminates *directly* and explicitly in the Divine Persons is a form of CSCP.

EX 316

Ex 316 describes spiritual consolation as follows:

> I call it consolation when the soul is aroused by an interior movement which causes it to be inflamed with love of its Creator and Lord, and consequently can love no created thing on the face of the earth for its own sake, but only in the creator of all things. It is likewise consolation when one sheds tears inspired by love of the Lord, whether it be sorrow for sins or because of the Passion of Christ our Lord, or for any other reason that is directly connected to His service and praise. Finally, I call consolation any increase of faith, hope and charity and any interior joy that calls and attracts to heavenly things, and to the salvation of one's soul, inspiring it with peace and quiet in Christ our Lord.

J. Ayestaran considers this a phenomenological description of the CSCP during the time following its infusion into the soul.[36] The CSCP, we maintain, does arise "by an interior movement which causes it [the soul] to be inflamed with love of its Creator and Lord." As we saw above, the CSCP does terminate directly in God. The rest of *Ex* 316, however, seems to describe accurately the "what I want and desire" consolations of each specific meditation. This section describes the CCCP and possibly the consolations of "the time that follows" the CSCP.

MISCELLANEOUS QUESTIONS ABOUT THE CSCP

The Frequency of the CSCP

In view of what we have already seen, it is not surprising that some commentators consider the CSCP as a very rare experience, essentially mystical, and given only to those most advanced in the spiritual life.[37] On the other hand, we agree with those commentators who stress the remarkable nature of the CSCP, but who see it as an experience belonging to the normal perspective of the spiritual life. The CSCP admits of various degrees of purity and intensity, but

---

[36] J. Ayestaran, *La experiencia de la divina consolación. Un estudio filosófico-teológico de las Anotaciones sobre los Ejercicios de los Hermanos Pedro y Francisco Ortiz* (Rome: Dissert. ad Lauream, 1964), pp103ff, 300ff.

[37] C. Judde, *Retraite spirituelle, appelée grande retraite de trente jours* (Lyon, 1865), II, p314; J.B. Scaramelli, *Le discernement des esprits*, trad. par A. Brassevin (Paris, 1893), p272; F. Suarez, p510.

does not necessarily belong to peripheral phenomena such as visions, locutions, stigmata, etc.[38]

We maintain, therefore, that the CSCP falls well within the framework of the normal course of events during the full 30 day Ignatian retreat. In this sense, the CSCP is hardly more extraordinary than the other expected consolations. An experience of the CSCP of varying purity and intensity is certainly to be expected as the normal crowning of the CCCP which the exercitant frequently receives during the Exercises. The Rejadell letter confirms that "it frequently happens."

Perhaps the CSCP occurs most explicitly and in its purest form during the Exercises. On the other hand, the horizon of every person's consciousness as Whither and the grace of Christ results in a core experience of the CSCP for everyone. The CSCP belongs to those primordial, core experiences which all persons share. Whenever a person comes fully to himself, fully possesses himself, but fully surrenders himself to the loving Mystery of his life calling him beyond himself, he experiences CSCP. The CSCP can be found anonymously as the mysticism of daily life. In a sense, the Exercises do nothing more than to amplify, to strengthen, and to deepen this anonymous mysticism of daily life (*Ex* 313).

Psychological Awareness of the CSCP?

How can the exercitant recognize and distinguish the CSCP from the CCCP and the consolations which follow in the wake of the CSCP? Many commentators find the solution in the "suddenness" of the CSCP.[39] *Ex* 330 and 336, however, say nothing about "suddenness." In fact, Ignatius' *Spiritual Journal* emphasizes the gentle quality of interior *loqüela*.

We maintain that when the exercitant discovers a *disproportion* between an expected "what I want and desire" consolation from the specific meditation and the actually given consolation which draws him entirely into God's love, he has reason to believe he is receiving

---

[38] K. Rahner, *Dynamic*, pp144ff, 151; W. Sierp, *Hochschule*, II, p472; G. Fessard, I, p258; H. Coathalem, *Commentaire du livre des Exercices* (Paris, 1965); A. Denis, IV, pp327ff.

[39] C. Judde, II, p304; F. Suarez, p510; W. Sierp, *Hochschule*, II, p458; M. Meschler, II, p326; J. Alvarez de Paz, *De Inquisitione pacis sive studio orationis* (Paris, 1876), VI, p653. For an excellent psychological approach to the problem, see: J. Bökmann, *Aufgaben und Methoden der Moralpsychologie im geistlichen Ursprung aus der Unterscheidung der Geister* (Köln, 1964), cf. esp. p126.

the CSCP.[40] The *disproportion* (something more than "what I want and desire"), therefore, *signals* the exercitant to take careful notice. The *quality* of the religious experience (its intrinsic evidence and the drawing entirely into God's love) is the *criterion* of the CSCP.

Paradoxically, the CSCP may not be immediately recognizable, because it is the fulfillment and completion of the CCCP. The disproportion is paradoxically proportionate to what can be expected to transcend the CCCP in this sense. We contend that the CSCP is the absolutely fundamental experience of every person. Once it moves more or less explicitly into awareness during the Exercises, therefore, it is experienced both as disproportionate, and yet, as somehow proportionate and fitting. Every person's deepest desire for fulfillment somehow anticipates and expects its actual fulfillment. The actual fulfillment, however, is "disproportionately proportionate" to the actual expectation.

The CSCP, therefore, may or may not seem to disrupt the normal course of the CCCP, because it is the proper continuation and fulfillment of the CCCP. The exercitant must discover in *all* of his experiences the CSCP as ever-present, at least as the implicit, supporting horizon and context for the CCCP.

The traditional commentaries, therefore, tend to emphasize that the exercitant can recognize the CSCP as it begins. To a greater or lesser degree, of course, this can be done. On the other hand, *Ex 336* warns the exercitant to distinguish the CSCP from "the time that follows it." This can be done only *afterwards*. We maintain with G. Fessard (p270, 288) that it is often only *after* a particular experience of God that the exercitant realizes God *was there*.

The CSCP can be recognized afterwards just as a person leaving a comfortable room experiences a temperature change for the worse. We agree with D. Gil (R,132) that during the CSCP, the exercitant experiences a greatly heightened interior unity, simplicity and presence. A return to his normal state is experienced as a loss. For many exercitants, it is only after the 30 day retreat that they realize just how rich and profound the entire experience had been.[41]

This is not surprising. Ignatius valued memory and the thinking back upon graces already received. His *Spiritual Journal*, his *Autobiography*, his letters, his underlining of certain passages he had written himself, his copying out of certain sections of Scripture, etc. all

---

[40] F. Suarez, p510; A. Gagliardi, p154; J.B. Scaramelli, p271; G. Fessard, I, p259.

[41] The *Official Directory* states that the exercitant may find what he desires only after the retreat, *MI* II, 1, p1167.

reveal an uncanny ability to recall and to reflect upon very special, past graces in order to extend their influence for as long as possible. *Ex* 43, 62, 64, 72, 118, 119, 204, 207, 208, 227, etc. indicate that Ignatius also expected the exercitant to look back upon and deepen graces already received. Much of the Exercises is a training in Ignatius' own amazing form of mystical memory.

Although some of the traditional commentaries stress God's sudden inbreak, we prefer to emphasize that the CSCP may or may not be recognizable at the start. The CSCP may be scarcely distinguishable from the CCCP. God, however, does not leave the person without drawing him entirely into His love and heightening his self-presence. After this experience, a loss is felt.

The CSCP can be recognized, therefore, not only by the disproportion which occurs at the beginning of the experience, but also by the experience of loss which characterizes the movement from the actual time of the CSCP to "the time that follows it."

The CSCP and the Unconscious

Typical of today's skepticism concerning the divine origin of the CSCP and religious experience in general is W. Meissner. He says of the CSCP:

> Ignatius regards the CSCP as an effect of grace. This assumption is at least questionable since the effect could be attributed to purely natural causes working through unconscious motivations.[42]

We also saw above that D. Gil is prepared to accept the unconscious as a possible source of the CSCP, because irruptions from the unconscious can have profound religious significance. He stresses that Ignatian discernment actually centers upon the religious significance of an experience, and not upon its origins. Are these positions acceptable?

First of all, if W. Meissner implicitly assumes that all of Ignatius' religious experiences can be explained in this way, he exceeds the limits of empirical psychology, as J. Maréchal has clearly shown.[43]

---

[42] W. Meissner, "Psychological Notes on the Spiritual Exercises," *WL* 93(1964), p188. For a more nuanced statement, see: J. de Guibert, *The Theology of the Spiritual Life*, trans. by P. Barrett (Sheed & Ward: New York, 1953), p136 and L. Poullier, "Les règles du discernement des esprits," *Les grandes directives de la retraite fermée* (Paris, 1930), p213.

[43] J. Maréchal, *Studies in the Psychology of the Mystics*. Trans. by A. Thorold (Benziger: New York, 1927), esp. chapter I, "Empirical Science and Religious Psychology," pp1-54.

The Christian position that a personal God of love communicates Himself immediately and directly must not be tacitly assumed to be impossible. Mysticism and the life of faith in general mean a greater or lesser awareness of creation's *graced* situation.

Secondly, has not the term "unconscious" become an all too often imprecise, catch-all term to avoid the issue of God's personal communication of Himself?

Thirdly, from what we have already seen, Ignatius definitely thought that he was dealing with God, not with religious meaning alone.

Fourthly, most mystics, including Ignatius, did err on occasion with respect to the origin and meaning of their religious experiences. If one assumes, however, that they were always wrong in claiming that God Himself was then acting in a special way, the limits of truly objective, scientific methodology are once more exceeded.

Fifthly, it is naive to presuppose that Ignatius and much of the Christian mystical tradition had no knowledge of the unconscious and hidden motivation.[44] They were very much aware of inordinate attachments, deep and hidden self-love, the different levels and dimensions of the one person, and of what often springs from a person's own habits and reflection (*Ex* 336). Even their angelology and demonology point to an awareness of forces which operate on the person "from without," that is, not issuing "solely from my own liberty and will" (*Ex* 32-3). Furthermore, Ignatius *discerned* the various movements in his soul. For example, one may dispute the actual origin of Ignatius' meat vision and snake-like vision, but the fact remains that he accepted the first as from God and the second as a demonic temptation only after very careful discernment.[45] Ignatius hardly attributed to God every psychic twitch he experienced.

Sixthly, one must not tacitly presuppose that the unconscious is a primordial cesspool which often degrades consciousness. J. Maréchal, among others, has shown the continuity between consciousness and the unconscious and stressed the riches and resources of this dimension.[46]

Seventhly, precisely because this area of the person is profound, rich and often unexplored, its irruption into consciousness could

---

[44] I. Hausherr, "Direction spirituelle en Orient," *DSAM* III, pp1026-27; K. Rahner, *Dynamic*, pp141ff.

[45] L. Beirnaert, "L'expérience fondmentale d'Ignace de Loyola et l'expérience psychoanalytique," *Expérience chrétienne et psychologie* (Paris, 1964), pp291ff.

[46] J. Maréchal, pp125-6.

strike the person as strange and mysterious. The unconscious, however, is merely one dimension of the one person, and what comes from that dimension will bear the marks of that person.[47] An adequate egocentric metaphysics, a metaphysics of self-appropriation, indicates that every person has at least an implicit, personal, holistic, non-reflexive knowledge of all that he is.[48] This means, however, that the unconscious could never be experienced *intrinsically* as a foreign element. For extrinsic reasons, of course, the unconscious and its irruptions are often experienced as "mystical," "divine," "angelic," or "demonic." This may be true psychologically and extrinsically, but not metaphysically and intrinsically.[49] Intrinsically, spirit means active self-identity and radical self-presence achieved in and through matter. Every person's deepest awareness is a global, holistic awareness of all that he is, and this includes the unconscious.

Eighthly, we agree with those Ignatian commentators who stress that the exclusively divine CSCP does not rule out human preparation, emotional undercurrents, concepts and reflection.[50] To stress a consolation without previous cause, a consolation in which God is immediately present, does not exclude mediation, nor an immediacy in context. The mediated immediacy of the CSCP is analogous to the mediated immediacy of an act of human freedom. Both occur in context, in and through other factors, but not from or because of those factors. The CSCP may break forth from the deepest dimensions of the human spirit, from that mysterious point in the human spirit prior to its division into intellect and will, from man's faculty of mystery where only God can come and go as He pleases. This does not mean, however, that the CSCP can occur without a context, adequate preparation or the concomitant involvement of the other dimensions and faculties of the one person. Ignatius

---

[47] J. de Tonquedec, p401.

[48] P. Scheuer, *op. cit.;* S. Strasser, *The Soul in a Metaphysical and Empirical Psychology* (Pittsburg, 1962); B.J.F. Lonergan, *Insight: a Study of Human Understanding* (Philosophical Library: New York, 1965).

[49] Psychological studies, for example, indicate that some insomniacs on a given night actually slept a total of five hours, yet hotly claimed only one or two hours. Metaphysically and intrinsically, they slept for five; psychological and extrinsically, for one or two hours. There is often a considerable difference between what we *actually* experience and what we believe we have experienced.

[50] P. Penning de Vries, *Discernimiento. Dinamica existencial de la doctrina y del espiritu de San Ignacio de Loyola* (Bilboa, 1967), p65; L. Gonzalez Hernandez, p144; A. Lefèvre, "Direction et discernement des esprits selon saint Ignace," *NRTh* 78(1956), p684.

stressed both the absolute gratuity of grace and the exercitant's careful preparation to receive that grace. The CSCP, for Ignatius, demands spiritual *exercises*, "every method of examination of conscience, of meditation, of contemplation, of vocal and mental prayer, and of other spiritual activity . . . to free itself of all inordinate affections . . . of seeking and discovering the Divine Will" (*Ex* 1).

Ninthly, we maintain that the unconscious cannot adequately account for the CSCP, because this experience draws the person *entirely* into God's love. Any movement capable of excluding all inordinate affections and unifying the entire person can come only from the person's radical principle of unity, the human spirit.

Tenthly, although any movement which unites the entire person must also include the unconscious, the unconscious alone cannot account for the exercitant's experience of wholeness, totality and self-presence. Ignatius expects the exercitant to be rid of *all* sadness (*Ex* 329) on occasion, to watch the *entire* course of his thoughts and to accept them only if *all* are good and *entirely* directed to what is right (*Ex* 333). Consolation from the evil one, moreover, is only *apparent* (*Ex* 314); only God and His angels can bring *true* consolation (*Ex* 329). Though the evil one may transform himself into an angel of light, the "serpent's tail" (*Ex* 334, *cola serpentina*) cannot be hidden. No matter how much deception the evil one uses, the experience does not ring true. The exercitant's direction of attention, moreover, must be *simple* (*Ex* 169); *all* of his intentions, actions and works must be directed to God's service and praise (*Ex* 46). Ignatius, therefore, emphasizes integrity and wholeness. His emphasis upon inordinate affections must be seen as a focus upon what hinders or destroys this wholeness. The CSCP is a radically integral, fully human experience, unifying and summing up the one person in all of his depths and dimensions.

Eleventhly, the CSCP is the supreme case of Ignatian *sentire*, that felt-knowledge which flows from the unification and harmony of all of the person's faculties. Although we basically agree with K. Rahner that this is not " 'feeling', 'instinct' " (p94, n9), but "an intellectual knowledge which is ultimately grounded in the simple presence to itself of the intrinsically intelligible subject which in the very accomplishment of its act has knowledge of itself, without that contrast of knower and known" (pp94-5, n9), we prefer to stress the holistic, body-person nature of the CSCP. Beginning in the presence of spirit to itself, the CSCP, however, can be explained only through the interior harmony and unity which results when the total body-person has become connatural to grace, when God's love has penetrated all of the layers and dimensions of the one person and unified this person to his very roots.[51]

Twelfthly, A. Brunner has called attention to the "super-conscious" (*Überbewusstsein*), or beyond-the-conceptual aspect of human consciousness.[52] This aspect of human consciousness is often confused with the unconscious, because it concerns the person's deepest interiority and horizon of consciousness.[53] This "super-consciousness" is what we mean by the human spirit's presence to itself in radical active self-identity. During the CSCP, the exercitant becomes more explicitly aware of his supernaturally and Christ-affected active self-identity. This special form of Ignatian felt-knowledge transcends discursive reasoning and is a type of "superconsciousness." For this reason, it may look like an irruption from the unconscious.

Lastly, we readily admit that the unconscious can, should and does play a role in consolation or desolation. We maintain, however, that the unconscious alone cannot draw the person totally into God's love. Precisely because the CSCP is the basic unifying experience of the one body-person, the unconscious is involved, but not vice versa. We do accept, however, the unconscious as a source of CCCP. A consolation which had its roots in the unconscious would have to be splashed against the horizon of meaning, totality and wholeness supplied by the basic, "super-conscious" consolation, the CSCP.

The CSCP: "Transcendence without Dogma?"

Intermingled with a highly disciplined, pragmatic secularity, and often secularism, is a new American Romanticism. One author calls this new American mystical movement a search for "transcendence without dogma."[54]

---

[51] P. Leturia, *Estudios Ignacianos*, (Rome, 1957), II, p153; G. Dumeige, "Ignace de Loyola II. Expérience et doctrine spirituelle," *DSAM* VII, p1284; J. Futrell, "Ignatian Discernment," *Studies in the Spirituality of the Jesuits* 2(1970), p56; J. Futrell, *Making an Apostolic Community of Love: The Role of the Superior According to St. Ignatius of Loyola* (St. Louis, 1971), p111, n12.

[52] A. Brunner, "Philosophisches zur Tiefenpsychologie und Psychotherapie," *StdZ* 144(1949), p92.

[53] A. Görres, "Ein existenzielles Experiment zur Psychologie der Exerzitien des Ignatius von Loyola," *Guardini-Festschrift*, hrsg. von H. Kuhn & H. Kahlfeld (Würzburg, 1967), p4.

[54] See: "Neue religiöse Subkulturen in den USA," *Herder Korrespondenz* 25(1971), p525. See also: A. Greeley, "The New American Religions," *The Concrete Christian Life*, ed. C. Duquoc, *Concilium* 69 (Herder & Herder: New York, 1971), pp111-23.

We maintain, however, that the supreme form of Ignatian transcendence, the CSCP, is not a "transcendence without dogma." The CSCP remains inextricably linked to the historical Jesus, to a love of the world, and to service in the visible Church.

We have already noted how the CSCP arises out of the meditations on the life, death and resurrection of Jesus Christ. As we shall see later on, Ignatius' mysticism begins and ends in the person of Jesus Christ, whose humanity, divinity and cosmic qualities Ignatius intimately experienced. Against those who would advocate emptying the mind of all created things, even Jesus Christ, in order to experience pure transcendence, Ignatius' CSCP remains intrinsically fused to the person of Jesus Christ. Ignatian mysticism does not pursue the apophatic way of negation and darkness, but Jesus Christ as the Way and the Light. For Ignatius, Jesus Christ is *the* "signal of transcendence" *par excellence.*[55]

Ignatian mysticism loves the world, because God can be found in all things (*Ex* 230-7) and all things are "bathed in the blood of Christ." As we shall see, Ignatius tacitly presupposes that Christ is the fulfillment and meaning of human existence. The CSCP, therefore, is dialectically linked to the full meaning and mystery of human, earthly existence in Jesus Christ.

The christocentric aspect of Ignatian mysticism means a mysticism of service in the visible Church. A profound worldly involvement in terms of love of neighbor and service are a necessary precondition and dialectical moment of the CSCP. For Ignatius, transcendence, service and Church are dialectically related.

With the exception, however, of the Rules for the Distribution of Alms (*Ex* 337-44), Ignatius gives no explicit instructions on the love of one's neighbor. In fact, during the time of the Exercises, he recommends that the exercitant separate himself from all his friends and worldly worries, because "the more the soul finds itself alone and away from men, the more apt it is to approach and be united with its Creator and Lord" (*Ex* 20).

On the other hand, the individual, private nature of the Exercises actually fosters a mysticism of service. The exercitant experiences deeply that he is to live only for the "sake of others in Jesus Christ."[56] The utter openness to the Mystery of God in Jesus Christ during the CSCP also means a great openness to one's fellowman.

---

[55]P. Berger, *A Rumor of Angels* (New York, 1970), esp. pp52-75.
[56]St. Ignatius, as quoted by L. Beirnaert, "Sens de Dieu et sens du péche. Besoins contemporains et spiritualité ignatienne," *RAM* 26(1950), p27.

The CSCP contains as a moment of its own accomplishment the finding of God in all things through the service of God in all things, especially one's neighbor. The CSCP produces a contemplative in action who loves his fellowman in his innermost core, because he has entered into God Who alone is allowed into this core.[57] The CSCP, therefore, as the exercitant's total openness to God's love, contains as a moment of its completion the exercitant's openness to his fellowman.

For Ignatius, the CSCP finds its completion and fulfillment in an ecclesial context. His transcendence is not without dogma, because the same Spirit who guides the exercitant's transcendence to Election also "guides and governs our Holy Mother Church" (*Ex* 365). The CSCP, therefore, is intrinsically linked to established, historical, ecclesial norms which may be used to measure the CSCP's authenticity (*Ex* 170). For Ignatius, even a vocation discovered not to be from God cannot be changed, if that choice is deemed immutable by the hierarchical Church (*Ex* 172).

Although we agree with H. Rahner (pp214-38) that Ignatian mysticism is ecclesial, "Roman" and "hyper-papal," this must not be overly simplified. For example, L. Mendizábal has shown that Ignatius expected *inner* obedience to papal authority, because the Pope was the interpreter of God's Will.[58] This went beyond the tradition of the great Scholastics to see the Pope more as the head of a social body, demanding *outer* obedience, but not inner, because only God was superior of man's intellect and will. On the other hand, R. Schwager has shown that Ignatius' papal mysticism sometimes meant getting the Pope to see things Ignatius' way.[59] Ignatius used every possible means at his disposal to prevent Le Jay and Canisius from being made bishops and to prevent Borgia and Laynez from being made cardinals. Ignatius had a felt-knowledge for more than the Pope's explicit wishes.

---

[57] K. Rahner, "The Apostolate of Prayer," *TI* 3, pp214ff. A good case can be made for saying that the CSCP is implicit in the act of love of one's neighbor. Cf.: K. Rahner, "Reflections on the Unity of the Love of Neighbor and the Love of God," *TI* 6, pp231-249.

[58] L. Mendizábal, "El 'hecho eclesiástico' de la obedience ignaciana," *Manr* 36(1964), pp403-20; "Sentido intimo de la obediencia ignaciana," *Manr* 37(1965), pp53-76.

[59] R. Schwager, pp133ff. See also: B. Schneider, "Die Kirchlichkeit des heiligen Ignatius von Loyola," *Sentire Ecclesiam*. Hrsg. von J. Daniélou und H. Vorgrimler (Freiburg i.B., 1961), pp268-300. An excellent study!

For Ignatius, however, the Church was far more than Church politics, rules and dogma. Because Ignatius was Christ-directed, he was also a man of the Church. Ignatius had mystically tasted that:

> In its origin and its witness to Christ, the Church is the historical sign of God's victorious will for Salvation, conquering all man's guilt. To this extent the Church is the 'sacrament' (i.e. the holy, effectual sign) in which the world's divinization appears and, in appearing, establishes itself. As the historical presence of God's unrevoked pledge of himself in Christ, the Church's testimony wherever it is expressed in a definitive witness on the part of its authoritative teaching office, is protected from slipping from God's truth.[60]

Ignatius' ecclesial mysticism, therefore, results from an incarnational, christocentric mysticism. The Church contains within itself the Mystery of God's salvation history which culminated in Christ.

It is within this total context that Ignatius understands the ecclesial moment of the CSCP. Ignatius' supreme form of transcendence and felt-knowledge, therefore, does not really result in "Rules for Thinking with the Church," but in a mystical "sense" of "being in the Church" (*Ex* 352, *Para el* sentido *verdadero que* en la iglesia *militante*, (emphasis mine).

---

[60]K. Rahner, "The Need of a 'Short Formula' of Christian Faith," *TI* 9, p125.

 Chapter III

The Anthropocentric Moment
of the Exercises and the
Ignatian Mystical Horizon

INTRODUCTION

This chapter proposes to demonstrate the anthropocentric aspect of Ignatius' mystical horizon by unfolding the intrinsic, anthropocentric moment of the Exercises. This moment reveals the unity, fusion and oneness of the exercitant's surrender to the loving Mystery of God in Jesus Christ and his "return" to himself, because this moment is the one core *movement*, the basic dynamic or rhythm of the Exercises containing the experiential translation and crystallization of Ignatius' mystical horizon.

The anthropocentric moment of the Exercises, therefore, centers upon the exercitant's self-discovery, self-presence, self-knowledge, self-acceptance, self-possession and self-emptying in the light of the Mystery of God in Jesus Christ. Essential to the inner rhythm and dynamics of the Exercises is the exercitant's radical return to himself as subject, the active disposition of his entire person, his creative self-presence, his presence to his own deepest mystery as man, a self-presence which sums up, concentrates and fulfills the expectations of his own created self-transcendence to surrender itself to loving Mystery in Jesus Christ.

By taking on the rhythm of Christ during the Exercises through the experience of consolations and desolations, the exercitant becomes more expressly aware of his basic horizon of consciousness. Although certain exercises center more on calling into play and strengthening one of the exercitant's faculties (his will, understanding, intellect, memory, emotions, affections, etc.), every exercise likewise sets in motion and fulfills, at least partially, his essential, basic thrust for self-identity, self-surrender and self-fulfillment. Throughout all of this, the exercitant's faculties are disciplined, awakened, deepened and strengthened in such a way that their inner unity, common root, and fundamental horizon are brought to the fore. The exercitant experiences what he is, who he is, and therefore, discovers God's specific Will for him. The surrender of the exercitant to the Mystery of God in Jesus Christ presupposes a moment of self-return, of active self-identity, of self-possession, a return to his own deepest mystery as man. Throughout this chapter, therefore, it is essential to see the various aspects we shall discuss as aspects of this *one, basic,* transcendental movement, a movement more explicitly evoked, deepened and strengthened by each of these aspects.

The *Principle and Foundation* Meditation

The introductory meditation of the Exercises, the *Principle and Foundation* (*Ex* 23), focuses simply, sharply and trenchantly on God, all created things and the exercitant. The exercitant is summoned to "use" or to "rid himself" of "all other things on the face of the earth" insofar as they help or hinder him "to praise, reverence and serve God our Lord." The emphatically theocentric thrust of this meditation renders all created things relative; "therefore we must make ourselves indifferent to all created things, in so far as it is left to the choice of our free will and is not forbidden."

This basic Ignatian meditation presents the entire Exercises in embryonic form.[1] It expresses in capsule form what must be seen and accomplished during the Exercises by someone who enters them with the courage and generosity Ignatius clearly expects (*Ex* 5). The *Principle and Foundation* meditation sets before the exercitant in general terms what he must understand, experience and accomplish, because:

> Spiritual Exercises are methods of preparing and disposing the soul *to free itself of all inordinate attachments,* and after accomplishing this, of *seeking and discovering the Divine Will* regarding the disposition of one's life. (*Ex* 1) (Emphasis mine)

This meditation, therefore, gives the exercitant a holistic view of reality and places him within this whole. Ignatius' skillful reduction

[1] See: H. Rahner, "Notes," p310; H. Carrier, "La 'caritas discreta' et les exercices spirituels," *ScE* 8(1956), p178; J. Calveras, "Tecnicismos explanados," *Manr* 1(1925), pp118-28; 307-20. W. Sierp, *Hochschule,* I, pp169ff has shown how the *Foundation* manifests itself throughout the Exercises in the form of the preparatory prayer, as in *Ex* 46. E. Przywara, *Deus,* II, pp185ff has shown the link between the *Foundation* and the *Third Degree of Humility,* the Election, the *Contemplation to Obtain Divine Love* and the "Take, O Lord, and receive" prayer.

of everything in terms of end and means manifests his concern that the exercitant experience his entire life as a contribution to the basic harmony or disharmony of God's one creation. By insisting right from the start on creation's meaning and goal, everything is seen and experienced as leading to or away from that goal. The exercitant begins to see and to experience his own harmony and disorder with respect to the very meaning and goal of all of creation.

Only if the exercitant sees and experiences the whole, therefore, can he really see and experience his own "inordinate affections." The vision central to this meditation ought to result in an absolutely basic, holistic experience against which all other experiences are relativized and placed in context. The *Principle and Foundation* offers the exercitant a basic unifying view within which everything else must be integrated, even his often obstinate individual tendencies. The explicitly theocentric emphasis reveals an implicit anthropocentric emphasis, insofar as the exercitant must integrate all he is and does with a view toward his final end.

Inordinate Attachments

The obverse side of Ignatius' theocentric emphasis upon God's Will, therefore, is his implicit anthropocentric emphasis upon the exercitant's integrity and wholeness. This comes to light most clearly in Ignatius' abhorrence of "inordinate attachments." The Ignatian battle is scarcely against the person's God-given nature, nor even against his lower nature. It is against the wrong directions and subjective deformities introduced by the exercitant through his misuse of creatures, his own freedom and his faculties.

Ignatius realized that inordinate attachments produce false loves which often coax the exercitant into harmony with them.[2] This vitiates an Election based upon reality, God's reality. God's true call, the vibrations from reality's deepest source, cannot be heard by the truncated, fractured, dissociated, "uncollected" person. The ability to hear God's word of truth and the true demands of reality depend upon a whole, integral, recollected, unified subjectivity. Self-seeking prevents the simplicity of direction required for truly seeking and finding God's Will (*Ex* 169).

Inordinate attachments, therefore, damage the anthropocentric moment of God's Self-communication, because true self-love in the form of subjective integrity is an essential moment in that communication. Inordinate attachments produce subjective "static" which

---

[2]*MI* II, 1, pp1153-5.

interferes with the reception of God's Self-communication. This explains Ignatius' frequent warnings against inordinate affections, especially as the exercitant approaches the Election.[3]

The Exercises aim, therefore, at the exercitant's healing, unification and integration to insure his complete "return" to himself. Communication with his true self is an essential moment of his reception of God's Self-communication. He cannot know God's Will unless he knows his true self. For this reason, Ignatius expects the exercitant to grow in an experiential ability to know, taste and deal with the slightest disorder in his person. To a greater or lesser degree of explicitness, the Exercises offer the exercitant the anthropocentric rewards of *Ex* 63:

> That I may have a thorough knowledge of my sins and a feeling of abhorrence for them. That I may comprehend the disorder of my actions, so that detesting them I will amend my ways and put my life in order.

The Role of the Intellect

To rid the exercitant of his inordinate attachments and to redirect him towards seeking and finding God's Will, Ignatius insists that the entire person, in all his depths, awakens, exercises and enters into a new reality, the reality from God's saving word. Ignatius begins this process by immediately directing the exercitant's intellect towards the truth.

From the beginning to end, the Ignatian experience is sustained, explained and guided by an intellect solidly rooted in the truths of salvation history. Ignatius cautions the retreat director to expose the "true essentials" of this history as faithfully as possible (*Ex* 2).

The solid, historical truths of the faith ground Ignatian love and service. Ignatian love and service are not empty enthusiasm; they respect the intellect's need for truth and are solidly anchored in the truths of salvation history.[4] The truths of salvation history insure a discrete, balanced love, generosity, enthusiasm and service.

Many commentators have shown that Ignatius translated into the Exercises his own personal experience of an intellectual light which had seized control of his depths to purify, heal, free and guide him.[5]

---

[3] See esp.: *Ex* 1, 16, 21, 63, 97, 169, 172, 179, 182, 184, 189, 212, 216, 325, 338, 339, 342. For the commentators who emphasize this point, see: W. Sierp, *Hochschule*, II, pp354, 448; J. Roothaan, p2, n2; M. Meschler, I, p227; *MI* II, 1, p1156, 1163; A. Bellecius, p232.

[4] G. Cusson, *Pédagogie*, pp184, 267; W. Peters, p27; W. Sierp, "Recta sentire in Ecclesia," *ZAM* 16(1941), pp32ff.

[5] J. Roothaan, pp26ff; G. Cusson, *Pédagogie*, pp47, 126; H. Carrier, pp171ff.

Many individual meditations in the Exercises aim at purifying the exercitant's intellect (*Ex* 2, 50, 63, 64, etc.). Intellectual purification also clears the way for the purification of the will and the senses. It firmly anchors the exercitant's affective-volitional dimensions in a clarity found only in a profound consideration of God's saving truth. The intellectual clarity born from intellectual effort, thinking over, reflecting, seeking out relationships, conclusions and meanings, etc., provides the exercitant with a truly trustworthy foundation for his later affective life.[6]

This intellectual anchoring in the historical truths and true essentials of the faith compels the Ignatian method to stay up to date. To be faithful to Ignatius, the retreat director must keep abreast of current exegesis and theology. Ignatius emphasized profound theological study because of an authentic conviction that love must know what and why it is loving. Authentic love presupposes intellectual harmony with the truths of the faith. A service rooted in discrete charity cannot be theologically blind.[7] The Exercises, therefore, give the exercitant an experience of intellectual light. This intellectual grounding, moreover, gives the exercitant the beginnings of Ignatius' own mystically "architechtonic" view of God and reality, his "dogmatic discretion," his taste for the theological interdependence of all the mysteries which he had experienced on the banks of the river Cardoner. One of the major goals of the Exercises is the imparting of an experience which mystically awakens the exercitant's intellect.

The Role of the Will

The Ignatian experience, of course, must go beyond the intellect. *Ex* 50, for example, directs the exercitant to *reason* more in detail upon the subject matter so that the *will* may move the *affections* more deeply. In *Ex* 43, the exercitant prays to *know* his sins so that he may be *free* from them. In *Ex* 63, he prays to *know* and comprehend so that he may *abhor, detest,* and be filled with horror. In *Ex* 104 and 130, he prays for an intimate *knowledge* of Jesus Christ in order to *love* and follow him better. In *Ex* 233, he prays for a deep *knowledge* of the many blessings he has received so that he may be filled with *gratitude,* and in all things love and serve the Divine Majesty.

---

[6] See: J.B. Lotz, "Die ignatianische Betrachtungsmethode im Lichte einer gesunder Wertlehre," *ZAM* 10(1935), p8; A. Haas, *GÜ*, pp134ff; W. Sierp, *Hochschule*, II, p367.

[7] See: H. Rahner, *Werden*, pp92ff; *Ignatius*, pp1; 70, n31; G. Cusson, *Péda-gogie*, p189, n3.

The exercitant, therefore, frequently prays for a twofold grace, one pertaining to the intellect and the other to the will in conjunction with the emotions. The experience of light must touch the exercitant's affective-volitional core to move him in all his depths. This twofold request for light in order to move the will and the emotions is a constant feature of the Exercises.[8]

Several key Ignatian mediations are specifically designed to purify and to test the readiness of the exercitant's will to choose only what is in keeping with God's Will. The *Three Clases of Men* (*Ex* 149-56), the *Three Modes of Humility* (*Ex* 165-7) and the *Colloquies* (*Ex* 63, 147, 157, etc.) uncover the exercitant's secret weaknesses, expose his hesitations, and lay bare his real motives and desires.[9] The unmasking of the exercitant's secret weaknesses, hesitations, real motives and real desires may prevent him from stumbling at the critical moment of the Exercises, the Election.

The Role of the Emotions

Ignatius had a great respect for religious emotions in his own spiritual life. From what we have already seen, Ignatius definitely expects to mobilize the exercitant's emotions throughout the Exercises. In fact, the exercitant must often pray specifically for pain, tears, shame, sorrow, affliction, horror, detestation, abhorrence, confusion, amazement, affectionate love, joy, gladness, peace, quiet and tranquillity. He must carefully pray at times according to the needs he *feels* within himself (*Ex* 109). Each Ignatian colloquy (*Ex* 53, 54, 63, 71, 109, etc.), moreover, prepares the exercitant to surrender to the more spontaneous desires and feelings of his heart.

Ignatius, therefore, does not underestimate the importance of the exercitant's emotional matrix and foundation for definite growth in the spiritual life. He clearly intends to reorient and Christianize the exercitant's spontaneous likes and repugnances. By having the exercitant feed emotionally on God's saving word, Ignatius restructures the exercitant's emotional life so that he *feels* differently about himself, God and all of creation.

Ignatius does not suppress emotions, but transforms them in accordance with God's truth. Ignatius instinctively knew that not only does the intellect influence the will, which then moves the

---

[8] See: L. Claßen, "Die 'Übung mit den drei Seelenkräften' im Ganzen der Exerzitien," *Ignatius von Loyola. Seine geistliche Gestalt und sein Vermächtnis* (=*Loyola-Gestalt*), hrsg. von F. Wulf (Würzburg, 1956); J.B. Lotz, p117; G. Cusson, *Pédagogie*, pp131ff; J. Roothaan, pp73-4, n2.

[9] H. Pinard de la Boullaye, *Étapes*, pp54ff; G. Cusson, *Pédagogie*, pp311ff; W. Sierp, *Hochschule*, II, pp218ff.

emotions (*Ex* 50), but also that the emotions influence how the exercitant thinks and wills. By changing the emotional ambiance of his intellect and will, the exercitant feels and experiences himself, God and all of creation differently. This means that he will also think and will differently.[10] In fact, the psychologically attuned Ignatius even realized that food (*Ex* 83, 89), sunlight or darkness (*Ex* 79, 130), bodily position during prayer (*Ex* 76), sleep (*Ex* 73, 84), corporeal penances (*Ex* 85-9) and the weather (*Ex* 130, 229) can subtly alter the way the exercitant thinks, wills, decides and acts.

Ignatius' *Third Method of Prayer* (*Ex* 258-60) also indicates his expectation of profound emotional motions and intense consolations during the Exercises. As W. Peters (pp172ff) has shown, this method of prayer helps the exercitant to deal with the intensity of these motions. He must not suppress, cut off or be carried away by them. This method of prayer integrates very intense consolations and motions with the exercitant's natural breathing rhythm. The integration of these intense consolations and motions into the exercitant's tranquil, natural breathing rhythm massages the different levels in his being with the healing power of God's saving word.

Several commentators have shown the profound role played by the mystical gift of tears during part of Ignatius' life.[11] Ignatius also expects the exercitant to shed tears during the Exercises (*Ex* 48, 56, 78, 89, 195, 199, 203, 316). Although tears do not constitute true sorrow, they do manifest and foster a faith rooted in more than spirit alone. Tears deeply affect the one body-person in all his depth. Tears shed while meditating upon the mysteries of the faith help to root out inordinate attachments at their very source; besides, they anchor the exercitant's faith both in his spirit and in his body.

The Role of Memory and Imagination

The Ignatian method does not neglect to reorient and to Christianize the exercitant's memory and imagination. The first prelude of almost every meditation explicitly directs the exercitant to recall to mind the history or the true essentials of the particular mystery at hand (*Ex* 2, 50-2, 102, 111, 137, 149, 191, 201, 219). Ignatius advises the exercitant to recall the sins of his past life (*Ex* 56) and to examine his conscience twice daily (*Ex* 25-31) through a

---

[10]The entire article by J.B. Lotz, is especially good on this point. See also: R. Schwager, pp90ff; J. Maréchal, pp86ff; A. Görres, pp7ff.

[11]See: I. Navatel, "La dévotion sensible, les larmes et les Exercices de Saint Ignace," *CBE* 64(1920), pp12ff; A. Görres, pp12ff; J. de Guibert, *Jesuits*, pp59-66.

lively and methodical use of memory. After each period of prayer, the exercitant must go over it in his mind to discover the reasons for the success or failure of his prayer (*Ex* 77). The exercitant must often repeat, recapitulate, recall or review a previous meditation to "dwell upon the points in which I have felt the greatest consolation or desolation, or the greatest spiritual relish" (*Ex* 62, 118, 227, 254, etc.). After recalling God's many benefits to him, the exercitant might be ready to surrender everything to God, including his memory (*Ex* 234).

Ignatius' first or second prelude, moreover, concerns "a mental image of the place" (*Ex* 47, 65, 91, 103, 112, 138, 151, 192, 202, 220, 232). He frequently directs the exercitant to see, to hear, to smell, to taste and to touch *in his imagination* what is taking place in the Christian mystery at hand (*Ex* 66ff, 92, 103, 106, 121ff, 143ff, 194ff). Even before falling asleep and immediately upon rising, the exercitant is to direct his attention to the specific meditation at hand.

It seems clear, therefore, that Ignatius fastens the exercitant's memory and imagination to the solidly incarnational foundation of Christian salvation history and symbolism. This, too, runs counter to the apophatic mystical tradition of negation and darkness. Never does Ignatius attempt to wean the exercitant from created things. There is no voiding of the mind to bury everything beneath a cloud of forgetting to reach God beyond a cloud of darkness and unknowing.[12] Ignatius' mysticism remains decidedly cataphatic and incarnational.

The Role of the "what I want and desire" Prelude

Ignatius also orients and Christianizes the exercitant's various faculties by awakening him to what he should really desire. Because inordinate affections unconsciously motivate the exercitant in all he does and chooses, they must be eliminated. The clear, simple and explicitly conscious desire of what one really wants, especially when this flows from the salvific effects of each meditation, purifies the exercitant of his inordinate affections by awakening him to the deepest desires of his true self.[13] Clear, explicit, Christian desires

---

[12]See: R. Barthes, "Comment parler à Dieu?," *Tel quel* 38(1969), pp37ff and A. Haas and P. Knauer, *Tagebuch*, pp147ff for an excellent treatment of Ignatian memory and his stress upon imagery. J. Maréchal, pp186ff, seems too impressed with the traditional apophatic mystics.
[13]See: *Ex* 20, 48, 73, 76, 87, 89, 130, 133, 168, 199, 203, 206, 227, 233, etc. See also: G. Cusson, *Pédagogie*, pp149ff, 159ff; W. Peters, p4.

force the exercitant to take conscious possession of his life, and even the unconscious direction of his life, in accordance with God's truth.

The preparatory prayer of each meditation asks for "the grace that all my intentions, actions, and works may be directed purely to the service and praise of His Divine Majesty" (*Ex* 46). This orients the exercitant in a basic, simple, yet general way. The second or third Ignatian preludes specify this general request by asking for a definite grace which varies with each particular meditation.

The exercitant must pray for "what I want and desire" (*Ex* 48). He requests: "joy with Christ rejoicing" (*Ex* 48), "tears, pain, and suffering with Christ suffering" (*Ex* 48), "an ever increasing and intense sorrow and tears for my sins" (*Ex* 56), "a deep awareness of the pain suffered by the damned" (*Ex* 65), "that I may not be deaf to His call, but prompt and diligent to accomplish His most holy will" (*Ex* 91), "an intimate knowledge of our Lord" (*Ex* 104, 113), "a knowledge of the deceits of the evil chieftain . . . and a knowledge of the true life . . . the grace to imitate Him [Christ] " (*Ex* 139), "the grace that I may be received under His standard" (*Ex* 147), "the grace to choose what is for the greatest glory of His Divine Majesty" (*Ex* 152), "sorrow, affliction, and confusion because the Lord is going to His passion on account of my sins" (*Ex* 193), "that I may feel intense joy and gladness for the great glory and joy of Christ our Lord" (*Ex* 221) and "a deep knowledge of the many blessings I have received " (*Ex* 233).[14] Note that the general preparatory prayer and the specific "what I want and desire" coincide at the *Contemplation to Obtain Divine Love* (*Ex* 233).

This "what I want and desire" prelude is the backbone of the Exercises. Its dynamism sets the exercitant's prayerful search in motion by focusing his deepest desires. This prelude also awakens his inordinate attachments, because they must now make room for God-given attachments. These very specific "what I want and desire" requests attempt to render the exercitant connatural with the saving truths of the particular meditation. Although derived from God's *a posteriori*, historical deeds and words, the "what I want and desire" grace from each meditation also corresponds to the exercitant's deepest and most authentic yearnings, for reasons we shall see later on.

The "what I want and desire" prelude coaxes the exercitant into line with the deepest desires of his true self, eliminates inordinate affections and subjective deformities, reduces subjective static and promotes his greatest growth. The "what I want and desire" as a

---

[14]*MI* II, 1, p1142; H. Coathalem, p291.

saving grace corresponds to and fulfills the anthropocentric demands of the fully recollected, integral person. As indicated by the frequent repetition of this prelude, however, the exercitant with his inordinate affections is not easily oriented to the deepest desires of his true self brought to light by the salvific effect of each meditation.[15]

The Role of Consolation and Desolation

The exercitant progresses during the Exercises if he receives the "what I want and desire" graces of each particular meditation. He must experience, during his meditations on the great truths of salvation history, various interior movements which Ignatius calls consolation (*Ex* 316). These consolations, in turn, must become an actual state of soul proper to each week of the Exercises.

The exercitant successfully completes the First Week by pruning the roots of his sinfulness, turning to Christ Crucified, experiencing detestation for his sins, confusion, knowledge of his disorders, etc. and by resolving to do something for Christ (*Ex* 53, 56, etc.). He successfully completes the next three Weeks if he knows, loves and serves Christ better by having suffered and rejoiced with Him (*Ex* 104, 193, 221, etc.).

Ignatius, moreover, clearly expects more during the Exercises than consolation. He knows that the generous exercitant will experience consolations, desolations and be moved by various spirits (*Ex* 6). He instructs the exercitant in "perceiving and understanding to some degree the different movements that are produced in the soul" (*Ex* 313), and perhaps in an even "greater discernment of spirits" (*Ex* 328ff).

If consolation is a sign of progress and guidance from God and the good spirit (*Ex* 318, 329), "in desolation the evil spirit guides and counsels" (*Ex* 318). In spite of this, however, desolation has many lessons to teach. Desolation can awaken a lax conscience (*Ex* 314), bring the exercitant's tepidity and sloth to light (*Ex* 322), test him and teach him that consolations are strictly God's gifts (*Ex* 322). And yet, Ignatius would always have the exercitant fight against this state of soul (*Ex* 319).[16]

[15] H. Coathalem, pp36ff, 47ff; W. Peters, p33. The Ignatian method is an intelligent, skillful striving for wholeness and does not suppress emotions, affections, thoughts, desires, etc. arbitrarily, as K. Jaspers supposes, as quoted in: A. Görres, p3. Note, too, that the *Official Directory* cautions against any kind of excessive strain, *MI* II, 1, p1144.

[16] See: J. LaPlace, "L'expérience du discernement dans les Exercices spirituels de Saint Ignace," *Chr* 4(1954), p38; F. Lawlor, "The Doctrine of Grace in the Spiritual Exercises, *TS* 3(1942), pp513-32; A. Steger, "La place de la grâce dans la spiritualité de saint Ignace," *NRTh* (1948), pp572ff.

We mentioned above the importance of the repetitions and résumés of previous meditations during the Exercises. During this time, the exercitant lingers upon those sections in which he experienced "the greatest consolation, desolation, or the greatest spiritual relish" (*Ex* 62, 118). The return to previous areas of special consolation and desolation helps the exercitant to pinpoint areas of harmony and disharmony within himself in the light of God's saving word. These consolations and desolations accentuate the exercitant's spontaneous, yet often hidden, likes and dislikes which may or may not be in accord with the demands of his true self.

Consolations and desolations manifest the exercitant's hidden affections which either help or hinder his basic anthropocentric dynamism to come to himself and surrender to the loving Mystery of God in Jesus Christ. Consolations and desolations are the positive and negative echoes of his own being to the deepest demands of his true self. The exercitant's consolations and desolations, his peace and disharmony, are the profound signs of his self-surrender to, or self-refusal of, the deepest anthropocentric demands of his own being, namely, to return entirely to itself and so surrender itself to loving Mystery.

While meditating upon the life, death and resurrection of Jesus Christ, the God-man who perfectly responded to and fulfilled the deepest demands of His own human nature, the exercitant's deepest nature is evoked and enlightened. The exercitant's consolations and desolations while meditating upon Christ's life, death and resurrection are a measure of the soundness or sickness of his own human nature. The generosity and progress the exercitant makes in knowing, loving and serving Christ indirectly deepens and strengthens his own human nature.

From this point of view, desolation can be understood as the repugnance which flows from the exercitant's deordination and resistance to the deepest demands of his own human nature. Desolation highlights the exercitant's often hidden resistance to full self-identity as well as those areas in the exercitant's being which prevent his authentic, human growth.

When the exercitant receives desolation instead of the "what I want and desire" consolation of a specific meditation, this also indicates hidden areas of resistance to God's healing grace. Desolation exposes his disorder and truncation, and allows him, through frequent repetition of the points in which he received these desolations, to work out and heal the inordinate attachments in much the same way that a person works out a cramp from a muscle.

These desolations point out those areas and aspects of his life and being which are not connatural to God's saving grace, his own deepest integrity and the demands of his true self.

One criterion for true consolation and desolation depends upon the person's *habitual* state of soul (*Ex* 314-15). Consolation and desolation mean different things to the sinner and to those striving to advance in God's service. Furthermore, precisely because the absolutely basic situation of every person is such that he is already touched by God's grace and objectively redeemed (the supernatural existential), touched by the life, death and resurrection of Christ (the christic existential) while at the same time remaining a sinner, subject to death and sin (the original sin existential), three basic existentials pull the one exercitant in two different directions.

This means, however, that one moment of God's grace will always be experienced as consolation *and* as desolation, because it will be in accord with his deepest self, but against his original sin existential. Because the supernatural and christic existentials represent the basic, deeper and more powerful existentials, consolation will always be experienced as the more "natural," more fitting, deeper and true experience. Desolation will be experienced as something which runs counter to the exercitant's basic authenticity. In this sense, desolation is somehow an "unnatural" experience.[17]

The Role of the Application of the Senses

Still another way in which the exercitant returns to dwell upon those aspects of a meditation in which he experienced "the greatest consolation, desolation, or the greatest spiritual relish" (*Ex* 62, 118) is through the *Application of the Senses* (–AS) exercise. Almost every day, for the exercise before dinner, Ignatius instructs the exercitant to apply the five senses to the day's previous meditations (*Ex* 129, 133-4, 227; note *Ex* 209). He once again sees, hears, smells, tastes and touches in imagination what is taking place in these saving mysteries.

It must be noted, however, that Ignatius' AS contains at least three levels: the simple consideration of the imitation of Christ or Mary in the use of the senses (*Ex* 247-8); a more interior AS on the mystery of hell (*Ex* 65-70); and an even more interior AS, wherein the exercitant sees, hears, touches, smells and tastes the soul, its virtues, the Divinity, and all else (*Ex* 121-4).

---

[17] For the theological metaphysics behind this opinion, see: K. Rahner, "Justified and Sinner at the same Time," *TI* 6, pp222ff; "The Historicity of Theology," *TI* 9, pp75ff; "Redemption," *TD*, pp395ff.

The AS, therefore, carries forward and completes the contemplative movement begun in the preparatory prayer, the preludes, the meditations and contemplations' various points, the repetitions and the résumés. The AS insures the slow and affective penetration of the exterior, *a posteriori*, historical, saving word of God into all the exercitant's dimensions. This awakens the inner, *a priori* word of God found in the exercitant's supernaturally elevated and Christ-affected transcendence to come to itself in full force to penetrate slowly and affectively the exercitant's many levels. The exercitant interiorly understands and savors (*Ex* 2), having become conscious with his entire body-person. He experiences an incarnational connaturality or holistic grasp of the entire saving mystery. He receives an affective intuition, an experiential knowledge, a sentiment of presence, a quasi-intellectual intuition anchored in an intellect and will enlightened by affective faith and animated by an affective love which permeates the entire body-person.[18]

Because Christ is the fulfillment of what it means to be human, and because He has touched everything through His life, death and resurrection, the AS completes its cycle in the presence of God's incarnate Word. The AS, therefore, plays a major role during the three weeks of meditations on Christ. The exercitant begins to make himself present to God's saving mystery in Christ by interiorizing it. At the next stage, he ought to receive an interior knowledge and tasting of its saving meaning. At the final stage, he should attain an incarnational, holistic, immediacy to the mystery best described in terms of the "spiritual senses." At this stage, just as the bodily senses are immediately present to the qualities of any sense object, the exercitant's "spiritual senses" are now immediately present to the Mystery of God's love in Christ.[19]

We totally agree with F. Marxer (pp63, 117, 162), therefore, that the final stage of the AS produces an experience initiated from, but not caused by, the outer senses. Holistic experiences of varying degrees and intensities during the last stage of the AS occur when the meditations on Christ have brought God's inner word to the exercitant into contact with itself. This produces a movement of grace from the exercitant's deepest core to his more external

---

[18] See: A. Gagliardi, p23; F. Marxer, pp39ff; H. Coathalem, p181; L. Roy, "Faut-il chercher la consolation dans la vie spirituelle? ," *ScE* 8(1956), p134. J. Maréchal's "Note sur la méthode d'application des sens dans les Exercices de S. Ignace," *Mélanges Watrigant*, pp50ff, on the other hand, is too rationalistic an explanation of the Ignatian AS.

[19] H. Rahner, *Ignatius*, pp187, 210; W. Peters, p35; *MI* II, 1, p781.

dimensions. Although the exercise begins with a progressive interiorization of the saving mystery, i.e., a movement from the outside to the inside, it ends with a movement from the inside to the outside. This last phase of the AS involves the graced body-person tasting in a holistic way at his very core the inner word of grace evoked and brought to itself through the outer, historical saving word of God.

Please note what is being said. Ignatius knew that the exercitant must interiorize the historical, *a posteriori* saving mysteries. But he also instinctively knew that the interior, spiritual senses experience and exteriorize that *a priori* dimension of the saving mystery in such a way that God's *a priori* word is the light, depth and horizon for properly understanding and experiencing the *a posteriori*, historical saving mysteries. The inner, spiritual senses are sensitive to God's grace which is present before and anticipates God's historical, saving grace. The ordered, integrated exercitant is sensitive both to God's inner and outer word.

Because inordinate attachments make it impossible for the exercitant at times to sense the deeper realities in his own being, one aspect of the AS centers upon the exercitant's purification by transforming his affective-spiritual dimensions through a spiritual-sensuous living, dying and rising with Jesus Christ.[20] The purified exercitant tastes the "true essentials" of the saving mystery, as well as its deepest interiority. The Ignatian AS, therefore, purifies, transforms, evokes and strengthens the exercitant's spiritual senses so that he can holistically experience and perceive at the most intimate point in his being the immediacy of God in Christ.

The Evocative Function of the Truths
of Salvation History

It seems clear, therefore, that the Ignatian method does far more than aid the exercitant to internalize a sublime, Christian value system, as W. Meissner (p187) too easily assumes. What distinguishes the Exercises from indoctrination is the twofold movement we saw above. Ignatius presents the exercitant with the objective, *a posteriori* truths of salvation history in such a way that he grasps not only their "true essentials," but also the *a priori* horizon against which these *a posteriori* saving events are experienced precisely as God's ways and deeds.

The *a posteriori*, saving truths of faith, for that reason, are tasted not only in themselves, but also inasmuch as they awaken, intensify

---

[20]F. Marxer, pp29, 169; G. Fessard, I, pp135ff.

and explicate the exercitant's supernaturally elevated and Christ-affected horizon of consciousness. These saving truths are then experienced precisely as *saving* and as truths of *faith*. The Ignatian method is a mystagogy into what is *already* hidden in the human heart, into what the exercitant continuously experiences on the fringe or as the undercurrent of all his experiences; moreover, he may ignore, repress or deny this haunting experience. The Exercises, therefore, expressly awaken the exercitant to what is already present in the depths of his being, present not by nature but by grace, a grace which embraces every person as the inescapable setting of his existence.[21] We are emphasizing that the Exercises do not merely bring something into the exercitant, but also light up, intensify and explicate what he already is, knows, lives and experiences, before the Church's external word reaches him.

The Exercises parallel, in a sense, the intrinsic, metaphysical dynamics of the act of faith itself. The external message of faith brings the *a priori* motive of faith, the light of faith, directly into relationship with itself. Because man is an historical being, the historical, *a posteriori* word of God is a necessary moment in the *a priori*, inner word's coming to itself. But it is only this inner word as the light of faith and interior connaturality with God that allows the person to hear the external word of God precisely as *God's* word.[22]

The external, *a posteriori*, historical word of God, however, does not merely explicate the *a priori*, inner word of God's anointing. Man is an historical being who from his very essence is referred to history in order to be what and who he is. History, therefore, is not merely the explication of the transcendental. And yet, the historical, *a posteriori*, external word of God corresponds to and fulfills the *a priori*, inner word of God's anointing. The inner word, moreover, anticipates this completion, although this completion is still experienced as a work of grace far surpassing its expectations. God's historical word expounds the inner word, intensifies it, explicates it, fulfills it and forces the exercitant to take a more explicit stand with respect to it. The *a posteriori* facts of salvation history are experienced as *saving* facts; hence, they strike profound, subjective chords in the exercitant.

Although God's historical word is a necessary moment in the inner word's coming to itself, this inner word dwells at the

---

[21] K. Rahner, "Nature and Grace," *TI* 4, pp168, 173, 178; "Faith," *TD*, pp166ff.
[22] K. Rahner, "Theology and Anthropology," *TI* 9, pp42ff; "Reflections on Methodology in Theology," *TI* 11, pp84ff.

exercitant's core and reaches its fulfillment as *his* fulfillment. Again, the Exercises are not ideology nor indoctrination. Anthropocentric fulfillment is not only a movement from the outside to the inside, but also one from the inside to the outside. Just as a person who describes his experiences to a psychiatrist is often told in different, yet enlightening and freeing terms what he already somehow knew, experienced, and lived, so, too, with the Exercises. The Exercises are a form of psychiatric therapy in which the exercitant comes to realize more explicitly and freely what he had always known and experienced in some way. Or, in a sense, the Exercises are like a loudspeaker which amplifies what is already there. This amplification of what was once only implicit, marginal, repressed or hidden often works a profound conversion and transformation.

Ignatius insures the required interaction between the objective truths of salvation history and the exercitant's subjective, inner anointing by instructing him to become connatural with the saving mystery at hand and with his own true self. Ignatius, therefore, removes the exercitant from his ordinary daily life as much as possible to plunge him into God's saving realities (*Ex* 18-20). As W. Peters (pp24ff) has noted, moreover, although the "points" (*Ex* 47) of each Ignatian exercise do refer at times to its individual parts or breakdown, "points" also refer to "the various activities of the exercitant" (p26). The exercitant must orient his memory, understanding, will, imagination, reason, emotions and reflections with the particular meditation at hand.

This also means that the Ignatian instructions concerning a "mental image of the place" are more than a "composition of place," as tradition would have it. W. Peters correctly insists that "the second prelude is not a composition of *place*, but a composition of *oneself*" (p30). The exercitant must put himself together to harmonize as deeply as possible with the specific, saving mystery. He "composes" himself by seeing, hearing, tasting, smelling, touching, considering and reflecting upon God's word. He focuses his entire being like a concentrating lens on the "true essentials" of the mystery, which also includes its spatio-temporal qualities. We agree with W. Peters that "composition implies inner harmony and unity as well as harmony with external circumstances" (p29).

In the light of the Mystery of God in Christ's life, death and resurrection, Ignatius also throws the exercitant back upon himself. He must review his entire life (*Ex* 56). He reviews each day methodically, often comparing hour by hour, or one day with another (*Ex* 24-31, 43). He must compare himself to all men, to the angels, and even to God (*Ex* 58-9, 258). He attempts to experience himself as the rest of creation does (*Ex* 60). In the presence of Christ on the Cross, he examines himself and asks: "What have *I* done for Christ? What am *I* now doing for Christ? What ought *I* do for Christ? " (*Ex* 53, emphasis mine). He is to pray to a God who became man *for him* (*Ex* 104, 116). He is instructed to contemplate certain mysteries as if *he himself were there* (*Ex* 114). He prays to Christ who goes to His Passion for *his* sins (*Ex* 193, 197, 206). He is asked what *he* should do about it (*Ex* 197, 206). He must "ponder with great affection how much God our Lord has done *for me*, and how many of His graces He has given *me*" (*Ex* 234, emphasis mine). He must see, hear, smell, touch, taste and then *reflect within himself* to derive profit (*Ex* 106-8, 115-6, 122-5, 194, 234-7).

Ignatius also expects that "as a result of his own reasoning or through the enlightenment of his understanding by Divine grace," the exercitant "may find something that will make it [the divine mystery] a little more meaningful for him or touch him more deeply" (*Ex* 2). The psychologically perceptive Ignatius knew that most persons are more delighted by what they discover for themselves than by what they hear from "discourse at great length" (*Ex* 2).[23]

This is one reason, therefore, why many Ignatian meditations, as repetitions, résumés and AS, are *continuations* of a previous meditation. They work over and deepen those points in which the exercitant experienced the greatest consolation, desolation, or spiritual relish (*Ex* 62, 118, 132, 148, etc.). The exercitant must not change anything during a meditation or hasten, as long as he is finding "what he desires" (*Ex* 2, 76, 89, 130, 133, etc.).

For this reason, the sober, concentrated presentation of the truths of salvation history demands a subjective moment of creative self-presence in which the exercitant comes to taste salvation history as the history of *his* salvation. The exercitant must percolate this saving history through his being in such a way that he is thrown back upon himself, radically called into question, then knows and possesses himself to give himself. Essential to Ignatius' method is the discovery and subjective tasting of the personal, subjective anticipation of the objective truths of salvation history. In the light of salvation history, he sees himself and experiences this history precisely as *his* salvation.

---

[23]*MI* II, 1, p1136. J.B. Lotz, *op. cit.*, is an excellent explanation of the Ignatian method of discovery.

For the proper interaction of the exercitant's God-anointed subjectivity with the objective, historical saving truths, the exercitant must experience himself as a unity-in-multiplicity, as a being with the deepest interiority which begins at an inviolable center and moves out in ever-varying degrees of "exteriorized-interiority" to exteriority.[24] Ignatius alerts the exercitant to his interiority and exteriority in various ways. As we saw above, he instructs the exercitant to recognize that certain thoughts come solely from his own liberty and will, whereas others come "from without" (*Ex* 32-3, 347). We maintain, moreover, that "from without" refers to a dimension outside of the exercitant's most intimate core. "From without" refers to his more "exteriorized-interiority" levels, and not to a dimension found outside of the exercitant himself in some spatial sense of the word.[25] Through the examination of his conscience, the exercitant learns to discern what comes from his very core from what comes "from without," i.e., from outside of his own freedom, from the different levels of his own "exteriorized-interiority" which do not belong to his inner core of freedom.

Because God alone can console at the exercitant's deepest core (*Ex* 330), consolation from God is his most *interior* experience. All consolation from God and His angels, moreover, is an interior movement which brings interior joy (*Ex* 316). God and His angels "bring *true* happiness and spiritual joy to the soul and . . . free it from *all* sadness and disturbance" (*Ex* 329, emphasis mine). The consolation from the evil spirit, however, is only "apparent" (*Ex* 314), always contains the "serpent's tail" (*Ex* 334), and works against the exercitant's advancement. It would seem, therefore, that false consolations (and desolations, too) do not begin at nor penetrate to the exercitant's innermost core, but always remain in his more "exteriorized-interiority" levels.

The Anthropocentric Moment and
the Mystery of God in Jesus Christ

From what we have already seen, Ignatius immerses the exercitant into his own radical mystery as man by plunging him into

---

[24] K. Rahner, "Unity-Love-Mystery," *TI* 8, pp230ff; "Some Thoughts on 'a good Intention'," *TI* 3, pp106ff; "Dialektik von Einheit und Vielfalt im Wesen des Menschen," *HPTh* II/1, pp22ff.

[25] See: W. Sierp, *Hochschule*, I, pp30, 145; II, p 412; A. Ambruzzi, p160; J.B. Scaramelli, p136; V. Mercier, pp418-9. On p177, Mercier says that the Rules for the Discernment of Spirits do not apply to unfree motions. We reject this view. We also disagree with A. Gagliardi, p107, and J. Clémence, p348, who seem to interpret Ignatius' "from without" phrase too literally.

the Mystery of God in Jesus Christ. As the exercitant gives more of himself to the great saving mysteries, he slowly realizes that the penetration into God's Mystery in Christ's life, death and resurrection, and the penetration of his own mystery as man, are intrinsically linked. The feedback result of his explicit surrender to the Mystery of God in Jesus Christ is a deepening, strengthening and fulfilling of what is most profoundly human in the exercitant's being. The initiation into the Mystery of God in Jesus Christ is no mere indoctrination, therefore. It corresponds to the exercitant's deepest desire for total, human self-fulfillment. The exercitant's conversion to the Mystery of God in Jesus Christ contains as a necessary moment of its accomplishment the total opening of the exercitant's being for his own "return" to himself in active self-identity.[26]

The exercitant's anthropocentric fulfillment is hindered by inordinate attachments (*Ex* 1), the flesh and the world (*Ex* 97). These are the immediate focal points of a dramatic struggle being fought against the "enemy of our human nature" which has its ultimate victory only in the Cross of Jesus Christ (*Ex* 95, 98, 142, 146, 155, 157, 173, 193, etc.).

That Ignatius designates Jesus Christ as the "true life" (*Ex* 139) which has been revealed by "the Creator who became man" (*Ex* 53), and Satan as "the enemy of our human nature" and "the enemy of our progress" (*Ex* 7, 136, 325, 333, 334, etc.) has great anthropocentric significance. Ignatius juxtaposes Jesus Christ and Satan to show clearly that we find our true humanity in the humanity of Jesus Christ (*Ex* 53, 195, 196, 219, etc.) and the death of this humanity in Satan. The two, real, although unequal, dialectical possibilities of human nature are: surrender to Christ in whom the fulfillment of human nature is already a reality and so can fulfill ours, or surrender to the mortal enemy of this nature who thwarts its progress.

Ignatius' explicit Christology and demonology contain a very powerful, albeit indirect, anthropocentric reference. Jesus Christ and "the enemy of our human nature," for Ignatius, are two realities which intrinsically affect the exercitant. The Ignatian drama is an anthropocentric drama which concerns the exercitant's fulfillment or destruction as man.

Ignatius instructs the exercitant, therefore, to enter the Exercises with great courage and generosity, offering God his entire will and the disposition of his person (*Ex* 5). His progress consists in the

---

[26] J.B. Metz, p80.

depth of his flight from self-love, self-will and self-interest (*Ex* 189). This movement manifests itself christocentrically when the exercitant begs to be taken under Christ's standard in its most intimate form (*Ex* 98, 147, 156, 168, etc.), asks what he is going to do for Christ (*Ex* 53), and offers his total self to the Lord (*Ex* 234). The flight from self-love, self-will and self-interest parallels Christ's, because "it is with reason that He will not have us withhold a part of ourselves, since He has so completely given Himself to us and desires to give Himself to us forever."[27]

Ignatius' method, therefore, implicitly rests upon an anthropocentric-christocentric Mystagogy which sees the existential self-dedication which Christ accomplished as corresponding to the basic desire of all human nature to surrender itself to Mystery. Ignatius' method stresses explicitly and implicitly that whoever gives himself to God without reserve comes to his true self, because he has imitated Christ's self-emptying, the perfect act of the perfect man.

In and through the meditations on Christ's life, death and resurrection, the exercitant secretly tastes in Him the fulfillment of his being. The explicit and personal reference to Jesus Christ places the exercitant before the only man in human history who answered with His life and His person the radical question which every man is and lives at the core of his being. The exercitant comes into contact with the perfect man who accomplished what every human heart longs to perform: total surrender to the loving Mystery which calls him beyond himself in self-fulfilling love. Accomplishing this surrender with a totality that stamped His entire person is the meaning of Christ's life and being. Every single phase of the Exercises, therefore, aims at that mysterious wholeness demanded by human nature, which, paradoxically, can be brought to itself and completed only in Christ.

When the exercitant, therefore, receives the Father-initiated CSCP which arises from the meditations on Christ's life, death and resurrection and which sums up, concentrates and fulfills the basic thrust of his being to surrender to loving Mystery, and when he responds to this consolation in such a way that he lives the Ignatian "Take, O Lord, and receive all my liberty, etc." (*Ex* 234) from the depths of his being, then he has reached the anthropocentric-christocentric goal of the Exercises. He has surrendered to the Mystery of God in Jesus Christ and to his own deepest mystery as man.

---

[27] *Letters*, p131. See also p84, 149, 167, 174.

 Chapter IV

The Christocentric
Moment of the Exercises
and the Ignatian
Mystical Horizon

INTRODUCTION

This chapter will explore the christocentric aspects of the Ignatian mystical horizon by unfolding the intrinsic, christocentric moment of the Exercises. Ignatius' encounter with and experiences of Jesus Christ had determined his all-embracing mystical horizon, his *a priori* stance towards reality, the actual way in which he thought and experienced everything. Jesus Christ dominated Ignatius' entire perspective. Ignatius tacitly presupposed Christ's central position in creation, in sustaining that creation and in salvation history. He also implicitly presupposed that the exercitant has been deeply touched by the life, death and resurrection of Christ. Ignatius knew that the exercitant is a Christ-directed being, for Christ is the absolute fulfillment of what the exercitant is as man.

THE CHRISTOCENTRIC GOAL OF
EACH WEEK OF THE EXERCISES

The First Week
The First Week of the Exercises focuses primarily on the history of sin and disorder and their ultimate consequence: hell.[1] Ignatius expressly desires the First Week to center on the consideration and contemplation of sin (*Ex* 4) to introduce the exercitant to the purgative way (*Ex* 10). The exercitant reaches the goal of the First Week when he understands and experiences the cosmic dimensions of sin

---

[1] See *Ex* 45-71. The Christocentrism of the *Foundation* meditation (*Ex* 23) will be treated on pp97ff.

and disorder (*Ex* 50), the beginnings of sin and disorder in human history (*Ex* 51), the power of sin and disorder in his own life (*Ex* 55-61), the personal disorder which sin can cause (*Ex* 62-3), and the ultimate consequences of sin as hell (*Ex* 65-71). Ignatius clearly expects the exercitant to receive profound sorrow, contrition and tears for his sins (*Ex* 4).

The strongly personalistic emphases of the First Week, however, are the key to understanding its profundity. Ignatius constantly refers the exercitant to Mary, the Father, or Christ crucified (*Ex* 46, 48, 50, 52, 53, 58-61, 63, 71, etc.). These references to persons, especially to Christ crucified, prevent an abstract consideration of sin and enforces the interpersonal and relational understanding and experiencing of sin. Sorrow, contrition and tears in the First Week must flow from a deep appreciation of "What have I done for Christ? ", and not from abstract theological principles. The exercitant of the First Week deepens his sense of sin, because he deepens his sense of the mercy and love of God in Jesus Christ. In and through the meditations of the First Week, he discovers that he is a redeemed sinner, subject to great mercy (*Ex* 60), and profoundly loved.[2]

Although the Father and Mary belong to one of the most important colloquies of the First Week, Christ crucified (*Ex* 53, 71) specifies the basic horizon and is the hermeneutical key for understanding this Week. The exercitant radically reviews his life in terms of the Creator who became man to die for his sins. He ponders the course of history in terms of before, during and after the life of Christ. In the presence of Christ crucified, the Father's love and mercy towards men, he experiences the contrition, sorrow and tears for his sins for which he so ardently pleads (*Ex* 4, 48, 50, 56, 63, 65, etc.). The exercitant reaches the high point and goal of the First Week when he truly cries out in wonder that he has been spared (*Ex* 60), sees the entire sinful cosmos as taken up in God's love and mercy, and surrenders himself in the colloquy of mercy to Jesus Christ.[3] The Christocentrism of the First Week heightens the exercitant's sense of himself as a sinner, but as a sinner redeemed in and

---

[2] L. Beirnaert, "Sens de Dieu et sens du péché. Besoins contemporains et spiritualité ignatienne," *RAM* 26(1950), pp18-9; Cf. also G. Cusson, *Pédagogie*, p197.

[3] H. Rahner, *Ignatius*, p59; L. Boros, "Dialektik der Freiheit. Gaston Fessards Erhellung der ignatianischen 'Exerzitien' durch Hegel," *WW* (1962), p188; W. Sierp, "Das Christusbild der ersten ignatianischen Exerzitienwoche," (="Christusbild"), *ThGl* 20(1928), pp814ff; G. Cusson, *Pédagogie*, pp166ff; E. Przywara, *Deus* I, p231.

through the Father's love and mercy in Jesus Christ. For these reasons, the First Week is just as much a "Jesus Week" as the other three.[4]

H. Rahner understands the First Week so christocentrically that for him, sin is intrinsically linked to the rejection of Jesus Christ. The angels sinned by rejecting the Incarnation of the Creator-become-man.[5] Sin for H. Rahner, therefore, is the radical "No" of the angels, men and the exercitant to the incarnation, life, death and resurrection of the Creator-become-man.

The profound Christocentrism of the First Week, therefore, provides the necessary prerequisites for a christocentric experience of sin and salvation and links the First Week with the meditation on the Incarnation, the major event in world history, as given in the Second Week (*Ex* 101ff). It also leads the exercitant to answer the question he raised in *Ex* 53, "What shall I do for Christ? ", in terms of the call of Christ in the *Kingdom* meditation (*Ex* 91ff), the example of Christ in the *Third Degree of Humility* (*Ex* 167), and an Election which explicitly and concretely specifies this call and humility into a particular way of life or a particular course of action.[6]

The Second Week

The Second Week corresponds to the illuminative way (*Ex* 10). Jesus Christ, therefore, is also the light of this week, but Christ as seen from the meditations on his life up to and including Palm Sunday (*Ex* 4). The Second Week concerns itself with the imitation of Christ. This imitation, however, is the fruit of a grace consistently prayed for: for the intimate knowledge and love of Jesus Christ (*Ex* 104, 130, etc.).

The high point and goal of the Second Week, then, is "an intimate knowledge of our Lord, who has become man for me, that I may love and follow Him better" (*Ex* 104). This knowledge, moreover, must flow into the most radical form of Ignatian service: to serve the Eternal Father in poverty, in abuses and in sufferings, as seen from Christ's example given in the *Third Degree of Humility* (*Ex* 167).[7] The following of Christ in poverty, in abuses and in

---

[4] W. Sierp, "Christusbild," pp812-3; Cf. also: H. Pinard de la Boullaye, "Jésus, dans les Exercices," (="Jésus"), *RAM* 18(1937), pp220-1; J. Solano, "Jesucristo en la Primera Semana de Ejercicios," *MiCo* 26(1956), pp165-76.

[5] H. Rahner, *Ignatius*, pp69ff. Cf. also: "Notes," pp312ff.

[6] H. Rahner, *Werden*, p45. Cf. also, *Ignatius*, pp106ff. Even for those not capable or willing to go beyond the First Week, the goal of this week is still Christocentric: frequent confession and Holy Communion (*Ex* 18).

[7] See: *Ex* 98, 104, 109, 130, 139, 147, 167, 168; Cf. also: J. Roothaan, p161, n1.

sufferings provides the hermeneutical key for understanding the Christocentrism of the Second Week.

The Third Week

The Third Week immerses the exercitant in the Passion of Jesus Christ (*Ex* 4). The exercitant is summoned to contemplate the Divinity which hides Itself and the most Sacred Humanity of Jesus which suffers so cruelly for the exercitant's sake (*Ex* 196).[8] Ignatius expects the exercitant to experience deep grief and sorrow because Christ is going to his death for the exercitant's sins (*Ex* 193, 197, 203, etc.). The suffering and dying Jesus dominates the entire perspective of the Third Week and provides the necessary hermeneutical key for understanding its goal and purpose.

The Fourth Week

During the Fourth Week, the exercitant participates in the Risen Life of Jesus Christ (*Ex* 4). He must contemplate the Divinity which appears and manifests Itself in the Resurrection (*Ex* 223). He reaches the high point and goal of this week when he experiences the intense joy and gladness for the great glory and joy of Jesus Christ (*Ex* 221, 229). In fact, Christ *is* his consolation during this week (*Ex* 224). The glorious and Risen Christ dominates the entire perspective of the Fourth Week.

THE EXPLICIT CHRISTOCENTRISM OF THE EXERCISES

The *Kingdom*, *Two Standards* and the *Three Degrees of Humility*: the Election of Jesus Poor, Suffering and Humiliated

One of the most deeply Ignatian meditations, and one which not only sums up the experience of Ignatius' early conversion, but also presents the main lines and major emphases of the Christology of the Exercises is the *Kingdom* (*Ex* 91ff).[9] In this meditation, Jesus is

---

[8] An exposition and critique of Ignatius' monophysite tendencies is beyond the scope of this work.

[9] Cf.: H. Rahner, *Werden*, p47; J. de Guibert, *Jesuits*, pp118-9; J. Nadal, as quoted by J. Conwell, *Contemplation in Action. A Study in Ignatian Prayer* (Washington, 1957), pp21ff, 46ff; G. Dirks, "Le 'De Regno Christi' et la personne du Christ," *RAM* 29(1953), pp317-26; G. Cusson, *Pédagogie*, p241; I. Zeiger, "Gefolgschaft des Herrn, ein rechtsgeschichtlicher Beitrag zu den Exerzitien des heiligen Ignatius," *ZAM* 17(1942), pp1-16. Zeiger has shown that the knightly ideal plays a considerable role in Ignatian spirituality. The

depicted as a living Leader with the means at His disposal of carrying out the Father's salvific Will. This Christ invites those who want to distinguish themselves by their *service* to follow Christ in the accomplishment of His task. The exercitant, therefore, is called upon to share the very life of Christ in much the same way that soldier and general often share the same life on the battlefield, and then the glory. The exercitant who wishes to prove himself a worthy knight makes an oblation that he will follow Christ poor, suffering and despised, if Christ so calls him.

The *Official Directory* describes the *Kingdom* as a foundation or prelude to the entire course of the Exercises, and as a summary of Christ's life and the mission entrusted to Him by the Father.[10] Because the *Kingdom* introduces the coming meditations on the life of Christ and concentrates within itself the main lines and basic dynamics of all these meditations, it is often considered to be a second *Foundation* meditation.[11] The abstract truths of the *Foundation* and its means and end schema are now seen in explicitly christocentric terms, the working out of salvation history in the life, death resurrection of Jesus Christ.

The *Kingdom*, therefore, remains one of the most fundamental meditations of the Exercises. It concentrates within itself Ignatius' main lines and christocentric emphases, evokes within the exercitant the desire to imitate, follow and serve Christ radically if necessary, and so prepares the exercitant for the very important work of the Election.[12] The exercitant learns in the *Kingdom* that he was created to serve the triune God reverently through the imitation of Christ poor, suffering and humiliated, and so enter into His glory. We agree, therefore, with G. Cusson (p340) that the experience fundamental to the *Kingdom* meditation provides the key for understanding the Exercises in their entirety.

The *Two Standards* (*Ex* 136-48) meditation continues, expands and forms an inner unity with the *Kingdom*. This meditation elucidates in greater detail what is proper to Christ's Kingdom, what is His manner of doing things, and that He has knowledge of the true life. The exercitant also discovers that the "evil chieftain" calls him and

---

relationship between Lord and vassal, in this view, is one of service based upon mutual trust and friendship, and not upon money.

[10] *MI* II, 1, p1148. Cf. H. Coathalem, p23.

[11] See: H. Pinard de la Boullaye, "Jésus," p221; J. Roothaan, p158, n1; H. Rahner, *Werden*, p93; F. de Hummelauer, pp6ff; G. Cusson, "Exercices," p1316.

[12] See: *MI* II, 1, p1162.

that the "evil chieftain" has his own methods and deceits. Using some of the Exercises' richest symbolism, the *Two Standards* accentuates the difference between Christ's Kingdom and its goal with that of the Kingdom and goal of the enemy of our human nature. This meditation introduces the exercitant to the basics of the discernment of spirits and is, in fact, a dramatic transposition of the Ignatian Rules for the Discernment of Spirits in their most profound sense.[13]

The *Kingdom* and the *Two Standards* set the stage for the dramatic nature of the Exercises. The exercitant finds himself before Jesus Christ who calls him to serve in the work of the redemption through spiritual or actual poverty, contempt and humility. Although the exercitant is called to serve with Christ, he must still pray and ask to be placed under Christ's standard (*Ex* 147). Ignatius wishes to make it absolutely clear to the exercitant that he is also exposed to the wiles and deceits of the "evil chieftain" who calls him to riches, honor and pride. The exercitant must be able to discern keenly the call of Christ and the call of the "evil chieftain," especially as he approaches the difficult task of the Election. These deeply Ignatian meditations are the two basic poles around which some of the deepest movements of the Exercises take place. These movements demand incisive discernment.

Note, however, that these two key meditations emphasize the exercitant's *being called*, and not his making an Election. The exercitant must beg not to be deaf to the call (*Ex* 91), to respond with the dispositions of a good knight (*Ex* 94), to be called to imitate Christ in bearing injuries, insults, all evils, etc. (*Ex* 98) and to be placed under the standard of Christ either in perfect spiritual poverty or in actual poverty (*Ex* 147). The deeply personal logic of these meditations should lead to a decision during the consideration of the *Three Degrees of Humility* to choose only those things (other factors being equal) which will make the exercitant more like Christ poor, suffering and despised.

The *Kingdom*, the *Two Standards* and the *Three Degrees of Humility*, therefore, do not stress the Election as such but the being called and the desire to be placed with Christ poor, suffering and despised. The inner dynamism of these three meditations, however, provides the foundation and context essential to the Election. Only in the context of the desire to be placed with Christ poor, suffering and despised does the Ignatian Election reveal its profundity.

[13]Cf.: V. Mercier, p314; I. Diertins, p303, n3; F. de Hummelauer, pp20ff; E. Przywara, *Deus* II, pp103ff; S. Lyonnet, "La méditation des Deux Étendards et son fondement scriptuaire," *Chr* 12 (1956), pp435-57.

The exercitant, moreover, does not stand before a row of possible choices, only one of which is in conformity with God's Will. He stands before the Christ of glory who calls Him to help in the redemptive work. The exercitant who desires to distinguish himself in the service of the Divine Majesty (*Ex* 97) will want to be placed under Christ's standard (*Ex* 147), and to follow Christ as intimately as possible.

What the exercitant really elects to do, therefore, is to respond to a call which places him under Christ's standard in the most perfect spiritual poverty, and perhaps even in actual poverty. The choice of a way of life or the reform of one's life, in short, the more explicit and concrete form of the Ignatian Election, actually depends upon the exercitant's ability, readiness and disposition to follow Christ poor, suffering and despised. The strength and purity of the exercitant's anthropocentric self-emptying can be measured by his desire to resemble Christ poor, suffering and despised, and to serve the Father in this way.

The goal of each week of the Exercises and the meditations on the *Kingdom*, the *Two Standards* and the *Three Degrees of Humility* provide the foundation, background and necessary horizon against which the more explicit and more concrete Election takes place. Only when the exercitant so disposes himself to be free from all inordinate affections (*Ex* 1), only when he resolves not to be deaf to the call of Christ (*Ex* 91), only when he sincerely desires to be placed under the standard of Christ in the most radical fashion of an ever greater service and praise of the Eternal Father through the following of Christ poor, suffering and despised is he ready for the actual, concrete Election. The radical Christocentrism of the Exercises demands that before the exercitant is ready to come to a concrete form of Election concerning his life in full or in part, he must first of all have elected to surrender himself as deeply as possible to the Christ who serves the Father and works out the redemption of man through poverty, sufferings and humiliations. The Exercises, therefore, rest upon and lead to a mysticism of service of the Eternal Father, and grasp that in the life of Christ poor, suffering and humiliated the profoundest and most efficient expression and means of service can be found.[14]

[14] See: J. de Guibert, *Jesuits*, chap. 17, "To Serve in Company with Christ,"; H. Schlingen, "Die Bedeutung der Betrachtung über die Liebe in den Exerzitien," *ZAM* 8(1933), pp33ff; R. Cantin, "Le troisième degré d'humilité et la gloire de Dieu selon saint Ignace de Loyola," *ScE* 8(1958), pp237-66.

The Triple Colloquy

The *Triple Colloquy* of the Second Week (*Ex* 147) contains the quintessence of everything we have said about the above three key meditations. It is extraordinary that Ignatius has the exercitant make this colloquy some 15 times (*Ex* 147-8, 156, 158, 161, etc.) before the *Three Degrees of Humility* meditation; moreover, he is to make this colloquy during the *Degrees* meditation itself (*Ex* 168). This colloquy likewise serves as the mode of colloquy to be made during the Third Week. It is also to be noted that the oblation prayed during the *Kingdom* meditation (*Ex* 98) contains many of the elements of the *Triple Colloquy*.

The *Triple Colloquy* explicitly welds together the Exercises' anthropocentric and christocentric dimensions. The exercitant's deepest desire and the specific nature of Ignatian Christology explicitly manifest themselves during this colloquy. The exercitant asks to be placed under Christ's standard in the most perfect spiritual or actual poverty. His one desire is to imitate and follow Christ poor, suffering and humiliated. The exercitant's anthropocentric self-emptying, therefore, reaches its goal when it is explicitly christocentric. True self-identity and self-surrender reveal themselves as the pure desire to imitate Christ in His self-emptying poverty, sufferings and humiliations. It is *this desire* which dominates the entire Ignatian perspective.

The Christ to be imitated, however, is still "the Eternal Lord of all things" (*Ex* 98) and the "Eternal King" (*Ex* 95) who calls the exercitant to His service. *This view of Christ* dominates the Exercises' perspective and gives even the individual meditations on the life, passion, death and resurrection of Christ their particular Ignatian stamp. This is the Christ who is obedient to His parents at Nazareth (*Ex* 134), who preaches in the temple (*Ex* 161), whose Divinity hides itself and whose Sacred Humanity suffers so cruelly (*Ex* 196), and who manifests His Divinity through the effects of the Resurrection (*Ex* 223). It is the "Eternal Lord of all things," therefore, who calls the exercitant to His service through the imitation of Him poor, suffering and humiliated. It is *this* Christ, the "supreme and true Leader" (*Ex* 139) with His standard and His way of life who provides the hermeneutical key for understanding the Exercises.

The Christomorphic Theme

The Ignatian imitation of Christ partially stems from his fascination with the christomorphic theme.[15] Ignatius' *Autobiography*

[15] R. Barthes, pp46ff.

points to an often very literal imitation of Christ. D. Mollat's fascinating article on the *Autobiography* points out that Ignatius' life shortly after his conversion literally resembled Christ's life in many important aspects.[16] The *Autobiography* also emphasizes Ignatius' desire to imitate Christ poor through a life of begging and to find his security and confidence only in Jesus Christ. When Ignatius began his studies, in order to progress more easily, he often imagined that the professor was Christ Himself and his fellow students the disciples. When Ignatius wrestled with the very difficult question of the Order's poverty, he noted that since Jesus was Head of the Society, this was a greater argument to proceed in complete poverty than all the other human reasons he had mustered.[17]

The Exercises also contain the christomorphic theme. In the matter of eating and drinking, Ignatius demands a harmony between inner disposition and outer behavior that is inspired by Christ's example. At table, the exercitant imagines himself in the presence of Christ and His disciples and observes how Christ eats, drinks, looks and speaks (*Ex* 214). When the exercitant gives alms, Christ is again the norm so that his way of life approaches as near as possible Jesus Christ's, "our model and rule" (*Ex* 344). The *Third Degree of Humility* offers the best example of the Exercises' christomorphic theme. Other things being equal, the exercitant is to desire and choose those things that will make him more like Christ poor, suffering and humiliated. The Ignatian imitation of Christ, therefore, is profound, penetrating and often literal.

The Christocentrism of the Application of the Senses

The AS plays a considerable role in the Exercises, because the exercitant is to use this method of prayer almost daily. Because most of the individual meditations are explicitly christocentric, the AS frequently focuses on the person of Jesus Christ. Because of the unity between the anthropocentric and christocentric dimensions of the Exercises, the proper object of the AS is Christ.[18] The exercitant

---

[16] D. Mollat, "Le Christ dans l'expérience spirituelle de saint Ignace," *Chr* 1(1954), esp. pp32ff.

[17] See: *St. Ignatius' Own Story.* (=*Autobiography*), trans. by W. Young (Loyola Univ: Chicago, 1956), p53; *SJ*, Feb. 23; F. Suarez, p52: "Nam conformitatem ad Christum putant esse sufficientem rationem amandi omnem abjectionem et humilitatis modum."

[18] See: *MI* II, 2, p510.

tastes in Christ the fulfillment, perfection and meaning of his own humanity. As Origen said:

> Christ is the source, and streams of living water flow out of him. He is bread and gives life. And thus he is also spikenard and gives forth fragrance, ointment which turns us into the anointed (*christoi*). He is something for each particular sense of the soul. He is Light so that the soul may have eyes. Word, so that it may have ears to hear. Bread, so that it may savour him. Oil of anointing, so that it may breathe in the fragrance of the Word. And he has become flesh, so that the inward hand of the soul may be able to touch something of the Word of life, which fashions itself to correspond with the various manifestations of prayer and which leaves no sense of the soul untouched by his grace.[19]

The first and last object of the spiritual senses, therefore, is none other than the World made flesh, Jesus Christ of the Gospels.[20] Through the AS, the exercitant opens himself to Christ's Divinity, His Spirit, His Humanity, the summit of created self-transcendence, and the perfection, meaning and goal of all things. The AS bestows upon the exercitant an instinct for the christocentric depth in all reality. Through the AS, moreover, the exercitant experiences in and through the Humanity of Christ that the man Jesus is "totally my God," that the Father is Father of "such a Son," that this "Jesus sits at the feet of the Trinity," and that Jesus is what it means to be fully human.[21] The AS, therefore, gathers together and unites the christocentric, anthropocentric and mystagogical tasting which flows from that interior understanding and savoring (*Ex* 2) of the intimate knowledge of Jesus Christ who has become man for me (*Ex* 104).

The Personal Knowledge of Jesus Christ

The emphasis upon the Christ of the Gospels gives the Exercises an eminently concrete character. The person of Jesus Christ dominates the entire perspective of the Exercises. The contemplation of this person is far more important than any event, incident, or doctrine presented in the Exercises. The contemplation of the person of Christ under certain aspects determines the grace to be asked for during a particular meditation or a particular week. Ignatius would have the exercitant flee from all self-love, self-will and self-interest (*Ex* 189) so that he may be filled with Jesus Christ.[22] One extremely

---

[19] Origen, quoted by H. Rahner, *Ignatius*, p200.
[20] H. Rahner, *Ignatius*, pp199ff, 184ff; F. Marxer, p62; A. Haas, *GÜ*, pp147ff.
[21] *SJ*, Feb. 23, 27, 28.
[22] *Letters*, pp150, 290, 292, 295, *passim*.

important Ignatian goal is to have the retreatant progress in the existential knowledge and love of Christ, especially Him poor, suffering and humiliated.[23] Part of the Ignatian genius shows itself in that Ignatius does not have the exercitant meditate upon abstract virtues, religious truths or dogmas, yet presents them all, but indirectly, in and through his strong emphasis on the intimate knowledge, love and service of the person, Jesus Christ, the man who is "totally my God."

The Intimate Knowledge of the Cosmic Christ

The Ignatian Christ is the Christ of Majesty, the "Eternal Word" (*Ex* 130). In the manger, on the cross, with His disciples, etc. the Ignatian Christ is never separated from the plenitude of being which unites Him to the Trinity. Ignatius strongly emphasizes that Jesus Christ is the *Creator-become-creature*. Jesus Christ is the Creator who became man (*Ex* 53), the "Eternal Lord" (*Ex* 65), the "Eternal Lord of all things" (*Ex* 98), the Creator and Lord who works in His creatures (*Ex* 16), the Lord and Savior who wants to communicate Himself to the devout soul (*Ex* 15), "the Eternal Word Incarnate" (*Ex* 109, 130), the Divinity who allows His Sacred Humanity to suffer (*Ex* 196), the Divinity who has risen from the dead and now acts as Consoler (*Ex* 223-4), and the exercitant's Creator and Redeemer. Be it in the Incarnation, on the Cross or in the Resurrection, Ignatius sees the Creator as having bridged the entire gap of possible love between Himself and the exercitant. The Creator has given Himself in the deepest possible way to the exercitant.

One of the foundational elements of Ignatian Christology, therefore, is Jesus Christ as man and as "Creator and Lord." Ignatius clearly expects the exercitant to experience deeply Jesus Christ as his "Creator and Lord."[24] The Eternal Lord of all things, the Creator and Lord, the Christ of Majesty, the eternal King who accomplished His mission through His life, death and resurrection and now calls the exercitant to share in His mission, dominates the Ignatian perspective. The exercitant must imitate Christ poor, suffering and humiliated, but the Christ whom the exercitant has also experienced as his Creator and Lord.

Ignatius had tasted deeply in his own life and successfully translated into his Exercises that the "Creator . . . although infinite, made

---

[23] L. Peeters, p24; W. Betrams, "Die Gleichzeitigkeit des betenden Christen mit den Geheimnissen des Lebens Jesu," *GuL* 24(1951), pp414ff.

[24] H. Rahner, *Ignatius*, pp63ff; D. Mollat, pp23ff; R. Hostie, "Le cercle de l'action et de l'oraison d'après le Père Jérôme Nadal," *Chr* 6(1955), p196.

Himself finite and willing to die."[25] The Exercises frequently refer to Christ as Creator and to the fact that we are His creatures.[26] The exercitant will discover through the meditations on the life of Christ that redemption essentially means the Creator Himself entering into His creation.[27] Ignatius frequently refers to the Society of Jesus as the *Societas Jesu Creatoris*, as O. Vercruysse has shown.[28]

The Ignatian experience of Christ, therefore, welds together in one stroke his deeply personal love of the man Jesus and his cosmic Christology. This cosmic, yet deeply personal love of Christ, flowed, no doubt, from a mystically experienced *communicatio idiomatum*.[29] Many commentators are convinced that when Ignatius uses the expressions "Creator," "Creator and Lord," "Creator and Redeemer," "Eternal Lord of all things," etc. that he is referring to the person of Jesus Christ.[30] The exercitant's intimate, existential knowledge and love of Jesus Christ must contain as a moment of its realization a penetration into the cosmic Christ: the *man* Jesus is totally the exercitant's *Creator, Lord* and *God.*

IGNATIUS' DEEPER, MORE IMPLICIT CHRISTOCENTRISM

Ignatius' Architechtonic View: All in Christ

Shortly after Ignatius' conversion, he mystically experienced and saw with the eyes of his spirit the humanity of Christ, how God had created the world, and how Jesus was present in the Eucharist. More importantly, however, he had received an architectonic insight into all of the truths of the faith.[31] What Nadal says about the essence of

---

[25] *Letters*, p56, *passim.*

[26] See: *Ex* 5, 16, 20, 330, 15, 50-3, 229.

[27] See: *Ex* 184, 229, 316, 230-8.

[28] O. Vercruysse, "Our Creator and Lord Jesus Christ," *Ignatiana* (Ranchi, 1956), pp245ff.

[29] H. Rahner, *Ignatius*, p15. Ignatius does not make the connection between his Jesus-mysticism and his Logos-incarnation mysticism very clear. We shall show the theoretical connection below.

[30] Haas and Knauer, *Tagebuch*, pp50ff, 131ff; M. Giuliani "Dieu notre Créateur et Rédempteur," *Chr* 6(1959), pp332ff; G. Cusson, *Pédagogie*, pp76ff; A. Haas, *GÜ*, p240, n11; W. Sierp, "Christusbild," p815; J. Solano, "Jesucristo bajo las denomincaciones divinas de S. Ignacio," *EstEc* 118(1956), pp325-42; G. Rambaldi, "Christus heri et hodie-temas cristologicos en el pensamiento ignaciano," *Manr* 28(1956), pp105-20.

[31] See: *Autobiography*, § 29-30.

Jesuit prayer describes Ignatius' experience rather well:

> It is a still higher gift when God bestows a grace and a most sublime illumination in which the supreme truths are all united together in one single embracing vision — and those who have experienced this feel that in this illumination they see and contemplate all else *in the Lord.*[32] (Emphasis mine)

Ignatius' mystical illumination on the banks of the river Cardoner also recapitulated and summed up all things in Jesus Christ.[33] The person of Jesus Christ became for Ignatius the very way in which and through which he grasped reality, his *a priori* stance, the very horizon against which and in which everything took its ultimate meaning. Ignatius mystically tasted that all things hold together in Christ.

When Ignatius says that the enlightened soul desires only Christ and Him Crucified, that Jesus Christ is the beginning, middle and end of all our good, that "all our wickedness shall be entirely consumed, when our souls shall be completely penetrated and possessed by Him," or that we should see all creatures as bathed in the blood of Christ, this is more than pious talk.[34] It expresses Ignatius' emphatic Christocentrism, his appreciation of the christocentric dimension of all things.

The position of A. Haas and P. Knauer strengthen this view.[35] They have discovered that Ignatius' phrase, "finding God in all things," must often be understood christocentrically. Ignatius frequently uses the word "God," when he clearly means "Jesus Christ." The phrase, therefore, often means "finding *Jesus Christ* in all things."

Ignatius translated this view and experience into the Exercises. He frequently turns the exercitant's attention to a creation-redemption cosmos, to "all the things on the face of the earth." This can be grasped, however, only in reference to Jesus Christ, the "Eternal Lord of all things."[36] Ignatius' cosmic and universal outlook derives its force and depth from its christocentric underpinnings, Jesus Christ, the "Eternal Lord of all things," through whom, for whom and in whom all things were created. Even the *Foundation* and the *Contemplation to Obtain Divine Love* must be understood christocentrically. The descent of all things from God, their reascent to

---

[32] J. Nadal, quoted by H. Rahner, *Ignatius*, p10.
[33] Haas and Knauer, *Tagebuch*, pp66-7; G. Cusson, *Pédagogie*, pp49ff.
[34] *Letters*, pp69, 83, 153, 268.
[35] Haas and Knauer, *Tagebuch*, pp131ff.
[36] See: *Ex* 23, 50-4, 58, 60, 71, 93, 95, 102-3, 106-8, 235-7.

Him, the proper use of creatures, the love and service of the Divine Majesty in all things, the self-giving of the Creator through His laboring "for me in all the created things on the face of the earth" (*Ex* 23, 230-4) find their proper horizon and context of meaning only in terms of Ignatius' architechtonic experience: *the seeing of all things as rooted and grounded in Jesus Christ.*[37]

God's Self-Communication and Redemption: Christocentric?

A section from Ignatius' *Catechism* says:

> After God our Lord had created heaven, earth and all things, and when the first man was in paradise, it was revealed to him how the Son of God had resolved to become Man. And *after* Adam and Eve had sinned they recognized that God had resolved to become man in order to redeem their sin.[38]

The explicit Christocentrism of the *Catechism*, the strong Christocentrism of each of the four weeks, the *Kingdom*, the *Two Standards*, the *Three Degrees of Humility*, the *Foundation*, the *Contemplation to Obtain Divine Love*, and the Ignatian titles for Jesus point, however, to a far deeper and less explicit Christocentrism which Ignatius tacitly presupposes.

Ignatius tacitly presupposes that God wills creation and the Incarnation as moments of His Self-giving into the realm of the non-divine. Creation takes place, therefore, because God desires a history of Love communicating Itself, a Self-communication which reaches its climax at the Incarnation. From this perspective, creation is the other which God brings into being so that He can give Himself.

The goal of creation, therefore, is the Incarnation, and everything prior prepares for it. Because of creation's incarnational orientation, it can never be understood as something neutral. As K. Rahner says:

> The actual order of creation (of man and the world) is founded even as a natural order on Christ (the *Verbum incarnandum et incarnatum*) and reposes on him, so that the world even in its natural state is in fact everywhere and always a Christian thing, even though it is possible to 'prescind' from this, and (another) world without Christ is possible.[39]

---

[37] H. Rahner, *Ignatius*, pp61ff. We agree with his exposition of the christocentric dimension of the *Foundation*. We have also applied his idea to the *Contemplation to Obtain Divine Love*.

[38] Quoted by H. Rahner, *Ignatius*, p78.

[39] K. Rahner, "Controversial Theology on Justification," *TI* 4, p211.

If the goal of creation is God's Self-communication to it, Jesus Christ is the point where God's active Self-giving and creation's acceptance of Him reach their apex. In Jesus Christ, a two-fold movement finds its completion. In the movement as seen from below, Jesus Christ, as creature, fulfills evolution's basic dynamism: the total surrender of created self-transcendence into the Mystery which calls it beyond itself. Creation evolves towards Christ, for in Him God's definitive Self-emptying and Self-communicating in the sphere of the non-divine occurs.[40] In the movement as seen from above, God accomplishes His Self-communication to creation, and creation arrives at that term demanded by the deepest dynamism of its essence: to be that in which and through which God becomes all in all.

From this point of view, Christ's humanity is the goal, perfection and accomplishment of the basic dynamism central to evolution's self-transcendence, especially man's active self-transcendence to surrender himself to what draws him beyond himself. Man, therefore, reaches his highest perfection (but one which is not absolutely demanded) when he surrenders himself so totally that he no longer belongs to himself, but becomes the otherness of God in the world. Human nature, therefore, is the possibility of God's existence in the world, because human nature in its transcendence "means being immeasurably open with regard to the *freedom* of the mystery, and being utterly abandoned to the necessity of allowing oneself to be disposed of."[41] When God exists in the world, man's greatest possibility of attaining the full meaning of humanity occurs.

This possibility, therefore, must be seen in Jesus Christ. In fact, viewed from above, man is possible and comes to be because God willed to express Himself and communicate Himself radically to His creation. Viewed from below, God can empty Himself into creation because of creation's (especially man's) inherent dynamism for active self-transcendence, the dynamism which draws creation to evolve to the point of being God's existence in the world.

The Incarnation, therefore, is the most radical form of created self-transcendence, and though unattainable from below, it fulfills precisely the deepest demands of this self-transcendence. Human nature, therefore, *is* precisely the ability to be God's existence in the world. Christology, therefore, is prior to anthropology, and man understands his own meaning only in Christ.[42] For these reasons,

[40] K. Rahner, "Christology within an evolutionary View of the World," *TI* 5, pp157-92.
[41] K. Rahner, "On the Theology of the Incarnation," *TI* 4, p110.
[42] *Ibid.*, pp116ff.

too, the deepest anthropocentric movement of every person, that essential return to himself in active self-identity and surrender to Mystery, is simultaneously a christocentocentric movement. In Christ, man experiences the meaning and deepest fulfillment of his own being and existence. During the Exercises, therefore, the exercitant experiences his salvation in Jesus Christ because of the intimate correspondence between his basic structure and dynamism and that of Christ's.

At the Incarnation, creation receives God's definitive Self-communication in love. God's absolute Will to this Self-communication is also a *redemptive*, salvific Will because of sin. God's covenanting Will, His Will to communicate Himself to the creature absolutely, lovingly and efficaciously, is central and primary. Sin is permitted, therefore, because in Christ, it is comprehended within God's Will to efficacious Self-communication. Redemption and the forgiveness of sins, therefore, are "merely" an inner moment of God's efficacious and absolute Self-communication to creation.

Christ is not simply someone ejected out of the Godhead to clean up man's messy situation. Christ is the real symbol and full expression of God's love for man, that in spite of sin, God has efficaciously given Himself to the evolving cosmos which He prepared as the condition for this Self-communication. Jesus Christ is proof that Love is God's primary motive for becoming man, and not the blotting out of sin. God did not need sin in order to give Himself. God's original Will was His own Self-giving in the Incarnation, and sins are forgiven as a moment within this efficacious Self-communication in love through Jesus Christ.[43] All men are offered God's divinizing and forgiving grace because of Jesus Christ. Man's basic situation with respect to divinization and salvation, therefore, is determined from the outset by two real existentials: he is in original sin through Adam and oriented to and redeemed by Christ.[44]

The Death of Christ

Solid theological opinion maintains that God's redemptive Self-communication to creation necessitated the *death* of Jesus Christ. Nowhere else does the impasse of sin, the blockage of God's radical Self-communication, the enclosure of the universe upon itself, the emptiness and loneliness of an existence which has refused the offer of God's Self-communication manifest itself so clearly as in death. Death underscores that the active self-transcendence of the cosmos

---

[43] K. Rahner, "Original Sin," *SM* IV, pp330ff.
[44] The two existentials, of course, are not equal.

and our ultimate surrender to the intimate presence of loving Mystery have been vitiated in their roots because of the misuse of human freedom.

Through man, creation becomes free, open and capable of surrender to the loving Mystery which is the source of its active self-transcendence. Through sin, man binds this freedom, establishes closedness and brings about autistic self-affirmation. Sin introduces a "coefficient of viscosity" into the evolutionary process, because it is a refusal to grow, to evolve, to surrender to the deepest dynamism of active self-transcendence. Sin is the will to be alone and to be the source of one's own values.

Because creation's entire thrust moves towards the Incarnation, everything in creation is christocentric, and, hence, mutually interdependent. With sin, however, creation has taken on a counterthrust. Creation reached the apex of self-transcendence in Christ, and because Christ took sin upon Himself, openness to God's Self-communication *and* its refusal by creation also reached their apex in Him. All the cosmic forces which had hitherto been able to vitiate the cosmos' active self-transcendence into God became concentrated in Christ to close off His own dynamic openness to loving Mystery. As K. Rahner says:

> What was the manifestation of sin, thus becomes, without its darkness being lifted, the contradiction of sin, the manifestation of a 'yes' to the will of the Father.[45]

Without losing any of the horror of the divine abandonment belonging to death, Christ said "Yes" to the Father's Mystery in spite of the concerted "No" lurking at the roots of creation's active self-transcendence.

This must be considered under two aspects. First of all, the man Jesus at His death came into contact with the intrinsic, radically unified, ultimate and deepest level of the world's reality. At death, a person enters into a "pancosmic" relationship with reality, i.e., when the spirit:

> Enter[s] into a much closer, more intimate relationship to that ground of the unity of the universe which is hard to conceive yet is very real, and in which all things in the world are interrelated and communicate anteriorly to any mutual influence upon each other.[46]

[45] K. Rahner, *On the Theology of Death*, revised by W.J. O'Hara (New York, 1967), p62.
[46] *Ibid.*, p19.

Christ became pancosmically present to the very core of reality at his death. In other words, he descended into hell — that aspect of reality locked in upon itself, isolated and autistically affirming itself. Christ's dynamic openness to the Father ripped open the "ground of the unity of the universe" closed it upon itself. From an anthropocentric point of view, Christ's human freedom at His death radically confronted the autistic core of reality closed in upon itself due to sin, and ripped it open again to loving Mystery. In Christ, the core of reality could never again be closed to God's love, because Christ Himself became this core.

Secondly, Christ's death is that event in which God fully and irrevocably communicates Himself to creation. The Incarnation, therefore, was not accomplished all at once, but had a history. The Incarnation began with the creation of the first creature and reached its decisive stage with Christ's triumphal death and resurrection. Thus:

> Christ, in his life and death, belongs to the innermost reality of the world . . . When the vessel of his body was shattered in death, Christ was poured out over all the cosmos; he became actually, in his very humanity, what he had always been by his dignity, the heart of the universe, the innermost centre of creation.[47]

At His death, therefore, Christ became the very heart of the universe. The invisible dynamism behind creation's active self-transcendence became visible. The divine Axis of evolution which had hitherto been experienced only as the "Whither" in transcendental subjectivity, as a non-thematic, implicit over- or under-tone of that subjectivity can now be experienced in thematic objectivity: in the humanity of Christ.

Man's Christic Existential

Through His death, then, Christ entered into the entire cosmos in its deepest core as a real, permanent, metaphysical determination.

---

[47] *Ibid.*, p66; See also: *TD*, "Death," pp115-20. This is the deepest reason for the Christocentrism of the *Foundation*. See also: M. Fiorito, "Cristocentrismo del 'Principio y Fundamento' de San Ignacio," *CyF* 17(1961), pp3-42; S. Gómez Nogalez, "Cristocentrismo en la teologia de los Ejercicios," *Manr* 24(1952), pp35-52; E. Royon, "Anthropologia, cristocéntria del Principio," *Manr* 39(1967), pp349-54.

Christ in His life, death and resurrection belongs to the very heart of the world's reality. K. Rahner says well that:

> Consequently, if the reality of Christ, as consummated through his death, in his death is built into the very unity of the cosmos, thus becoming a feature and intrinsic principle of it, and a prior framework and factor of all personal life in the world, that means that the world as a whole and as the scene of personal actions has become different from what it would have been had Christ not died. And so possibilities of a real ontological nature were opened up for the personal actions of all other men which would not have existed without the death of our Lord.[48]

Touched by the life, death and resurrection of Christ, reality is now christic to its very core. To be concerned with the world and with the human is to be concerned with Christ who is their core and depth. God has done something to every person and to the cosmos in Christ, and for this reason the deepest experiences of all men are christic. The overtone or basic horizon of all human action is christic. In and through Christ, the finite has reached an infinite depth. The finite no longer contrasts with the infinite, but is that which the infinite Himself has become to open a way for the finite into the infinite. The life, death and resurrection of Christ have given the affairs of men a divine depth.

To accept fully the cosmos or humanity is ultimately to accept their dynamic Whither and their grounding in Jesus Christ. In the realm where man finds himself, a realm with God as the Whither or basic, dynamic drive of evolution (christocentric) and the humanity of Christ at the deepest center of its unity (christic), he is deeply touched by grace. Prior to any subjective attitude, man has been called by God and touched by Christ. God has loved all men in and through Christ, and this determines every man's existential situation. This objective, ontological modification of man flows from two different, but intimately connected, sources. The first is *christocentric* in that it flows from the Whither of man's transcendental subjectivity, that he always lives by the Holy Mystery which calls him to His love in self-surrender, even when he is not explicitly conscious of it. As K. Rahner says:

> Antecedently to justification by grace, received sacramentally or extra-sacramentally, man is already subject to the universal salvific will of

---

[48]*Ibid.*, pp65-6.

God, he *is* already redeemed and absolutely obliged to tend to his supernatural end ... it is an objective, ontological modification of man.[49]

The second source is *christic* in that it flows from the life, death and resurrection of Jesus Christ. All men are called and touched not only through the Mystery of God as the Whither of transcendental subjectivity, but also through the humanity of Christ, which is now at the heart of all reality. As K. Rahner says:

The grace which justifies and divinizes us, as in fact it is granted to us, is essentially so much the grace of the Incarnate and the Crucified that grace and Incarnation are two inseparable elements of the one mystery of God's self-communication to his creature.[50]

To experience the depth of the human and the cosmic is to experience the Mystery of God and the humanity of Christ. The very horizon of all activity has been changed and affected by the Mystery of God and the humanity of Christ as the all-supporting ground of all reality. The "contact lenses" of the human spirit, that by which it sees and experiences reality, are tinted by the Mystery of God and the humanity of Christ. This *a priori* horizon dominates the outlook of every person. This horizon flows from two existentials which produce a mysterious activation at the person's core, gracing him with a fundamental relevation and a christic anointing.

Admittedly, this deeper Christocentrism cannot be found explicitly in the Exercises. The explicit Christocentrism of the Exercises and other Ignatian writings, however, point to and demand a deeper Christocentrism which Ignatius tacitly presupposes. Many Ignatian commentators, moreover, have emphasized Ignatius' deeper and more implicit Christocentrism.[51]

The Exercitant as a Christ-directed Being

Because the source, meaning and goal of creation's active self-transcendence is Jesus Christ, and because Christ's life, death and

---

[49] K. Rahner, "Existential, Supernatural," *TD*, p161.

[50] K. Rahner, "Christocentrism," *TD*, p78.

[51] See: K. Rahner, *Spiritual Exercises*, trans. by K. Baker (New York, 1965); H. Rahner, "The Christology of the Exercises," and "The application of the senses," *Ignatius*, pp53-135, 181-213; E. Przywara, *Deus* I, II, III; Haas and Knauer, *Tagebuch*; Fessard I, II; A. Haas, *GÜ*; G. Cusson, *Pédagogie*, esp. pp380-6; L. Bakker, esp. pp306-7.

resurrection have touched all things, the exercitant is christocentric and christic in his Christ-directedness. This means that every person:

> Possesses an ontic and spiritual-personal capacity for communicating with Jesus Christ in whom God has forever made the countenance of a man his own and has opened the reality of man, with an unsurpassable finality, in the direction of God.[52]

The Exercises bring together the exercitant's and Christ's personal centers. The exercitant experiences in Jesus Christ, "the eternal Lord of all things" who has to do with "all the things on the face of the earth," someone with universal and cosmic significance, someone who has mysteriously anointed his interior core long before the exercitant had ever approached Him, someone who contains within Himself the meaning of all things, is the center of all things, and mysteriously activates the basic dynamic of all things, including the exercitant's. In Christ, the exercitant encounters a person to be intimately known, loved and served, but someone who also holds the key to his and the cosmos' origin, meaning and fulfillment.

The Ignatian method produces a powerful interaction of outer and inner word, of personal encounter with Christ in and through the Scriptures and the exercitant's christocentric and christic existentials. The exercitant comes to experience that Christ is the secret core of all reality and the source, meaning and goal of created self-transcendence. The exercitant tastes interiorly that:

> Jesus, the Man, not merely *was* at one time of decisive importance for salvation . . . he is *now* and for all eternity the *permanent openness* of our finite being to the living God of infinite, eternal life; he is, therefore, even in his humanity the created reality for us which stands in the act of our religion in such a way that, without this act towards his humanity and through it (implicitly or explicitly), the basic religious act towards God could never reach its goal.[53]

During the Exercises, therefore, the exercitant savors that the most powerful dynamic of his being has been fulfilled in Jesus Christ, and that the link connecting him to Christ is the secret essence of all reality, including the exercitant's own.

---

[52] K. Rahner, "The Dignity and Freedom of Man," *TI* 2, pp240-1.
[53] K. Rahner, "The Eternal Significance of the Humanity of Christ for our Relationship with God," *TI* 3, p44.

The Unity of the Anthropocentric and Christocentric Moments

It is absolutely essential to see this chapter's connection with the previous chapter on the Exercises' anthropocentric moment. We saw there that the Exercises present the objective truths of salvation history in such a way that the exercitant comes to himself in self-identity and self-surrender. The exercitant not only assimilates objective truths, but also experiences the stirring up in his being of *a priori* factors which deeply correspond to those objective truths. The outer, historical word sets in motion, deepens, illuminates and explicates the inner word.

From this chapter's point of view, the meditations on the life, death and resurrection of Jesus Christ set in motion, deepen, illuminate and explicate the exercitant's christic anointing and christocentric thrust which are actually the source, meaning and fulfillment of everything he is as man. The anthropocentric moment of the Exercises, therefore, is christocentric and vice versa, because the exercitant's deepest self-identity as man is that he is a Christ-directed being. His active self-return is accomplished by an act which refers him to Christ.

Ex 53 exemplifies this well. The exercitant imagines himself before Christ crucified. He is then to meditate *upon himself* and to ask: "What have I done for Christ ... what ought I to do for Christ? " The movement is from Christ to self to Christ. All of the exercises, no matter how explicitly theocentric or christocentric, demand as a moment of their self-accomplishment an anthropocentric return. The exercitant experiences his identity as a Christ-directed being, reflects upon what he has seen and heard, and listens to the subjective echoes produced by the objectively presented meditations. In and through the light of Jesus Christ, he comes to know himself, to possess himself, to surrender himself and to experience that Jesus Christ is *his* Creator, Savior and Lord, for reasons which have to do with his deepest identity as man. The exercitant tastes that what he is all about is answered in the "intimate knowledge of our Lord" (*Ex* 104).

The exercitant interiorly savors that the anthropocentric and the christocentric moments of the Exercises are actually different aspects of his one fundamental dynamism as man: self-identity in Christ and surrender to Mystery. Throughout the Exercises, the exercitant stands before a God who has emptied Himself to the point of death on a cross. In and through these meditations, the exercitant is led to his own self-emptying, a surrender to God which takes the anthropocentric form of a "flight from self-love, self-will and self-interest" (*Ex* 189) and reaches its christocentric peak as a fundamental option in favor of Christ poor, suffering and humiliated. True Ignatian poverty is man's total, transcendental openness in self-surrender and self-communication to Mystery, specified and made concrete by a full, explicit openness to Christ poor, suffering and despised. The exercitant finds his fulfillment in Christ when he experientially discovers that the more he empties himself and surrenders himself to Mystery, the more human he becomes.

The anthropocentric moment is christocentric, therefore, because when the exercitant empties himself as Christ did, his fulfillment and identity as man mysteriously take place.[54] The Exercises' explicit Christocentrism awakens the exercitant to the reality he is and was even prior to his explicit encounter with Christ. He discovers that the deepest desire and dynamism of his being have been fulfilled in Christ; moreover, this desire and dynamism call him to Christ for perfect self-emptying. Christ has answered the very question the exercitant is and lives by being man.

THE CHRISTOCENTRISM OF THE IGNATIAN ELECTION

Sentire en nuestro Señor

F. Marxer has convincingly shown that the Ignatian formula, *Sentir en nuestro Señor*, specifically characterizes his attitude of prudence, discernment and Election.[55] When Ignatius uses the expression "what I feel in the Lord," he means that his judgment of a matter and decision of an issue result from an experience of the situation in relation to his core experience of Jesus Christ. Nadal summed up well the Ignatian secret concerning the Election.[56] The exercitant must so enter into Jesus Christ that he can pass judgments and dispel temptations in Him. He must so dwell in Christ that in every situation, he has a sense for what Christ himself would do or decide.

---

[54] J. B. Metz, "Religious Act," *SM* V, pp287, 289-90. See also: K. Rahner, "Mystik," *LThK* VII, p744.

[55] F. Marxer, pp132ff, 153ff; M. Giuliani, "Dieu notre Créateur et Rédempteur," *Chr* 6(1959), p335.

[56] J. Nadal, quoted by R. Hostie, pp209-10: "Vtile et hoc est: personam Xpi agere, quaise in te sentias Xpum, et hoc statu vel sensu indices vel dissipes tentationes in ipso . . . Ita inueuiendus est Xpus, vt in re qualibet sentiamus quid his Christum in nobis habitantem sentiremus."

Ignatius, moreover, has developed a method which renders the exercitant sensitive not only to the historical person of Christ as seen from the revealed word, but also to his own christic existential and christocentric thrust. Ignatius steeps the exercitant in a primordial experience of the Mystery of God in Jesus Christ which is the basic meaning of the totality of the exercitant's life. It is within this experienced totality that individual decisions find their rectitude. The exercitant becomes so penetrated by the light and love of Jesus Christ that his christocentric thrust and christic existential become a more dominant, explicit factor in his experience. Ignatius evokes the christocentric and christic undertones and overtones of all experience through the meditations on the life, death and resurrection of Christ. Since all things are mysteriously summed up in Jesus Christ, the more the exercitant comes to know and love Him, the more sensitive he becomes to the basic dynamism and true center within all reality. Through a connaturality with Christ, initiated by the outer word and fulfilled by the inner word, the exercitant is able to discern spontaneously what is not from Christ, what does not promote true progress, what is the real enemy of his human nature, and the reverse. Ignatius expressly aims at imparting to the exercitant such a deep connaturality with Christ that he decides things in Him in much the same way that an old married couple instinctively knows the things that please or displease the other.

Ignatius' powerful method of supernatural logic, then, stems from a passionate knowledge and love of Christ which indirectly evokes the exercitant's christocentric thrust and christic anointing. Every choice and discernment flows from an "incarnational" or "hypostatic" tact which guides the exercitant.[57] When Ignatius had difficult questions to decide, it is well known that he often decided them in accordance with his priestly mysticism. He prayed over the questions during Mass and had others say Mass for his intentions.[58] Christ often appeared to him when he was struggling with these difficult questions.[59] Ignatius has translated to the Exercises his sensitivity to the Incarnate Word and the sacramental depths and significance of His life. The discipline of the Election springs from a

---

[57] E. Niermann, "Spirituality," *SM* VI, p164; K. Rahner, "Mystik," *LThK* VII, p745; H. Rahner, *Ignatius,* pp214ff.

[58] J. de Guibert, *Jesuits,* pp46ff; Haas and Knauer, *Tagebuch,* p129; H. Rahner, "La Storta," pp28ff, 215ff; *Letters* pp88, 93, 145, 152, 165; A. Sequia Goicoechea, *La Santa Misa en la espiritualidad de San Ignacio* (Madrid, 1950).

[59] See: *Autobiography,* § 101.

mysticism centered on Jesus' flesh.[60] Everything flows from, is governed by and is regulated according to a primordial experience of Jesus Christ. The profoundest criterion which Ignatius offers in the Exercises for coming to a true Election "without any admixture of flesh or other inordinate attachments" (*Ex* 172), or for discerning true from false consolations (*Ex* 313-44) is how the Election and the resulting consolation harmonize with this primordial experience of Jesus Christ.

J. Sudbrack's Critique

According to J. Sudbrack (p224), Ignatian commentators have overemphasized the element of Election in the Exercises to the detriment of their encounter-with-Christ-in-the-Scriptures dimension. Although commentators should stress the Exercises' encounter-with-Christ-in-the-Scriptures dimension, Sudbrack has still overlooked the *interior* unity which exists between the Election and the meditations on the life, death and resurrection of Christ. The Exercises are far more than a series of scriptural mediations or an encounter with Christ in the Scriptures in some haphazard way. They use the Scriptures to evoke, strengthen, illuminate and deepen the exercitant's christic anointing and christocentric thrust. Consolation, discernment and election flow naturally from the Ignatian christocentric *method*.

Ignatius does not present the exercitant with meditations whose inner and outer logic can be explained merely from the exegesis of his day, as Sudbrack maintains. First of all, as we have seen above, the Exercises place these meditations in the context of definite Ignatian emphases: the Christ of the *Kingdom*, the *Two Standards*, the *Three Degrees of Humility* and the *Triple Colloquy*. These key meditations flow more from Ignatius' knightly life-style than from the exegesis of his day.

Secondly, the *consolation* Ignatius received while meditating upon specific scenes explains their inner logic to a great extent. It is well known that Ignatius selected important passages from books, "the words of Christ he wrote in red ink and those of our Lady in blue."[61] Ignatius' conversion, his basic ability to discern spirits and his first election sprang from his reading of Scripture and pondering

---

[60]*SJ*, Feb. 15. Th. Baumann's, "Compagnie de Jésus. Origine et Sens Primitif de ce Nom," *RAM* 37(1961), p58 tells of how Ignatius shocked his dinner guests. He maintained that it was a very special gift of God to be a Jew, for then one would be related to Christ in the flesh.

[61]*Autobiography*, p11. See also chapter I, n16.

the great things the saints had done for God. He noticed that certain thoughts gave him a quickly fading joy, while others consoled him for long periods of time. The inner logic of consolation, discernment and election was the Ignatian principle of selection for the particular meditations, and not the exegesis of his day.

Thirdly, as H. Rahner says:

> The Exercises are never only a series of meditations, also not a blue-print of the spiritual life, but reveal their meaning through their goal: in an Election transforming one's life, to find God's Will in peace through the greatest possible assimilation to Christ. The center of the Exercises, therefore, is the "Call of Christ the King" to participate in the battle between Christ and Satan.[62]

The Exercises, therefore, are basically a method of seeking and finding God's Will for the exercitant through a particular series of meditations with an inner logic. The dynamic logic of the Exercises guarantees the maximum possible interplay between Scripture and the exercitant's christic anointing and christocentric thrust. This logic insures that the encounter with Christ is also a self confrontation at the deepest possible level. The exercitant tastes that his deepest anthropocentric movement is also christocentric, and vice versa, for to be elected to serve Christ is to be elected to surrender oneself and to be fulfilled and completed as man. Through the dynamics inherent in the Exercises, the exercitant is often called to elect in some specific way, perhaps an entire way of life, to exteriorize, to make utterly actual in his life, his transcendental, interior election of openness to the Mystery of God in Christ. The actual Ignatian Election is the *exteriorized-interiority* of this deeper election.

---

[62]H. Rahner, "Exerzitien," *Lexikon der Pädagogik* I (Freiburg i.B., 1952), p1106.

Chapter V

The Mystagogical Moment of the Exercises and the Ignatian Mystical Horizon

INTRODUCTION

We have seen that in and through the meditations on the life, death and resurrection of Jesus Christ that the exercitant discovers and tastes his christocentric orientation and his own deepest mystery as man. We propose now to explicate the mystagogical aspect of the Ignatian mystical horizon by unfolding the intrinsic mystagogical moment of the Exercises. The mystagogical moment of the Exercises awakens the exercitant to the ever-present, yet most often implicit, experience of triune grace. This moment evokes, deepens, explicates and strengthens the exercitant's deepest experiences of Mystery, Truth and Love which flow from his trinitarian existentials. The Exercises make more thematic and explicit the exercitant's relationship with and experience of a God who is Father, Son and Holy Spirit.

THE MYSTAGOGICAL EXPERIENCE
AND JESUS CHRIST

In the last chapter we purposely omitted certain important elements of the christocentric moment of the Exercises in order to treat them from the mystagogical perspective of this chapter. The more subjective, mystical horizon offered by Ignatius' *Spiritual Journal* provides an excellent hermeneutical instrument for understanding some of the less obvious, but more important elements of the christocentric moment of the Exercises.[1] This more subjective,

---

[1] The explicit trinitarian references in the *Autobiography* (esp. § 28, § 68 and § 100) and the Exercises indicate that the trinitarian experiences found in the *Spiritual Journal* are not discontinuous with Ignatius' earlier experiences. The trinitarian experiences in the *Spiritual Journal* are rather the blossoming and

mystical horizon also highlights and brings into focus the intrinsic relationship between the christocentric and mystagogical moments of the Exercises.

Ignatian Mediator Mysticism

A careful reading of the *Spiritual Journal* discloses Ignatius' extreme sensitivity to the role of mediators in man's relationship with God. He called upon and experienced Jesus Christ, His Mother Mary, the angels, the holy fathers, the apostles and the disciples as mediators. Moreover, Ignatius knew quasi-instinctively which mediator to call upon to present his prayers and petitions to the Eternal Father at any given time (*SJ*, Feb. 15). The profundity with which he had grasped God's Incarnation and its cosmic implications grounds Ignatius' "mediator mysticism."[2] The Exercises, of course, participate in this "mediator mysticism," especially in those colloquies and meditations which take place in the presence of the entire heavenly court.[3]

The Ignatian mediators, however, do not rank equally. Several important places in the *Spiritual Journal* refer to "my mediators," and the context seems to indicate Jesus and "our Lady."[4] Ignatius frequently called upon Jesus, our Lady or both of them together to act as his mediators (*SJ*, Feb. 8). They are the Ignatian mediators *par excellence*.

Ignatius had had visions of our Lady and had experienced her as the one from whom the Eternal Father would be pleased to receive his prayer (*SJ*, Feb. 15). Many of the most important graces he had received passed through her as the door or the gateway (*SJ*, Feb. 15). Most significantly, however, she is the Mother of Jesus Christ, because Ignatius had mystically experienced that *her flesh was in that of her Son* (*SJ*, Feb. 15).

---

more mature form of the trinitarian experiences which Ignatius had tasted from the very beginning of his conversion. We intend to use these more mature trinitarian experiences to illuminate the Exercises. Cf. also: J. de Guibert, *Jesuits*, chap. 1, 13; S. *Ignace mystique d'après son Journal Spirituel* (Toulouse, 1938); J. Daniélou, "La spiritualité trinitaire de saint Ignace," *Chr* 11(1956), pp328-48. We strongly recommend A. Haas and P. Knauer's excellent translation and commentary, *Tagebuch*. For our purposes, however, we shall use *The Spiritual Journal of Saint Ignatius*, trans. by W. Young, *WL* 87(1958), pp195-267. References in my text will be given as *SJ* followed by the date of entry.

[2] Haas and Knauer, *Tagebuch*, p126.
[3] See esp.: *Ex* 53, 63, 74, 98, 147-8, 151, 157, 199, 232, etc.
[4] Cf.: *SJ*, Feb. 7, 10, 13, 16; Mar. 12.

Our Lady plays, of course, an important role in the Exercises. During the First Week, she is called upon to obtain from her Son and Lord many important graces for the exercitant (*Ex* 63). During the Second Week, she frequently appears in the key meditations (*Ex* 102ff, 111ff, etc.), is addressed as "Thy glorious Mother" in the heavenly court (*Ex* 98), and plays a major role in the important *Triple Colloquy* (*Ex* 147). The first contemplation of the Fourth Week centers on Jesus' appearance to "His Blessed Mother" (*Ex* 218ff). Because she is first and foremost the Mother of Jesus who comes from her flesh, however, the Mariology of the Exercises ought to be explicated with this specifically in mind.

Jesus Christ is *the* Ignatian mediator. He is the Son who intercedes with the Father (*SJ*, Feb. 5, 8, 13-15, 18), sent the apostles to preach in poverty (*SJ*, Feb. 11) and has his interests set in order by the Father (*SJ*, Feb. 16). Ignatius frequently asked the Son to confirm him (*SJ*, Feb. 18-9) or to present his prayers to the Father (*SJ*, Feb. 24-6). Jesus is frequently the object of his love and tears (*SJ*, Feb. 27, Mar. 3, 14); profound movements of consolation and loving reverence often terminated in this Son (*SJ*, Mar. 7).

Ignatius had also experienced and explicated Jesus' two-fold Sonship. The Ignatian Christ is always the Son of the Virgin Mary according to the flesh and the Son of the Eternal Father. The *Spiritual Journal* almost always uses the word "Jesus" to designate the God-*man* and Savior *in the flesh*. It prefers the word "Son," however, to refer to the Second Person of the Blessed Trinity.[5]

This two-fold Sonship appears in the Exercises as well. Ignatius frequently refers to Jesus Christ specifically as the Son of Mary and the Son of the Eternal Father.[6] The Ignatian Christ is always the "Eternal Word Incarnate," the Second Person of the Blessed Trinity and the one who comes from Mary's flesh.

Much more important for our present considerations, however, is Ignatius' experiences of Jesus presenting him, placing him, drawing him to and being the means of union with the Most Holy Trinity (*SJ*, Feb. 27, Mar. 3). In Jesus' "shadow," Ignatius saw the Most Holy Trinity, was increasingly drawn in love and experienced an intensified union with the Most Holy Trinity (*SJ*, Mar. 3, Feb. 27). With Jesus as mediator, the most frequent and most important Ignatian experiences in the *Spiritual Journal* pivot around the Trinity, the Three Persons and the Divine Essence.

[5] Haas and Knauer, *Tagebuch*, p112; J. de Guibert, "Mystique ignatienne," *RAM* 19(1938), p114, n3.
[6] Cf.: *Ex* 63, 64, 95, 102, 106ff, 109, 110ff, 130, 134, 135, 219, etc.

In view of the usual trinitarian timidity of many Ignatian commentaries, Jesus' mediator function with respect to the Most Holy Trinity ought to be accentuated. For example, could not *Ex* 63, 64, 95, 135, 147, 148, 102, 106ff (to give just a few) be explained so that Jesus' "shadow" manifests the Most Holy Trinity more explicitly?

Jesus Christ: Entrance into the Trinity

In and through Christ's humanity, Ignatius experienced that He was also his God:

> I thought in spirit that I saw just Jesus, that is, the humanity, and at this other time I felt it in my soul in another way, namely, not the humanity alone, but the whole Being of my God, etc. (*SJ*, Feb. 27).

Ignatius mystically tasted the reciprocal interpenetration of God and man in Jesus' person. He reached the deepest interiority of Jesus' mystery when, in and through His humanity, he had grasped that Jesus was totally his God. With his spirit's interior eyes, Ignatius saw Jesus as the Son proceeding from the Divine Essence (*SJ*, Mar. 6), as the Son who along with the Father sends the Holy Spirit (*SJ*, Feb. 11), as a Person in the Most Holy Trinity (*SJ*, Feb. 21) and as the One at the feet of the Trinity (*SJ*, Feb. 28). The most significant elements of Ignatian Christology result from his profoundly trinitarian orientation.

In the last chapter we saw, from the Exercises, the Ignatian insistence that Jesus is the "Creator who became man" (*Ex* 53), the Second Person who was about to become man (*Ex* 102), and the "Eternal Word Incarnate" (*Ex* 109). The exercitant must contemplate in Christ "how the Divinity ... leaves the Most Sacred Humanity to suffer so cruelly" (*Ex* 196) and "the Divinity ... appears and manifests Itself so miraculously in the most holy Resurrection" (*Ex* 223).

Both the *Spiritual Journal* and the Exercises indicate, therefore, that Ignatius experienced the man Jesus in the Eternal Word and the Eternal Word in the man Jesus, and that he expected the exercitant to do the same. Ignatius could mystically begin in the Trinity and end in the humanity of Christ, or he could begin in the humanity of Christ and end in the Trinity. Ignatius' Mystagogy is christocentric and his Christology is mystagogical. He experienced both an "ascent" as well as a "descent" Christology. His trinitarian experiences often led to Christ and his christocentric experiences often led to the

Trinity. In the "shadow of Jesus," he felt more closely united to the Trinity (*SJ*, Mar 3), and vice versa (*SJ*, Mar 4, 5).

This relationship between Jesus and the Trinity can be experienced during the Exercises. We saw above that the consolation or grace demanded in each individual meditation ("what I want and desire") is usually a christic consolation, a very specific consolation with previous cause (=CCCP). This christic consolation, however, often gives rise to a mystagogical overshadowing, a consolation which draws the exercitant entirely into the love of God. This consolation without previous cause (=CSCP) overrides the christic dimension of the CCCP by going beyond it and yet fulfilling its basic dynamism. The CSCP is the deepest christic experience possible precisely because of its mystagogical dimension. A true experience of Jesus Christ must contain within itself as a moment of its own realization an experience of the triune God as Mystery which gives Itself as Revelation and Love. The christic CCCP leads to the trinitarian CSCP. The trinitarian CSCP maintains a dialectical relationship with a christic CCCP both before and after. In and through the transparency of Jesus during the CSCP, the exercitant experiences the triune God.

The Exercises methodically place the exercitant in the explicit "shadow" of Jesus to evoke, deepen and make more explicit the ever-present experience of trinitarian grace. The person of Jesus cannot be understood nor even experienced properly apart from a profound trinitarian horizon. The exercitant ought to be instructed, therefore, that part of the increased sensitivity he acquires in perceiving, understanding and discerning various motions (*Ex* 313, 328) ought to be a *trinitarian* sensitivity. In and through the meditations on the life of Christ, the exercitant should experience a God who is Father, Son and Holy Spirit. Although we are convinced that the exercitant arrives at a far more profound experience of the Trinity than the tradition has reckoned with, the tradition's trinitarian timidity in explicating the Exercises has not led to the more desirable explicit trinitarian experience. Had the traditional commentaries seen the Exercises in terms of the more subjective, mystical, trinitarian horizon provided by the *Spiritual Journal*, we suspect that much of today's spirituality would not be so stamped with hidden Unitarianism and trinitarian timidity.

THE MYSTAGOGICAL EXPERIENCE OF
THE ETERNAL FATHER

The use of the *Spiritual Journal* as a hermeneutical instrument for a better understanding of the Exercises uncovers another vital dimension in which the traditional commentaries are often sadly deficient. This vital dimension is the *Father*-centeredness of the Exercises. The tradition may have overlooked or understated the Father-centeredness of the Exercises because of their much more explicit Christology. As we shall see, however, the Person of the Father provides the proper horizon for understanding the Ignatian Christ and the Exercises themselves. The Exercises are a method of evoking, deepening, strengthening and making more explicit the ever-present experience of the Father.

The Father-Centeredness of the
Ignatian *Spiritual Journal*

Ignatius' *Spiritual Journal* quickly reveals the Father-centeredness of Ignatius' own mystical life. It describes his frequent visions of the Father (*SJ*, Feb. 5, 8, 11, 14, Mar. 7, 10, 11, etc.). Ignatius' prayers, consolations, devotions and tears often terminated at the Father (*ibid.*); besides, the Father Himself often showed him what mediator to call upon (*SJ*, Feb. 14). Occasionally it was the Eternal Father who restored Ignatius to his previous condition of grace and devotion (*SJ*, Feb. 13) by allowing Ignatius to have free access to Him (*SJ*, Feb. 14). Ignatius often asked the Father to confirm him (*SJ*, Feb. 18, 19). The Father placed Ignatius with His Son (*SJ*, Feb. 23). Ignatius had experienced Him as *the Father of such a Son* (*SJ*, Feb. 24). Ignatius experienced and saw the Being of the Father revealed in conjunction with the Being of the Godhead Itself (*SJ*, Mar. 10, 11, 12, Apr. 2). Ignatius' most significant mystical experience and the one most strikingly Father-centered was his profound experience of the *Father as the Source of the other Persons* (*SJ*, Feb. 29, Mar. 2, 6, 10, Apr. 2).[7] Ignatius had mystically seen with the eyes of his spirit that the Father is the Source and Origin of the entire Godhead. He had grasped the Father as the Principle, Source, Origin and Root of the other Persons. The mystery of the other Persons in the Trinity was tasted in terms of Their relation to the Father. The mystery of the Trinity began and ended

---

[7] Haas and Knauer, *Tagebuch*, pp107ff.

with the Person of the Father. We might say, then, that if the Exercises rest upon a very profound and very explicit Christology, the *Spiritual Journal* rests upon a very profound and very explicit Father-centeredness.

The Father-Centeredness of the Exercises

The focal point of the Exercises may be the person of Jesus Christ, but the Person of the Eternal Father is the all-embracing horizon surrounding this focal point. Jesus Christ is not only the "Eternal Lord of all things," but also the *one sent by the Father* to accomplish His Will. The exercitant is specifically asked not to be deaf to the call of the Eternal King, to serve Christ in the most intimate manner possible, "and thus to enter into the glory of My Father" (*Ex* 95).

The person of Christ cannot be understood apart from this mission of service to His heavenly Father (*Ex* 135, 272). The exercitant must experience Christ's deepest meaning of total service to the Father's Will. Although the Exercises do not emphasize that the *Father* will place the exercitant with His Son, he must earnestly petition the Father, Christ and our Lady to place him under Christ's standard (*Ex* 147-8).[8]

The Eternal Father is also addressed during the First Week as the One who may grant some of the critical consolations and graces belonging to that Week (*Ex* 63). The Eternal Father likewise plays a major role in the frequently repeated and very important *Triple Colloquy* (*Ex* 147-8, 156, 159, 199, etc.). Some of the individual meditations, too, are specifically concerned with Christ praying to His Eternal Father (*Ex* 201, 290), being about His Father's business (*Ex* 272), being called the Father's Beloved Son (*Ex* 273), driving the sellers from His Father's house (*Ex* 277), asking His followers to give glory to His heavenly Father (*Ex* 278), dying in His Father's hands (*Ex* 297), or telling His followers to baptize in the name of the Father, the Son and the Holy Spirit (*Ex* 307).

The role played by the *Our Father* prayer during the Exercises also underscores Ignatius' Father-centered mysticism. The *Our Father* prayer concludes most of the individual meditations and col-

---

[8] H. Rahner, "La Storta," pp127ff has shown that Ignatius had said that it was the *Father* who had placed him with Jesus Christ. Other Ignatian witnesses shifted this Father-centered emphasis. Cf. also: *Autobiography*, § 96; *SJ*, Feb. 23; R. Roquette, "Essai critique sur les sources relatant la vision de saint Ignace de Loyola à La Storta," *RAM* 33(1957), pp34-61, 150-70; T. Baumann, "Die Berichte über die Vision des heiligen Ignatius bei La Storta," *AHSJ* 27(1958), pp181-208.

loquies, stressing once more the importance of the Eternal Father for understanding the person and mission of Jesus Christ. The *Second* and *Third Methods of Prayer* (*Ex* 249-60) recommend the *Our Father* as the first prayer to be used. The words "Our Father" are specifically given as the example of words to be relished, thought about, etc.

Ignatius expects the exercitant to experience consolations which come and go (*Ex* 322); consolations which will teach him that he has no control over God and His gifts (*Ex* 322); consolations which, when remembered, will provide strength during future trials (*Ex* 320, 323-4); consolations which actually spring from a less obvious experience of the ever-present grace of God (*Ex* 320)[9]; or consolations in which the Creator Himself enters the soul and then leaves it (*Ex* 330). This consolation without previous cause contains as a moment of its own realization an experience of Him who is pre-eminently the One "without previous cause," the Eternal Father. Intrinsic to the Christ-initiated CSCP is an experience of the Eternal Father as the One "without previous cause," the *Principium sine principio*, the Origin without origin.

The basic rhythm of these consolations aids the exercitant to let God be God, to adore Him as the ineffable Mystery who communicates Himself as merciful and forgiving, but as the God-above-us, the One who cannot be manipulated. The exercitant enters into an Origin without origin, a Mystery who gives Himself but always remains incomprehensible, a creative Power that accomplishes its work quietly and patiently. He grasps a Mystery who gives Himself in loving seriousness and who is the beginning of the exercitant's future. In short, the exercitant experiences *God as Father*.[10]

In and through the meditations on the life, death and resurrection of Jesus Christ, the exercitant, therefore, experiences *the Father* of our Lord Jesus Christ. He will discover Jesus Christ as the person in whom the Father definitively addresses Himself to the exercitant. The true experience of Jesus Christ contains as a necessary moment of its accomplishment a taste of the Eternal Father, of Jesus as the Way to this Father. The Eternal Father is Jesus' proper context, for without this context, the exercitant's experience of Jesus remains essentially truncated. It is very easy to overlook the Father as

---

[9] For an excellent treatment of *Ex* 320, see: W. Sierp, *Hochschule* II, pp437ff; E. Raitz von Frentz (hrsg.) and A. Feder (übersetz), *Geistliche Übungen. Ignatius von Loyola.* (Freiburg i.B., 1951), p166, n1; G. Fessard I, p242.

[10] K. Rahner, "God our Father," *Grace in Freedom*, trans. and adapted by Hilda Graef, (New York, 1969), pp196-202.

horizon when concentrating upon Jesus as the Exercises' focal point. But Jesus is always the Son of such a Father and the one sent by the Father. It is precisely in the experience of the Father that the exercitant reaches the person of Christ in His final depths.

THE MYSTAGOGICAL EXPERIENCE OF THE HOLY SPIRIT

Difficulties

The almost total lack of explicit references to the Holy Spirit during the Exercises is most unusual and striking. It is most likely that Ignatius carefully avoided explicit references to the Holy Spirit, because Church authorities had frequently suspected him of being an Alumbrado.[11] When Ignatius was told by the Dominican interrogating him that he could speak about the things he had only through study or through the Holy Spirit, Ignatius strongly disapproved of this method of interrogation.[12] The Exercises, too, did not escape from the Alumbrado stigma. It is no wonder, then, that the Exercises contain so few references to the Holy Spirit. The few that do exist, moreover, occur in a context that clearly removes them from the danger of Illuminism.[13]

L. Bakker (p303, n31) has shown from a study of *Ex* 263, 268 and 274 that Ignatius purposely paraphrased certain Gospel texts and purposely omitted certain phrases to avoid mentioning the Holy Spirit. He has noted, too, that a comparison of the very early Cologne recension of the Exercises (c. 1539) with that of the *Autograph* or the *Vulgate* also brings out Ignatius' conscious elimination of Holy Spirit references. In the Rules for the Discernment of Spirits for the Second Week, we read in the first rule in the Cologne recension: "It is characteristic of the devil, moreover, to act contrary to such joy and consolation *of the Holy Spirit.*"[14] In the sixth rule of the same recension, we read: ". . . and just as little by little [the devil] labors to depress him and cheat him of the sweetness and joy *of the Holy Spirit.*"[15] The *Autograph* and the *Vulgate*, however,

---

[11] G. Dumiege, p1284; L. Bakker, pp300ff. In the appendix of H. Böhmer's *Studien zur Geschichte der Gesellschaft Jesu* I (Bonn, 1914), the inquisition texts relative to Ignatius can be found. They provide fascinating reading.

[12] *Autobiography*, p47, § 65.

[13] Cf.: *Ex* 263, 273, 304, 307, 312, 365.

[14] Quoted by L. Bakker, p305, n36. Bakker's emphasis.

[15] *Ibid.* Bakker's emphasis.

have omitted all references to the Holy Spirit in connection with joy and consolation.

Explicit References to the Holy Spirit

In general, because of their more private nature, the *Directories* are far more explicit and daring in their references to the Holy Spirit than the official versions of the Exercises. The *Directories* were meant for the personal use of retreat directors and were not submitted to Church authorities for approval. These *Directories* definitely expect the exercitant to be moved and led by the Holy Spirit, to discern through the Holy Spirit's guidance and to receive the Holy Spirit's gifts of interior peace, spiritual joy, faith, hope, love and tears.[16]

Likewise, the more personal nature of Ignatius' letters allowed him to be more explicit about his views concerning the Holy Spirit. Two of his letters to Borgia indicate that Ignatius expected people to be moved and directed by the Holy Spirit. He says:

> It is my hope that the same *Divine Spirit* who has hitherto guided your Lordship . . . Since the same *Divine Spirit* could move me to this action for certain reasons and others to the contrary for other reasons.[17] (Emphasis mine)

Very frequently in Ignatius' letters, as J. Van den Berg (pp60-3) has convincingly shown, the Holy Spirit is emphatically mentioned in a context of *election*, *discretion* and *consolation*. The Holy Spirit, therefore, plays a rather important role during the Exercises by aiding and supporting the exercitant in the matters of election, discretion and consolation.

The *Spiritual Journal* attests, too, that the Holy Spirit had played an important role in Ignatius' mystical life. He had experienced and seen how the Holy Spirit is a Person in the Trinity with His source in the Father (*SJ*, Feb. 21, Mar. 6). He had mystically tasted the Holy Spirit as the One sent from the Father and the Son to help him discern, examine and distinguish (*SJ*, Feb. 11). He frequently prayed to the Holy Spirit and received numerous gifts of loving reverence, devotion and tears (*SJ*, Feb. 11, Mar. 22). Especially in his later years, as Lainez and Nadal have noted, Ignatius received some of his

---

[16]Cf.: *MI* II, 1, p949, 974; *MI* II, 2, p73. The Polanco *Directory* (*MI* II, 2, p311) is very similar. Cf. also: J. Alvarez de Paz, pp628, 639-40.

[17]*Letters*, pp181-2, 258.

most important gifts from the Holy Spirit; he could also find the Holy Spirit almost at will.[18]

The Experience of the Holy Spirit and the Exercises

When the Exercises are read against the horizon of Ignatius' own mystical life, the importance of the Holy Spirit for the exercitant's consolation, discernment, election and experience of Christ becomes apparent. The Exercises contain as a necessary moment of their accomplishment a profound experience of *God as Holy Spirit.* Now that the dangers and the exaggerations from Illuminism are scarcely present, the exercitant must be explicitly told that the Exercises will evoke, deepen, strengthen and make more explicit the ever-present experience of the Holy Spirit.

Ignatius boldly presupposes that God will work directly with the exercitant and communicate His Will, if the exercitant surrenders himself entirely (*Ex* 15, 16, 20, 5). The Holy Spirit will govern and direct the exercitant to his salvation (*Ex* 365). The exercitant will be moved and led by a love from above which will entirely draw him into this love (*Ex* 184, 330). Through the Holy Spirit's help, the exercitant must learn to recognize, perceive and understand "to some degree the different movements that are produced in the soul" (*Ex* 313).

Although some of these movements are rather obvious in those who are making progress (*Ex* 314-17), Ignatius awaits impulses that are "gentle, light and sweet as a drop of water entering a sponge" (*Ex* 335). Gentleness, lightness, sweetness and quietness characterize the deeper forms of consolation from the Holy Spirit.[19] The more profound the experience, the more directly it comes from the Holy

---

[18] *M.Nad.* IV, p645: "Intellexi postea ego ab eodem P. Ignatio versari illum in personis diuinis, ac inuenire uaria dona et distincta a distinctis personis, sed in hoc contemplatione maiora dona invenit in *persona Spiritus Sancti,* tum etiam illud intellexi ipsum" (Emphasis mine). And from *FN* I, p138: "Otras cosas diversas me ha contado de visitaciones que ha tenido sobre los misterios de la fe, como sobre la Eucharistia, sobre la persona del Padre especialmente y pór un dierto tiempo después, creo, sobre la persona del Verbo; y últimamente sobre la *persona del Espïritu Sancto*" (Emphasis mine). Cf. K. Truhlar, "La découverte de Dieu chez saint Ignace de Loyola pendant les dernières années de sa vie," *RAM* 24(1948), pp313-37.

[19] Ignatius, of course, attributes this form of consolation to the "good angel." This imagery, however, can be used to describe the action of the Holy Spirit. Perhaps Ignatius selected this safer phrase (from Dionysius the Carthusian?) to prevent Alumbrado misunderstandings. Cf. esp. L. Bakker, pp300ff. The remarks to follow have their roots in F. Crowe's article, "Complacency and Concern," *Cross and Crown* 11(1959), pp180-90.

Spirit, the more subtle and quiet it is. These profound experiences from the Holy Spirit are not easily described in imagery which captures the imagination.[20] In an age prone to confuse the coarser forms of experience resulting from drugs, sex and pseudo-Pentecostalism with true religious experience, it is absolutely essential to accentuate the re-creative value of this "gentle, light and sweet" experience of the Holy Spirit.

Ignatius' image of the drop of water entering the sponge proffers an excellent description of the more subtle forms of consolations from the Holy Spirit. These consolations bring stillness, not dullness. They evoke being, not action; communion, not interaction; mystery, not problem; interiority, not exteriority; depth, not superficiality; fidelity, not duty; love, not desire; quiescence, not concern; and joy, not frivolity. They refresh and deepen the exercitant through their actionless existentiality, creative passivity and interiority. These important consolations given to the exercitant by the Holy Spirit affect him in his deepest interiority, increase his creative self-presence, allow him to discover and taste the true depths of the christocentric meditations and plunge him into the Father's Mystery and the Holy Spirit's Love. The exercitant must be made explicitly aware of the intrinsic link between his most profound consolations and the Holy Spirit. Indeed, one important aspect of the Exercises is to bring the exercitant mystagogically into a more explicit and thematic awareness and experience of the Holy Spirit *as Holy Spirit*.

The Exercises rest upon the assumption that God will communicate more than His gifts to the exercitant. Ignatius expects God to communicate *Himself* as *the Gift* to the devout soul (*Ex* 15, 16, 20, etc.). Throughout the Exercises, the exercitant will discover just how much God wishes to give *Himself* as Divine Love to him (*Ex* 230ff). He is to become aware of the many hidden ways in which God has already given Himself as Divine Love to him (*Ex* 233ff). God's Self-communication as Gift will always remain the exercitant's strength and foundation, although he may not always be able to perceive it as such (*Ex* 320, 322, 324).

This Self-communication, however, may be powerfully explicit and draw the exercitant entirely to Itself in Love (*Ex* 330). God's Self-communication aims at the exercitant's innermost core. God is active there not only as Gift, but also as the Power to accept this Gift. The Holy Spirit is God-in-us, the Father's Self-donation and

---

[20]G. Bardy, "Discernement des Esprits. Chez les Pères," *DSAM* III, p1250. Extraordinary mystical phenomena, however, such as raptures, visions, etc. are the exception.

Gift of Himself. The Holy Spirit reveals the Father's incomprehensibility, and so the distinction between God-in-us and God-above-us.[21] The Father gives Himself in and through the Holy Spirit, yet remains the sovereign, incomprehensible Mystery, God-above-us. It is the nature of the Holy Spirit to be God-in-us, the Gift of the Father's Self-communication.[22] The Holy Spirit binds the exercitant to the Father through Christ. The Father through Christ in the Holy Spirit has united Himself personally and dynamically, but not ontologically, with the Church and its individual members. Ignatius expects this to show itself during the Exercises (*Ex* 365).

The real purpose of God's Self-communication as Gift and Love-Given to the exercitant, however, is more than a simple God experience. Ignatius expects God to communicate His Will to the exercitant (*Ex* 1, 169ff), perhaps in a way beyond question (*Ex* 175). Ignatius frequently prayed: "I ask the Divine Majesty to grant us the fullness of His grace, so that we may know His most holy will and perfectly fulfill it."[23] Ignatius presupposes that the same Holy Spirit who guides the Church will direct the exercitant (*Ex* 365). The exercitant, therefore, through the experience of the Holy Spirit as Gift, must seek and find God's Will for him. As the *Official Directory* advises, all of the exercitant's efforts are to be directed towards finding God's Will for him.[24]

The Exercises have to do with an experiential knowledge of God's Gift, an existential knowledge arising from the Holy Spirit's touches and the touches of the enemy of our human nature, a special knowledge born from struggle, a special enlightenment from above which enables the exercitant to discover God's Will for him.[25] The exercitant will receive inner instructions from the Holy Spirit throughout the Exercises. It is no wonder that several Ignatian commentators view the Exercises as a method to expose the exercitant to a God who will work in and with the exercitant by communi-

---

[21] K. Rahner, "Trinity," *SM* VI, pp300-1.

[22] M. Schmaus, "Holy Spirit," *SM* III, pp58-9.

[23] *Letters*, p86. This is a common closing formula for many of Ignatius' letters.

[24] *MI* II, 1, p1127. Cf. also *Ex* 6, 15, 16, 20, 21, 76, 91ff, 118, 130, 135, 136ff, 163, 164, 169-89, 330, 336, etc.; *M.Nad.* IV, pp843ff; M. Giuliani, Se décider sous la motion divine," *Chr* 4(1957), pp165-86; J. Calveras, "Es lícito querer saber la voluntad de Dios por via directa? ," *Manr* 14(1942), pp247-69.

[25] Cf. esp.: *M.Nad.* IV, p844; L. Claβen, p290; F. Wulf, *Loyola-Gestalt*, p47; M. Giuliani, "Les motions de l'esprit," *Chr* 4(1954), p68; A. Steger, "Der Primat der göttlichen Gnadenführung im geistlichen Leben nach dem hl. Ignatius von Loyola," *GuL* 21(1948), pp97ff.

cating an interior knowledge, tasting and relishing of His Gift and His Will.[26]

The Experience of the Holy Spirit and Jesus during the Exercises

The Exercises clearly rest upon a core experience of the Holy Spirit, especially in connection with their emphasis on consolation, election and confirmation. The Holy Spirit, moreover, grounds the immediacy of the exercitant's relationship to Christ. A true experience of Jesus Christ contains as a moment of its realization an experience of Him as *the bearer of the Holy Spirit* and of Him as *the one who with the Father sends the Spirit.* The profound experience of Jesus Christ which the Exercises expressly evoke is possible only in and through the Holy Spirit. As H. Mühlen says of the Holy Spirit: "He is the Self unmediated, self-mediating Immediacy of our presence to Jesus Himself."[27] The Holy Spirit, therefore, *is* the exercitant's immediacy to Jesus. An experience of Jesus Christ is always at the same time an experience of the Holy Spirit, and vice versa.

If the exercitant is to grasp the mystery of Christ in all his depth, he must be led to grasp what the early Church had grasped: Jesus Christ is the bearer of the Holy Spirit and the one who with the Father sends the Spirit. Much of the Christology of the New Testament springs from a radical Pneumatology. The New Testament writers knew that the bestowal of the Holy Spirit gave Jesus his eschatalogical office.[28] The Holy Spirit could never be looked upon again as simply the *ruach Jahwe* of the Old Testament. The Holy Spirit was primarily *the Spirit of Jesus Christ.* The early Christians had experienced Jesus Christ in and through their experience of the Holy Spirit.

When the exercitant begs for the grace to "know more thoroughly the eternal Word Incarnate" (*Ex* 130), he is also implicitly asking for the grace to experience the Spirit of Jesus Christ. "The

---

[26] Luis de LaPalma, *Via Spiritualis. Qualem in Libro Exercitiorum Spiritualium Monstrat B.P. Ignatius Loiolaeus,* trans. from the Spanish by J. Nonell (Barcinone, 1887) 2 vols., II, p90; P. Ferrusolae, p172; A. Gagliardi, p95; A. Bellecius, p244; A. Denis, I, p61, III, p109; W. Sierp, *Hochschule,* I, pp81, 174; L. Bakker, pp106ff; G. Fessard I, p244; E. Przywara, *Deus* II, p139; G. Cusson, *Pédagogie,* pp218ff; F. Marxer, p41; K. Rahner, *Dynamic, passim;* W. Peters, p1; H. Urs von Balthasar, *Herrlichkeit,* I, p398; P. Penning de Vries, p66; I. Iparraguirre, "Ignace de Loyola," *DSAM* VII, p1270.

[27] H. Mühlen, "Das Christusereignis als Tat des Heiligen Geistes," *MS* III/2, p514.

[28] *Ibid.,* pp521, 531.

Logos is indeed the origin-become-time [*zeitgewordene Ursprung*] of the Holy Spirit."[29] When the retreat director explains the essentials of each meditation to the exercitant (*Ex* 2), he ought to develop their latent Pneumatology. Jesus was conceived through the Holy Spirit and endowed with the Holy Spirit at his baptism (*Ex* 262, 273). The exercitant must be instructed to see and experience the Holy Spirit in all of Jesus' activities. Perhaps the entire Third and Fourth Weeks should be developed more along the Johannine lines of the intrinsic link between Jesus' passion, death, resurrection and the giving of the Holy Spirit. The exercitant can expect, moreover, a mystagogical experience of the Holy Spirit through the christocentric meditations and a deepening of his experience of Jesus Christ through the immediacy of the Holy Spirit as Gift and Love-Given.

THE MYSTAGOGICAL EXPERIENCE OF THE TRINITY

The *Spiritual Journal* and the Trinity

An appreciation of Ignatius' profound trinitarian mysticism, therefore, is absolutely essential for the proper understanding of his Exercises. As his *Spiritual Journal* attests, Ignatius frequently prayed directly to the "Most Holy Trinity" or the "Three Divine Persons." The *Spiritual Journal* very frequently mentions the "Most Holy Trinity" or the "Three Divine Persons" as the object of respectful worship, love and reverence, tears, ecstatic love, deep interior movements, confirmation, special visions and graces of various kinds.[30] Even a lifetime of study would not have sufficed to give Ignatius what he had received from his trinitarian illuminations (*SJ*, Feb. 19). He had interiorly encountered the Divine Persons and penetrated to the core of Their common Essence (*SJ*, Feb. 21, 29; Mar. 2, 6, 11). He had frequently received graces concerning the "Single Essence" (*SJ*, Mar. 3, 6), the "Divine Essence" (*SJ*, Mar. 8, 25, 27; Apr. 2), the "Divine Being" (*SJ*, Mar. 11), and the "Being of the Most Holy Trinity" (*SJ*, Mar. 12). Ignatius had mystically penetrated to the heart of the mystery of the trinitarian "circuminsession" (*SJ*, Feb. 21).

---

[29]*Ibid.*, p541.
[30]Cf. *SJ*, Feb. 11, 12, 13, 18, 25, 29; Mar. 7, 12 for explicit references to the "Three Persons." Cf. *SJ*, Feb. 18, 19, 20, 21, 22, 24, 25, 26, 27; Mar. 2, 3, 4, 5, 6, 7, 9 for explicit to the "Most Holy Trinity."

The Exercises, Titles for God, and the Trinity

The "Three Divine Persons" are also expressly mentioned several times in the key meditation of the Second Week, the Incarnation (*Ex* 102, 106-9, 128). The entire Second Week, in fact, focuses upon the trinitarian mystery in the sense that the "Three Divine Persons" overshadow the events of that week and form the proper backdrop for understanding the week itself. The Incarnation contemplation, moreover, becomes the pattern for the preparatory prayer and preludes of the other exercises of that week and the Third Week (*Ex* 159, 204).[31] It is only within the horizon of the "Three Divine Persons" that the Second Week meditations on Jesus Christ as the Eternal Word Incarnate find their proper context.

The trinitarian horizon in the Exercises appears in a less explicit, but nevertheless very real way when Ignatius refers to God as "His Divine Majesty."[32] From the context in the Exercises and its use in the *Spiritual Journal*, Ignatius is referring to the Trinity when he uses the expression "Divine Majesty."[33] The same holds true for the Ignatian expression "God our Lord" during the Exercises.[34] Its context in the Exercises and its use in the *Spiritual Journal* clearly point to the Trinity.[35]

Although it is hardly our intention to examine every Ignatian expression for God, the context and use of such expressions in the Exercises as "Infinite Goodness" (*Ex* 52), "God" (esp. *Ex* 58-9; compare *SJ*, Feb. 18), "Divine Justice" (*Ex* 60), the "Divinity" (*Ex* 124), "His Divine Goodness" (*Ex* 151, 157), and the "Divine Power" (*Ex* 363) seem to refer to the Most Holy Trinity. These expressions, and the ones we saw above, flow from Ignatius' trinitarian mysticism and indicate a far greater trinitarian explicitness in the Exercises than the tradition has thus far elucidated.

---

[31] Cf. *MI* II, 2, p509.

[32] Cf. *Ex* 5, 18, 46, 146-8, 155, 167, 168, 183, 233, 235, 240, 248, 330, 368, 370.

[33] *SJ*, Feb. 17, 19, 26, 27; Mar. 2, 3, 4, 5, 10, 16; Apr. 2. On the other hand, *Ex* 146-7 seem to refer to Jesus Christ as "Divine Majesty."

[34] *Ex* 3, 16(3x), 18, 23, 25, 38, 39, 43, 48, 75, 77, 89, 92, 135, 137, 150, 151, 153, 155, 165, 169(8x!), 174, 175, 177, 179, 183, 185, 189, 232, 234, 336, 338, 339, 343. In *Ex* 38, 39, 135, 137, 155, 343, however, Ignatius *may* be calling Jesus Christ "God our Lord."

[35] *SJ*, Feb. 17; Mar. 10; Apr. 2, 3. *SJ*, Mar. 12, 14, 16 are utterly clear on this point.

Loving Reverence and Thankfulness

The Exercises are an initiation not only into the experience of the Father, Son and Holy Spirit, but also into the more general experience of God as One. The Ignatian experiences of loving reverence and thankfulness result from a profound mystagogical tasting of God as One. As he penetrated to the very core of the Godhead, Ignatius was infused with a very special gift, a mysticism of loving reverence. He considered this grace of loving reverence as one of the most important graces of his life (*SJ*, Mar. 14). The second half of the *Spiritual Journal* recounts time and time again that the dominant element of his mystical experience of the triune God in Unity was such reverence. The Exercises, too, indicate that Ignatius expected the exercitant to share this mystagogical experience of loving reverence in the presence of the one God.[36]

Ignatius' attitude before the all holy and mysterious God was not only one of loving reverence but also one of thankfulness. He may have explored the heart of the Godhead, but he had also discovered that this all holy and mysterious God can readily be found in His creation. This God communicates Himself to the exercitant and has descended to work for him in all the created things of the earth.[37]

An encounter with such a God means not only loving reverence but also thankfulness through apostolic service. This God can and must be sought, found and served in all things. The exercitant's thankfulness incarnates itself as apostolic service, as his spontaneous, original and comprehensive response to a God who gives Himself in all things. The exercitant experiences that everything he is and has is an incarnation of God's love for him. Aware of the many blessings he has received, finding God in all things, the exercitant becomes not only contemplative and reverent, but also contemplative in action and thankful through service.[38] Ignatius' mysticism and the spirituality proper to the Exercises do not let everything dissolve into the

---

[36] *Ex* 3, 52, 58, 59, 67, 74, 75, 92, 165, 258, 289, 370.

[37] *Ex* 43, 60, 61, 71, 322, 233-7, 5, 234, 189, 53, 98.

[38] J. Daniélou, "La vision ignatienne du monde et de l'homme," *RAM* 26(1950), p14; J. de Guibert, *Jesuits*, chap. 17; I. Iparraguirre, "Spirituality," *SM* VI, p163; E. Iserloh, "Gott finden in allen Dingen. Die Botschaft des heiligen Ignatius von Loyola an unsere Zeit," *TThZ* 66(1957), pp67-79; J. Stierli, *Loyola-Gestalt*, pp167-8; E. Coreth, "In actione contemplativus," *ZKTh* 76(1954), pp55-82; L. Verny, "In actione contemplativus," *RAM* 26(1950), pp60-78; M. Giuliani, "Trouver Dieu en toutes choses," *Chr* 6(1955), pp172-94; A. Merk, "Gottesliebe und Gottesdienst in den Exerzitien des heiligen Ignatius," *ZAM* 7(1932), pp117-34. For a good study of how the Exercises transformed the Church's orthodoxy into orthopraxis, see: J. Lortz, *Die Reformation in Deutschland* II (Freiburg i.B.,[3]1949), pp141ff.

mystic act. They seek and find God in all things through reverent, thankful service. The reverence of apostolic service is the thankful response of the person who has experienced God present and working for him in all things. Before such a God, reverence and thankfulness through apostolic service are the correct responses.

Trinitarian Existentials and the Experience of Mystery, Love-Given and Revelation

Ignatian commentators are undoubtedly correct, therefore, when they emphasize the trinitarian dimension of Ignatius' mystical life.[39] The trinitarian timidity and implicit Unitarianism of many traditional commentaries, however, have failed to see the trinitarian riches found in the Exercises. Still less have they grasped the intrinsic link between the basic dynamics of the Exercises and the exercitant's *a priori* experience of the Trinity. The Exercises are basically a method of evoking, amplifying and making more explicit the trinitarian experience which haunts every person. In and through the christocentric meditations, the exercitant is awakened to his deepest, yet most often only implicit, experience of the triune God. The Exercises serve as the exterior, *a posteriori* word, the amplifier, which calls the inner, *a priori* word to blossom and become more explicit.

Because of God's Self-communication, the basic, core, ground experience of every person is an experience of the Father, Son and Holy Spirit. God gives Himself *as Father, as Son* and *as Holy Spirit* and is Father, Son and Holy Spirit. The immanent Trinity is the Trinity of the economy of salvation, and *vice* versa.[40] This means that every person has a special relationship to God *as Father, as Son* and *as Holy Spirit*. Every person's core experience is of a God who gives Himself as He is: Father, Son and Holy Spirit. Man's basic situation is a trinitarian situation, because he has been anointed in his roots by the Trinity. Man is basically a Trinity-oriented being, a being having trinitarian existentials. He possesses a basic experience of the Trinity, whether or not he expressly notices it. This core

[39]Cf.: *M.Nad.* IV, pp651-2; H. Rahner, "La Storta," pp208ff; R. Richard, "Deux traits de l'expérience mystique de saint ignace," *AHSJ* 25(1956), pp431ff; G. Cusson, *Pédagogie*, pp74ff.

[40]K. Rahner, "Remarks on the Dogmatic Treatise 'De Trinitate'," *TI* IV, pp87ff. Cf. also: K. Rahner, "Theos in the New Testament," *TI* I, pp79-149; B. Fraigneau-Julien, "Réflection sur la signification religieuse du mystère de la St. Trinité," *NRTh* 7(1965), pp673-87; J. Dedek, *Experimental Knowledge of the Indwelling Trinity. Historical Study of the Doctrine of Thomas* (Mundelein, Ill., 1958). A good summary of Ignatius' trinitarian theology is to be found in his Sign of the Cross instructions, *MI* I, 12, p667.

experience, however, may be suppressed, falsely interpreted, partially altered or truncated through these false interpretations, but it can never be totally eliminated. The great world religions, moreover, attest to this by a threefold religious sense: a vertical religious sense of awe and worship, a horizontal religious sense of meaning and conscience, and an interior religious sense of depth and enstasy.[41]

Although God has communicated Himself in the most profound and intimate manner possible, He always remains Father, God-above-us, the Uncontrollable, Distance, the ever-greater God, Mystery, Silence, the Nameless, Darkness, the Holy, Depth, Source and the Abyss.

This God, however, is not only the non-manipulatable, silently hovering Mystery, the distant and unreachable point, the never-to-be grasped Whither of transcendental subjectivity.[42] He is also the One who has given Himself as Holy Spirit and can be experienced as God-in-us and as the Nearness, Gentleness, Caress, Kiss, Sanctity, Blessedness, Intimacy, Peace, Wisdom, Love-Given and Gift of this Mystery. This Mystery heals, justifies and eternally blesses by giving Himself as Gift and the Power to accept this Gift. Behind all human knowledge, love and experience stands the infinite Mystery of the Father as Abyss, Origin and Ground of all things. But this aloof and only asymptotically approachable God has come to man in absolute Intimacy and Immediacy. The exercitant must be taught to experience the Father's Intimacy, Immediacy, Unconditional Acceptance, Love, Gift and the Power to accept this Gift. This is an experience of the Holy Spirit.

The Father, however, also reveals Himself as He gives Himself. The Self-communication of Mystery in Love necessarily brings with it the Father's Self-expression, His Son and Word. The Father gives not only His Gift of Love; He also imparts His Word, the Light through which man experiences Mystery's Darkness as meaningful and revealing. The blessed Darkness has enlightened man with His Revelation which is primordial, healing and intimate. The blessed Silence has spoken His Word of Truth at the core of every person. The Father imparts His Son to be God-with-us, the Truth and Image of His Mystery, the Life of the ever-greater God, the Reflection of

---

[41] L. Cantwell, "Threefold Religious Sense," *Theology of the Trinity*, Theology Today Series, (Notre Dame, 1969), pp67-80.

[42] K. Rahner, "Mystery," *SM* IV, pp135ff; Cf. also: K. Rahner, "Revelation," *SM* V, pp353ff; "God is no Scientific Formula," *Grace in Freedom, op. cit.*, pp191ff; "Gnadenerfahrung," *LThK* IV, p1002; "Mystik," *LThK* VIII, pp743ff; H. Pinard de la Boullaye, "Expérience religieuse," *DThC* II, pp1786-1868.

the Holy, the Light of the blessed Darkness, the Word of the Silence and the Nameless, and the Way to the Source, the Depth and the Abyss. The Father's Word of Truth enlightens man with a basal, non-conceptual, existential knowledge which is architechtonic, preconceptual, non-thematic, rich and ravishing, ecstatic and enstatic, frightening yet intimate, a felt-knowledge which sees through love.

God, therefore, is the Whither of, the Gift to and the Enlightenment of man's core, of his transcendental subjectivity. The experience of God as Mystery, Love-Given and Revelation is the horizon experience of every person, because God the Father, while remaining the unoriginated Mystery, communicates Himself as Word and Gift. God's Self-communication to man, however, is historical and *a posteriori* as well as transcendental and *a priori*, for God's Word was made flesh and sent the Holy Spirit. As K. Rahner says:

> Inasmuch as history mediates transcendence, the Son sends the Spirit; inasmuch as transcendence makes history, the Spirit effects the incarnation of the Logos; inasmuch as the appearance in history implies the manifestation of reality, the incarnate Logos is revealed as the self-utterance of the Father in truth; inasmuch as God's coming among us in the center of our life signifies his love and ours, the Pneuma is revealed in his intrinsic reality as love.[43]

Through the christocentric meditations of the Exercises, God's historical Word of Love and Truth evokes, deepens and strengthens the exercitant's horizon experience of Mystery, Love-Given and Revelation. The exercitant awakens to the silent Mystery who reigns over him, with him and in him. The Exercises are a mystagogy into the experience of a God Who has communicated Himself as Mystery, Revelation and Love, as God-above-us, God-with-us, and God-in-us, as Father, Son and Holy Spirit, and is Father, Son and Holy Spirit in Himself.

---

[43]K. Rahner, "Revelation," *SM* V, p350.

Chapter VI

The Three Times of Election:
An Illustration of the
Ignatian Mystical Horizon

INTRODUCTION

It seems evident that although Ignatius frequently experienced the exceptional and extraordinary qualities of mystical graces, these were not his primary interest. Ignatius' main concern centered upon finding God's Will for him in and through those graces. The closing sentence in many of Ignatius' letters summarizes well his concern as well as his spirituality: "May God our Lord deign to give us all His abundant grace ever to know and fulfill His most holy will."

The Ignatian Exercises, therefore, hardly focus upon religious experience for its own sake. They are far more than diverse forms of prayer, carefully selected meditation themes, and a time for spiritual renewal. Spiritual exercises of this type have existed since the beginning of Christianity.[1] Ignatius' genius and originality, however, reveal themselves in another way. Ignatius discovered the intrinsic relationship between consolation, desolation and Election, and so was the first in the history of spirituality to give systematic instructions for finding the individual Will of God through the discernment of spirits.[2] As K. Rahner says, the Exercises are:

> . . . an attempt, especially in the Rules for the Discernment of Spirits, to provide and give practice in a formal, systematical method of discovering this individual will of God. We should even like to risk the assertion that they are actually the first and so far the only detailed attempt at such a systematic method.[3]

[1] M. Viller, "Le XVIIe siécle et l'origine des retraites spirituelles," *RAM* 9(1928), pp139-62, 359-84.

[2] A. Chollet, "Discernement des esprits," *DThC* IV, pp1380ff; J. Pegon, "Discernement des esprits. Période moderne," *DSAM* III, pp1271-2.

[3] K. Rahner, *Dynamic*, p115; See also: L. Poullier, "Les règles du discernement

The Ignatian Election is the heart and masterpiece of the Exercises. The explicit Election matter (*Ex* 169-89) dominates the Exercises' center. The *Directories* which began with Ignatius himself dedicate almost one-third of their space to the Election.[4] The Exercises prepare the exercitant to take on the disposition of Christ and to be united with the Father in such a way as to be called to a particular way of life or a specific reform of his present way of life. They consist in a drama of the divine call and a mysticism or discipline of Election.[5] The success of the explicit Election depends, therefore, upon the quality of the exercitant's spiritual experience throughout the Exercises. The exercitant must be so plunged into the life, death and resurrection of Jesus Christ that he is capable of electing Jesus poor, suffering and humiliated, or at least the second degree of humility.[6]

If the Election is really the heart of the Exercises, then the Ignatian horizon ought to manifest itself most clearly in it. We maintain, therefore, that the Ignatian Three Times for Election clearly manifest the anthropocentric, christocentric and mystagogical aspects of the Ignatian horizon. The Election flows from an experience of radical self-identify given to the exercitant through his meditations on the life, death and resurrection of Jesus Christ which may draw him entirely in self-surrendering love to the Mystery of God in Jesus Christ.

THE FIRST TIME OF ELECTION

General Description
Ignatius describes the First Time for Election as follows:

> The first occasion is when God our Lord moves and attracts the will so that the devout soul, without question and without the desire to question, follows what has been manifested to it. St. Paul and St. Matthew did this when they followed Christ our Lord. (*Ex* 175)

The First Time for Election, therefore, is a God-initiated, totally supernatural, irresistible, luminous revelation which so influences the

---

des esprits," *Les grandes directives de la retraite fermée.* (Paris, 1930), p200; C. Bernard, "Signification des exercices de saint Ignace," *RAM* 45(1969), p244.

[4] E. Raitz von Frentz, p12.
[5] H. Bremond, pp26ff, 93. See also: G. Fessard I, p93.
[6] C. Bernard, p244. See also: E. Raitz von Frentz, p38.

person that he responds "without question and without the desire to question." This exclusively divine experience so overwhelms the person that his response to Christ is as spontaneous and total as that of St. Paul and St. Matthew. When God alone calls, when the Creator works directly with the creature, as Ignatius clearly expects (*Ex* 15), the exclusively divine experience will remain divine even after it is appropriated by the person. The God-component of this experience drowns out every form of human echo to this experience, "for every divine call is always pure and clean and without any admixture of flesh or other inordinate attachments" (*Ex* 172). This accounts for a human response "without question and without the desire to question."

Frequency of the First Time of Election

A number of commentaries based upon the *Directory* of 1599 emphasize that the First Time Election is "miraculous," "extraordinary," "prophetic," "rare," "a truly supernatural revelation," and that it would be foolish pride and an illusion to imagine that it could be obtained.[7] And yet, both Ribadeneyra and Gonzalez indicate that Ignatius himself *frequently* decided according to the First Time.[8] Some commentators, moreover, offer considerable evidence that Ignatius' Cardoner experience as well as his Meat Vision involved First Time Elections,[9] two experiences which we shall examine later on. Ignatius' La Storta vision also exemplifies an experience of being-elected according to the First Time. Some 15 years after Cardoner, Ignatius received the grace of the *Two Standards*, the powerful experience of being elected and called to serve Christ poor, suffering and humiliated. As he says in his *Autobiography:*

> One day, a few miles before they reached Rome, while he was praying in a church, he felt such a change in his soul, and saw so clearly that God the Father placed him with Christ His Son, that he would not dare to doubt that the Father had placed him with His Son.[10]

---

[7] A. de Ponlevoy, *Commentaire sur les Exercices spirituels de saint Ignace* (Eureux, 1889), pp282ff; K. Rahner, *Dynamic*, pp127-8; V. Mercier, p295; I. Diertins, I, p175; A. Denis, III, p84.

[8] *FN* II, p415.

[9] L. Bakker, *passim*. See also: R. Silos, "Cardoner in the life of St. Ignatius of Loyola," *AHSJ* 33(1964), pp3-43; R. Cantin, "L'illumination du Cardoner," *ScE* 7(1955), pp23-56.

[10] *Autobiography*, p67.

The exclusively divine nature of the experience, the strong element of passivity, of being elected, and the irresistible certitude accompanying the experience make it highly likely that La Storta was a First Time Election experience. It must be admitted, however, that the "would not dare to doubt" is not as strong as "without the desire to question."

In addition, L. Bakker (pp209ff, 281ff) has noted that at least until 1539, Ignatius clearly expected exercitants to experience the First Time of Election. The Rejadell letter of 1536 lucidly says:

> For it *frequently* happens that our Lord moves and *urges* the soul to this or that activity. He begins by enlightening the soul . . . by speaking interiorly to it without the din of words, lifting it up wholly to His divine love and ourselves to His meaning *without any possibility of resistance* on our part, even should we wish to resist.[11] (Emphasis mine)

Furthermore, Ignatius' own *Directory*, written not many years later, definitely expects the First Time Election:

> Upon entering on the three or four times of election . . . Should the director observe that the retreatant is not moved *in the first*, he should insist he pass on to the second.[12] (Emphasis mine)

The 1590-91 *Directory* also states that many of the first Jesuits were called by means of a First Time Election.[13] Even the conservative *Directory* of 1599 notes the possibility of a First Time Election.

> And although such miraculous vocations do not happen now, *still there are some we both read of and see*, which, to some extent, seem to approximate to these apostolic vocations; in point of illumination and satisfaction of soul, and certain manifestation of the divine will, to a degree that eliminates all possible doubt.[14] (Emphasis mine)

Iparraguirre and Raitz von Frentz note, too, that M. Olave, C. de Torres, P. Manareo, Stanislaus and Aloysius are examples of vocations experienced according to the First Time of Election.[15]

---

[11] *Letters*, p22.
[12] *Autograph Directories of Saint Ignatius of Loyola* (=*Autograph Directories*), (Program to Adapt the Spiritual Exercises: Jersey City, NJ), pp7, 9.
[13] *MI* II, 2, p698.
[14] *Directory to the Spiritual Exercises of our Holy Father Ignatius.* Authorized translation (=*Official Directory*), (London, 1925), pp106-7.
[15] E. Raitz von Frentz, p41; I. Iparraguirre, *Historia* I, pp200-1.

G. Fessard (pp74ff) maintains the fascinating view that the First Time is not all that miraculous and special, because Matthew's call from Christ was no more miraculous than the one refused by the rich young man. To concentrate, therefore, upon Paul's extraordinary and miraculous call would be false.

The Risen Christ indeed appeared to Paul in an extraordinary and miraculous way. Nevertheless, can Christ's direct call of his apostles really be considered as normal and natural? Furthermore, as we have seen above, Ignatius definitely expected his exercitants to receive Christ's call during the Exercises in a manner similar to Matthew's. Ignatius mentions the First Time Election, therefore, not because of a "liking for system than for its practical importance," as K. Rahner (pp127-8, n25) states, but because some of his exercitants were so elected. Just as the CSCP is the prime example of the consolation from above against which all other consolations are to be measured, so too is the First Time Election the norm for all other elections. Could it be that Ignatius had all Jesuit Novices and Tertians make the entire Exercises, although they had already long made their choice, with the hope that they would now experience Christ's call according to the modality of the First Time?

The Meat Vision

Another striking example of a God-initiated, irresistible, certainty-filled experience in Ignatius' life is the famous meat vision. According to the *Autobiography:*

> While he was carrying out his abstinence from meat, *without any thought of changing it*, one morning as he got up, a dish of meat *appeared* before him, as though he actually saw it with his eyes. But he had *no antecedent desire* for it. At the same time he felt within himself a *great movement of the will* to eat it in the future. Although he remembered his former resolve, he *could not hesitate* to make up his mind that he ought to eat meat. Relating this to his confessor later, the confessor told him that he ought to find out whether this was a temptation. But he, examine it as he would, *could never have any doubt about it.*
>
> At this time *God treated him* just as a schoolmaster treats a little boy when he teaches him. This perhaps was because of his rough and uncultivated understanding, or because he had no one to teach him, or because of the *firm will God Himself had given him* in His service. But he clearly saw, and always had seen that *God dealt with him* like this. Rather, he thought that *any doubt* about it would be an offense against His Divine Majesty. (pp21-2, emphasis mine)

The meat vision exhibits many features characteristic of an experience of the First Time and the CSCP. God Himself initiates both the First Time Election and the CSCP. Ignatius explicitly speaks of the God-initiated quality of the meat vision: "God treated him . . . as . . . a little boy . . . God dealt with him like this." Furthermore, to doubt the divine origin of his experiences "would be an offense against His Divine Majesty." The experience of God acting, the "from above" or mystagogical element characteristic of the First Time and of the CSCP clearly belong to the meat vision.

During the First Time Election and the CSCP, "God our Lord moves and attracts the will . . . for it belongs to the Creator to enter the soul, to leave it, and to act upon it." During the meat vision, Ignatius "felt . . . a great movement of the will," and experienced "the firm will God Himself had given him." Note, too, that "a dish of meat *appeared*." The passivity of the will, its being acted upon by God is a dominant feature of the First Time Election, the CSCP and the meat vision.

The CSCP underscores an experience "without previous cause, that is, without any previous perception or knowledge of any object from which such consolation might come to the soul through its own acts of intellect and will." Although Ignatius does not describe the First Time Election in this way, it, too, seems to come about "without previous cause." St. Paul and St. Matthew hardly expected what Christ did to them; they experienced a stunning reversal of their lives "without previous cause." Ignatius' meat vision occurred although he "had no previous desire." The experience totally reversed a previous resolve and was clearly without previous cause, for Ignatius had been "without any thought of changing." The "without previous cause," therefore, belongs to the First Time Election, the CSCP and the meat vision. All three seem to involve a powerful movement contrary to what went before.

The meat vision yielded Ignatius an unusually profound certitude. "He could not hesitate to make up his mind; he could never have any doubt about it; any doubt . . . would be an offense." The certitude of the First Time Election is "without question and without desire to question." The certitude of the CSCP is unshakable, because the experience has "no deception in it; proceeds only from God our Lord," and draws the person "wholly to the love of His Divine Majesty." The First Time Election, the CSCP and the meat vision all possess radical, unshakable certitude.

The meat vision, however, seems to stand closer to a First Time Election than to the CSCP, because only the CSCP draws the person "wholly to the love of His Divine Majesty." During the First Time Election, God may move and attract the will in ways not involving being drawn "wholly to the love of His Divine Majesty." On the other hand, it seems obvious that St. Paul and St. Matthew were so drawn. The love element which characterizes the CSCP and perhaps even the First Time Election cannot be found in the meat vision.

Ignatius' Cardoner Experience

The most important experience in Ignatius' life took place on the banks of the river Cardoner. Ignatius describes the event in this way:

> The eyes of his understanding began to open; it was not that he beheld any vision, but rather he comprehended and understood many things, about the spiritual life as well as about faith and learning. This took place with an illumination so great that all these things appeared to be something new. He seemed to himself to be another man and to have an understanding different from what he had previously . . . He received a great clarity in his understanding; in such a manner that as he gathered together all the helps he had received from God and all the things he had known in the whole course of his life right up to his sixty-second year — even though he should gather all these into one, it seems to him that they did not come up to as much as those he received at that one time.[16]

L. Bakker (pp99ff, 259ff) perceptively explicates the Cardoner experience in this way. Ignatius received his greatest grace at Cardoner and valued it even more than the meat vision. It was not a vision, but a rapture of such force that it had to be a consolation that "God alone" could give, although the words "without previous cause" nowhere appear. Still, as L. Bakker (p105) says, the Cardoner experience is "the *existential* example of *consolation* without previous cause and with that of every true consolation." After Cardoner, Ignatius easily discerned true from false consolations, as exemplified by his rejection of the serpent-form vision because of its diminished color, his distaste for Erasmus because of diminished fervor and his decision to reject consolations which prevented him from sleeping. Laynez, Nadal and Polanco call Cardoner the "birthday of the Exercises"; moreover, Ignatius then received the gift of the discernment of spirits. Ignatius' architechtonic experience uncovered the link

---

[16] Quoted by J. de Guibert, *Jesuits*, pp30-1.

between consolation and Election as well as the salvation of oneself and a universal apostolate because Cardoner involved a First Time Election: to go to Jerusalem to live poorly, to preach to the Muslims, to visit the holy places and to experience sufferings and unjustice. Profound union with Christ, the third degree of humility and the intrinsic link between the great christocentric meditations of the Exercises and the Election resulted from Cardoner.

Although we agree in substance with Bakker's fine exposition, our emphasis is different. The Cardoner experience differs from the First Time Election and the CSCP because nothing is said about God moving and attracting the will or drawing the person wholly to His love. This experience is an example of Christian *satori*, of Christian enlightenment in which the understanding, and not the will, predominates: "The eyes of his *understanding*," "he *comprehended* and *understood*," "he seemed . . . to have an *understanding* different," and "he received great clarity in his *understanding*." Illumination, and not love, stands out: "An illumination so great" and "a great clarity." Perhaps this experience, in addition to Manresa, is the source of Ignatius' emphasis upon "thoughts" as a key element in discernment, an important point constantly overlooked by commentators.

Cardoner changed not only what Ignatius had previously known and seen, but also *how* he knew and saw. Ignatius' particular mystical horizon was born. The holistic, architechtonic quality of the experience put everything in a new light and unified everything, but not to the exclusion of particulars, for "he cannot point out the particulars of what he then understood, *although they were many*."

Cardoner, on the other hand, is clearly an example of the God-initiated, irresistible, certainty-filled experiences we have already discussed. It resembles the First Time Election and the CSCP. Cardoner transformed Ignatius into "another man" with a new understanding. His Cardoner experience was as stunning and profound a conversion as that demanded by the First Time Election and exemplified by St. Paul and St. Matthew. Although the specific words "without previous cause" and "drawing it wholly to the love of His Divine Majesty" are lacking, the reality is present. This stunning reversal of Ignatius' life was clearly without previous cause, for it far exceeded anything he had thought about and desired. Furthermore, if this experience surpassed the sum total of 62 years of graces, Ignatius could hardly "question or desire to question" the source of this experience. And as a new man, he now belonged "wholly" to the service of Christ.

The Relationship between the First Time
of Election and the CSCP

Because Ignatius gave no rules nor instructions for the First Time Election, Ferrusola (pp381-2) advises the exercitant not to spend much time in considering this type of Election. Many commentators, however, point out that *Ex* 330 and 336 belong to any explanation of the First Time, because the CSCP belongs to it.[17] The exact relationship between the First Time and the CSCP, on the other hand, remains a rather controversial subject, as L. Bakker (p89) notes.

Both the First Time Election and the CSCP clearly involve the immediate action of God in the person's core; moreover, they are experiences in which God alone is at work. Although the First Time does not specifically mention the word "consolation," *Ex* 316 describes consolation as "an interior movement . . . that is directly connected to His service and praise." The First Time, therefore, is clearly a God-initiated consolation. The First Time also takes place without previous cause, although these exact words are not used. The First Time involves a God-initiated movement which is disproportionate to what can be expected or prayed for by the exercitant. Although the First Time does not expressly use the phrase "drawing it wholly to the love of the Divine Majesty," this did happen to St. Paul and St. Matthew, Ignatius' own examples of the First Time. Although the certainty issuing from the First Time appears to be more profound than that from the CSCP ("without question and without the desire to question" vs. "there is no deception in it"), the CSCP, too, leaves almost no room for questioning. If this consolation comes from "God alone" and draws the entire person into God's love, what remains left for the person to doubt? The First Time and the CSCP clearly have very much in common.

G. Fessard (p76) stresses that the difference between the First Time and the CSCP "consists simply in that the one, the vocation of Paul and Matthew, embraces or specifies the future of one's life, which the other [CSCP] leaves more or less indeterminate." The Ignatian texts, however, are not that clear. When Ignatius focused upon St. Paul and St. Matthew, did he have in mind their fundamental conversion to Christ or their response to Christ's specific

---

[17]H. Coathalem, pp214ff; L. Bakker, p93; G. Fessard, I, p74; L. Gonzales Hernandez, p150; W. Sierp, *Hochschule* II, p360; J. Clémence, p355, n34.

command? Paul and Matthew's First Time Election could be interpreted as their total openness to Christ, an openness, however, yet to be specified in definite ways throughout their daily lives. They were moved and chosen to follow Christ, but were not the details of this discipleship to be specified only later? The CSCP also seems to involve a fundamental, indeterminate, unspecified conversion experience, a consolation which draws the entire person into God's love. Insofar as both involve a total, radical openness to serve Christ, and nothing more, both are identical.

Ignatius seems, however, to have something more specific in mind, because the "devout soul" is expected to follow "what has been manifested to it." He is told that after the CSCP "the soul makes various plans and resolutions which are not inspired directly by God" (*Ex* 336). In this case, the First Time Election would be a CSCP plus an explicit, God-guaranteed specification of His Will. The First Time would include the CSCP as a God-given communication which totally opens the exercitant to God's love in Christ plus a direct, explicit manifest command to do something specific for Christ — eat meat, enter religious life, become a Dominican, etc. The CSCP, on the other hand, would be a God-given communication to the person which draws him entirely into His love. Nothing explicit, thematic or specific, however, would be given. The CSCP is, therefore, a basic transcendental conversion to Christ. As this transcendental experience becomes categorical, it becomes the First Time Election. *That* God communicates Himself and *what* He *explicitly* communicates belong to the First Time. The CSCP centers only on *that* God communicates Himself and need not involve an actual election. The CSCP might even include an *implicit, non-thematic* specification of *what* He wills, a core consolation plus a non-verbal or non-conceptual tendency to specify His Will. During the First Time, however, God controls the core experience and the echoes it produces throughout the different levels in the person's being. During the CSCP, on the other hand, God controls only the core experience, and may *begin* to control the echoes, yet the echoes eventually arise from the good angel, the enemy of our human nature or ourselves (*Ex* 336). The CSCP can be the basis for Election, whereas the First Time is always an actual election or being-elected. The First Time, then, is the CSCP in its ideal development from a God-given core experience, and nothing else, to a God-given core experience with God-given echoes. The First Time always includes a CSCP, but not vice versa.

THE SECOND TIME OF ELECTION

General Description

Ignatius describes the Second Time of Election as follows:

> The second occasion is present when one has developed a clear understanding and knowledge through the experience of consolations and desolations and the discernment of various spirits. (*Ex* 176)

The *Official Directory* of 1599 comments as follows:

> The second "time" or occasion is of a more ordinary kind. This is when the mind is acted on by inspirations and internal motions so efficacious, that, without any intellectual effort or reasoning, or with scarcely any, the will is borne on to the service of God and to the state of perfection ... In the first and second "times" of Election, the will leads, the intellect follows, drawn by the will's attraction, without any discursive process of its own, yet without hesitation. (pp107-8)

The Second Time of Election centers upon development, clarity, knowledge, discernment, experience, the more ordinary, inspirations, internal motions, the lack of discursive reasoning and the ability of the will to attract the intellect. Lacking the extraordinary and miraculous characteristics of the First Time, the Second Time is "of a more ordinary kind," and definitely to be expected by the exercitant. Lacking the immediacy and intensity of the First Time, the Second Time comes about only after a long process of experimentation. Ignatius expects the exercitant to *develop* "a clear understanding and knowledge." Note, too, that both "discernment" and "inspirations," as well as "experience" and "internal motions" can be expected. Although the *Official Directory* emphasizes the internal motions, the will's leading of the intellect and the lack of discursive reasoning, the Second Time cannot be reduced merely to a time of religious affectivity. Ignatius clearly expects this *and* "clear understanding and knowledge." Although this Time lacks the certitude of the First Time, the experience of the tides of consolation and desolation allows the exercitant to piece together God's Will for him with "a clear understanding and knowledge."

The Second Time, moreover, has the same goal as the First Time: the divine call which comes from above. It, too, seeks, the pure moment of the pure movement from above. The Second Time, however, faces the reverse problem of *Ex* 336. *Ex* 336 would have the exercitant carefully distinguish "the exact time of such consolation"

(CSCP) from "the time that follows it." The Second Time, on the other hand, must begin from "the time that follows it" to find "the exact time of consolation." It is like an echo in search of its source or the focusing of a lens to concentrate many rays into a single point.

Ignatius' *Directory* states that the Second Time takes place:

> By proceeding in his meditations on Christ our Lord, and then observing to what God moves him when he finds himself in consolation. And the same when he finds himself in desolation. (pp9-10)

The Second Time pieces together a First Time which has dissipated and scattered itself into consolations and desolations which must be understood and discerned according to the Rules for the Discernment of Spirits (*Ex* 313-36). The shattered ray of light and love from above must be put back together again. The Second Time seeks what went before through what it has now. What has been lost in intensity and immediacy is made up by tides of positive and negative evidence, the tides of consolations and desolations which arise from the meditations on the life of Christ.

Intellectual and Affective Discernment

The Second Time of Election demands of the exercitant a truly spiritual experimentation. While meditating upon and contemplating the life, death and resurrection of Jesus Christ, he will experience consolations, desolations, inner motions and the thoughts which spring from these, "for just as consolation is contrary to desolation, so the thoughts that spring from consolation are the opposite of those that spring from desolation" (*Ex* 317). Thoughts, therefore, as well as internal motions must be discerned.

K. Rahner (pp102-3) puts this rather well:

> Even within this second mode of making the Election and within the stirring of spirits, rational reflection can and must develop as an indispensable element in the motion of the spirits. After all, these stirrings do not consist of merely indifferent, blind drives like hunger, thirst and so on. They consist of thoughts, acts of knowing, perception of values, etc. They themselves contain an objective conceptual element, they can be expressed and verified.

Too few commentators, however, mention that the Second Time and the Rules for the Discernment of Spirits deal with understanding, knowledge, thoughts, the unmasking of "false reasonings, seemingly serious reasons, subtleties" (*Ex* 315, 324); that there are *thoughts* which spring from consolation and desolation which have to be discerned (*Ex* 317); that the evil spirit *counsels* during desolation (*Ex* 318); that God gives "true knowledge and understanding" (*Ex* 322); that the evil one may suggest "good and holy thoughts" (*Ex* 322); that "we must pay attention to the course of our thoughts" (*Ex* 333-4); and that the exercitant is to obtain experience and knowledge" (*Ex* 334). Ignatius was not only aware that consolation and desolation resulted from certain thoughts, but also that certain thoughts resulted from consolation and desolation.

The Ignatian method, therefore, contains an intellectual criterion. Because the CSCP is an experience which God alone can give and is free from all deception, it, too, is the norm against which all thoughts are to be measured. Because the CSCP draws the person wholly into God's love, the exercitant's intellect is illuminated by this love and made new in a way analogous to Ignatius' "new understanding" at Cardoner. This understanding allows the exercitant to discern those "good and holy thoughts that are in conformity with the disposition of a just soul" (*Ex* 332), yet lead to "something evil . . . or less good than the soul had previously proposed to do" (*Ex* 333), and to reject them accordingly. The exercitant thus more easily detects and recognizes the evil one "by his deceptions and by the bad end to which he leads" (*Ex* 334).

Ignatius' own life clearly illustrates the use of intellectual discernment. In the hospital, as he relates in his *Autobiography* (pp17-24), he frequently saw a serpent-form which gave him great delight and consolation. But while thanking God before a cross for his Cardoner experience, he had the same serpent-form vision:

> But he noticed that as it stood before the cross it did not have that beautiful color as heretofore, and *he understood very clearly*, with a strong assent of his will, that it was the evil one. (p24, emphasis mine)

Ignatius rejected this vision, not because of diminished consolation, but because he "understood very clearly . . . that it was the evil one."

The *Autobiography* (pp21, 39-40) also relates that Ignatius rejected great illuminations and spiritual consolations which made him lose sleep or interfered with his studies, because "he gave it some thought" and "step by step he came to recognize that it was a temptation." *Discrete* charity is a hallmark of Ignatian spirituality.

The affective component of discernment, on the other hand, faces this major problem: Are the consolations and desolations which flow from the meditations on the life, death and resurrection of Christ with reference to a possible object of Election true or false? If they result from a congruence or disharmony between the exercitant's fundamental religious orientation and the possible object of Election, they are true. If they flow from a congruence or disharmony between the exercitant's inordinate attachments and the possible object of Election, they are false.

This method clearly presupposes a basal experience, a touchstone experience, an experience of exclusively divine origin free from all deception. The CSCP is this experience and the first principle of Ignatian supernatural logic. Because the CSCP is from God alone, it is the measure and standard for all other experiences. Once the exercitant has received this consolation, he can measure all other consolations and desolations against it.

While meditating on Christ, the exercitant prays over a possible object of Election. The *Directories* suggest: the way of the counsels or the precepts, in the world or religious life, which religious order, when to enter, which profession in the world, how to live this profession, etc.[18] To this could be added any specific decision to be made, such as the yearly retreat resolutions made by so many. The exercitant must then pay very close attention to the emotional-volitional tonality of his prayer and the affective horizon surrounding his thoughts. He must listen to the echoes his tentative Election produces in his being. Do "these thoughts weaken, disquiet or disturb the soul by destroying the peace, tranquillity, and quiet which it had before" (*Ex* 333)? If so, "this is a clear sign that they proceed from the evil spirit" (*Ex* 333). If these thoughts suggest something "distracting" (*Ex* 333), or "little by little" cause him to "fall from the state of sweetness and spiritual delight he was enjoying" (*Ex* 334), they are to be rejected. If the emotional-volitional tonality of these thoughts enhance, strengthen, deepen and are in harmony with the exercitant's CSCP, this is a clear sign of God's Will for him. The synthesis, congruence, meshing, harmony, or lack thereof, of the CSCP and the possible object of Election indicate God's Will for him.

Ignatius' own life illustrates this method. As the *Autobiography* (pp10, 14) relates, while Ignatius was convalescing from his canon ball injury, he frequently daydreamed about vain, worldly things and also about a life similar to St. Francis' and St. Dominic's. He noticed that:

> While he was thinking of the things of the world he was filled with delight, but when afterwards he dismissed them from weariness, he was

[18] See: *Autograph Directories*, pp10-11; *Official Directory*, pp103-6.

> dry and dissatisfied. And when he thought of going barefooted to Jerusalem ... and performing the other rigors he saw that the saints had performed, he was consoled, not only when he entertained these thoughts, but even after dismissing them he remained cheerful and satisfied ... learning from his experience that one kind of thoughts left him sad and the other cheerful. Thus, step by step, he came to recognize the difference between the two spirits that moved him, the one being from the evil spirit, the other from God. (p10)

The *Autobiography* (pp24-5) also notes that the thought that he was a just man depressed him more than a severe fever from which he was suffering, whereas "he found so much joy and so much spiritual consolation in the thought of dying that he melted into tears."

It would seem, moreover, that Ignatius' prohibition against the reading of Erasmus in the Society of Jesus sprang from the affective component of discernment.

> He observed something totally new and strange: whenever he picked up and began to read a book from Erasmus, his ardour disappeared and his devotion grew cold. If he read further, this change increased, so much so, that if he had finished a certain section, it seemed to him that also his earlier fervour was lost, that his spirit became deaf and his heart exchanged for another and that he was no longer the same person he was before the reading. When he had noticed this a few times, he finally threw the book away and developed such an aversion and disgust for the book and the author's other books that he later never wanted to read them again and that he likewise did not allow them to be read in the Society of Jesus, except for a few well-chosen sections and with great caution.[19]

THE THIRD TIME OF ELECTION

General Description
Ignatius describes the Third Time of Election as follows:

> The third occasion is in a time of tranquillity. Here one considers first for what purpose man is born, which is to praise God our Lord and to save his soul. Since he desires to attain this end, he chooses some life or state within the bounds of the church that will help him in the service of God our Lord and the salvation of his soul. I said 'a time of tranquillity,' when the soul is not agitated by diverse spirits, and is freely and calmly making use of its natural powers. (*Ex* 177)

[19]P. Ribadeneyra, *Vida de Ignacio de Loyola*, (Madrid, 1868), lib. I, c13.

The Third Time, therefore, stands out as a time of "tranquillity." A. Gagliardi (pp146, 152ff) maintains, however, that because God has withdrawn his sensible graces and left the soul to itself, this is a state of desolation! He says, too, that since the subtraction of fervor was done by God, it is the good desolation described in *Ex* 320 and 322. H. Pinard de la Boullaye simply calls it a "time of dryness."[20] W. Peters (p126) argues that a period of tranquillity indicates "something wrong" which the director must investigate, because Ignatius clearly expects the exercitant to experience consolations and desolations and to be moved by various spirits.

We agree with those commentators, however, who see this tranquillity as *consolation*, as the "peace and quiet in Christ our Lord" of *Ex* 316, as the "peace" of *Ex* 315, and as the "peace, tranquillity, and quiet" of *Ex* 333.[21] Although this Time lacks the high crests of consolation and the deep troughs of desolation, it is still a period of consoling peace, quiet and tranquillity in Christ.

Although the words, "Here one considers first for what purpose man is born, which is to praise God our Lord and to save his soul," evoke the *Principle and Foundation*, we disagree with W. Peters (pp121, 126) that the Third Time's "spiritual climate [is] totally different from that of the second week" or that "the Third Time lies outside the long retreat." During the Third Time, the exercitant surpasses the "we must *make ourselves indifferent*" of the *Principle and Foundation*, for he is expected to "*remain indifferent* and free from all inordinate attachments" (*Ex* 179, emphasis mine). This definitely indicates an exercitant who has progressed beyond the First Week. *Ex* 189 states, too, that one can amend and reform his life and state by "using the *Exercises* and *methods* of making a choice" (emphasis mine). In addition, the Third Time focuses on exactly the same object as the first two Times: "some life or state within the bounds of the Church," and not merely a mutable choice, as W. Peters (p126) maintains and as *Ex* 171, 173-4, 178 seemingly support.[22] The Third Time, therefore, belongs to the Exercises and may be used for both the choice of a way of life and for amending and reforming one's life and state.

---

[20] H. Pinard de la Boullaye, *Exercices spirituels selon la méthode de saint Ignace* (Paris, 1950), I, p216.

[21] P. Penning de Vries, p89, n2. See also: I. Diertins, I, pp177-8; 185, n1.

[22] For the contrary opinion, see: L. Bakker, pp243ff; J. Roothaan, p211, n1; A. Denis, I, pp88ff; E. Raitz von Frentz, p102, n1.

The Two Methods of the Third Time

Ex 178 says: "If a choice has not been made on the first or second occasion, below are given two methods of making it during the third occasion." Ignatius clearly unites the first two Times and opposes them to the Third Time in a way that seems to indicate his preference for the first two Times. Ignatius' *Directory* also seems to indicate a hierarchy of preference:

> Should the director observe that the retreatant is not moved in the first, he should insist that he pass on to the second... When in the second time no decision has been made ... let the third time be used. (pp9-10)

Ignatius would have the exercitant pass on to the Third Time only if the First and Second Time are lacking. L. Bakker (p285) has noted, however, that the *Vulgate* translation of the Exercises reverses this order:

> *Unless* the Election takes place during the first or second time, there is recourse to the third, in the following two ways. (Bakker's emphasis)

This could mean that during Ignatius' more mature years, he preferred the Third Time of Election. But it is more likely that the *Vulgate* text was more conservative, because it was the translation of the Exercises submitted to Church authorites for approbation.

Ex 179 echoes the *Principle and Foundation* meditation, although, as we said above, the exercitant must now "*remain* indifferent and free from any inordinate attachments," instead of making himself indifferent. The "tranquillity" of the Third Time enables the exercitant not to be "more inclined or disposed to take the thing proposed than to reject it" and "to be like the equalized scales of balance." The exercitant has already received the grace of indifference prayed for in *Ex* 23. He prepares himself, however, to transcend this tranquillity so that he can "feel" what is "more for the glory and praise of God our Lord." This evokes the atmosphere of the Second Time and perhaps even the First Time, indicating the Third Time's tendency to look to the other two Times for support and confirmation.

Ex 180 clearly shows how the Third Time looks to the First Time for support and confirmation. Although the exercitant is expected to examine "the matter thoroughly and faithfully with [his] understanding," the sentence, "I must ask God our Lord to deign to move my will and to reveal to my spirit," indicates an activity definitely surpassing the rational and participating in the mystical, God-initiated quality of the First Time. In the mystical order, the will leads, a fact which may have prompted the more conservative *Vulgate* to reverse the order to: "Enlighten my spirit and move my will," as some commentators have noted.[23]

Ex 181-2 emphasize the exercitant's rational activity. He must "reason," "weigh," "consider and weigh," "examine and consider," and "consider which alternative appears more reasonable. Acting upon the stronger judgment of reason and not on any inclination of the senses," he must, therefore, eliminate inordinate affections from his judgment, perhaps in a way which evokes the use of the intellectual aspect of the discernment of spirits.

Ex 183 counsels the exercitant to "turn with great diligence to prayer in the presence of God our Lord and offer Him this choice that His Divine Majesty may deign to accept and confirm it." Although commentators tend to make light of this moment of acceptance and confirmation by God, or mention perfunctorily that the *Vulgate* calls for God to "stabilize" the Election,[24] Ignatius clearly expects the Creator to work directly with the creature (*Ex* 15) by accepting and confirming his Election through a felt-knowledge and movements of consolation and desolation. We agree, therefore, with M. Giuliani that the acceptance and confirmation of the Election is scarcely *pro forma*, but a major moment of the Election and one at the heart of the Ignatian mystical Election.[25] This underscores, too, the tendency of the Third Time to seek the moment from above of the Second and First Times and to surpass exclusively rational activity.

Ex 184 introduces the exercitant to the second method of the Third Time, the "ultimate resource," according to the Ignatian *Directory* (p10). By appealing to "the love which moves me and causes me to make this choice should come from above," Ignatius once more evokes elements of the First Time. Elements of the Second Time are also evoked, because "before I make my choice I will *feel* that the greater or lesser love that I have for the thing chosen is solely for the sake of my Creator and Lord." Once again the Third Time looks beyond the purely rational to the more affective and mystical moments of the first two Times.

---

[23] J. Roothaan, pp212-3, n2; W. Sierp, *Hochschule* II, p368.

[24] A. Gaudier, pp283ff, 296ff.

[25] M. Giuliani, "Une nouvelle traduction des 'Exercices'," (="Traduction") *Chr* 27(1960), p405; J. Pegon, p1273; H. Pinard de la Boullaye, "Sentir," pp423ff.

Ex 185-7 advises the exercitant "to consider some man that I have never seen, and in whom I wish to see complete perfection," or "to consider that if I were at the point of death," or "to examine and consider how I shall be on the day of judgment." The exercitant chooses "for the greater glory of God" and his salvation with these situations in mind. By removing the exercitant from his present situation, Ignatius hopes to make him more objective. It is often easier to judge what is good for another than for ourselves. To judge for another or to consider some future situation helps to eliminate the present affect of inordinate affections and may help our true self to come into play. By making a decision for a stranger, seeing ourselves at the moment of death or on judgment day, we obtain a certain distance from ourselves, and, paradoxically, a deeper, more objective connaturality to means and end, and to the Eternal Now in our now. This connaturality also evokes elements of the Second Time.

These two methods of the Third Time demand much more than a purely human effort based on rational considerations of a syllogistic kind by which the exercitant moves from universal principles to the individual Will of God. The Third Time is incomplete in itself and seeks after elements from the first two Times. The Third Time demands rational activity, supernatural prudence made possible by indifference and religious affectivity, passionate love of God above all else, and a tranquillity which is Christ's peace. We find it strange that the Third Time is so often considered "rational" and "natural."

THE "PREFERRED" TIME?

The Preferred Time in the Ignatian Tradition

Writing on the Three Times for Election, L. Bakker (pp281ff) has clearly demonstrated that Ignatius expected and preferred the First Time, at least until 1539. Between 1539-41, he emphasized a more gradual calling and stressed the Second Time of Election. After this, however, the Third Time became prominent.

J. Roi (pp305-23) has convincingly summarized the Jesuit tradition after Ignatius concerning the Three Times of Election. Both Polanco and Dávila considered the First Time extraordinary and the Second Time more ordinary. Theologically, the Second Time is superior to and more excellent than the Third Time, because the motions and consolations may come directly from the Holy Spirit. If the light received during the Second Time suffices to find God's Will, there is no obligation to go on to the Third Time. Because the experience of consolations and desolations does not strike each exercitant with the same force, and because Satan often clothes himself as an angel of light, it is useful, safer, more prudent and often necessary to move to the Third Time to let reason shine its light on the Election. Polanco and Dávila emphasize, however, the insufficient certitude of the Third Time and the need to finish the election process with the Second Time.

J. Roi further notes that the *Official Directory* of 1599 recommends that the exercitant should *always* pass from the Second to the Third Time. Miron, too, had made this an obligation. Roi emphasizes that the *Official Directory* contradicts itself; at one point, the Second Time is called superior; at another, the Third Time.[26] The Jesuit General Mercurian, moreover, solidified the tendency to prefer the Third Time over the Second Time. He underscored the Third Time's rational elements and called the Third Time "admirable" and the Time of "true wisdom" (Roi, p317).

The Preferred Time and
Recent Commentators

The shift in the tradition from a solid appreciation of the Second Time and its ability to check the Third Time, to a distrust of the Second Time in favor of an excessively rationalistic interpretation of the Third Time which began in the *Official Directory* and solidified with Mercurian, provides the basis for the split one finds in Ignatian commentators. Many commentators stay with the later tradition and emphasize the necessity, safety, value and superiority of the Third Time.[27] Many recent commentators, however, stress the earlier Ignatian tradition.[28] They maintain that the Second Time is *the* Time Ignatius had in mind. The entire dynamics of the Exercises point to the atmosphere of the Second Time. The Second Time should be a check on the Third Time, for it is more certain, gives the exercitant clear understanding and may even be more ordinary. Commenting on Ignatius' letters and *Diary*, L. Bakker (pp284ff) has convincingly shown that Ignatius almost always experienced the

---

[26] J. Roi, p317. R. Rouquette's, "Le Directoire des Exercices: histoire du texte," *RAM* 14(1933), p395 praises the *Official Directory* as a masterpiece of unity and balance. J. Roi's position, however, is more nuanced than this.

[27] W. Sierp, *Hochschule*, II, p360; A. de Ponlevoy, p286; J. de Guibert, *Jesuits*, pp536ff; E. Przywara, *Deus* II, p189; A. Denis, III, pp83ff; A. Gaudier, pp28ff; F. Hettinger, p124; A. Bellecius, p246.

[28] K. Rahner, *Dynamic*, pp95ff, 100ff; H. Rahner, *Ignatius*, pp127ff; W. Peters, p121; J. Pegon, p1268; J. Clémence, pp355ff; M. Giuliani, "Traduction," p409.

Second Time, or at least the Third Time confirmed by strong movements of consolation and desolation.

THE THREE TIMES OF ELECTION AND
THE IGNATIAN MYSTICAL HORIZON

The Interpenetration of the Three
Times of Election

Writing on Ignatius' later life, M. Giuliani has cogently shown that the Three Times of Election were so much a part of Ignatius' life that he passed from one to the other with incredible ease.[29] We maintain, moreover, that Ignatius could do this because the ideal Election contains an interpenetration or fusing of the Three Times which the Exercises explicate as three distinct Times only for clarity. In the concrete, however, the Three Times are not three distinct ways of finding God's Will, but actually aspects of one core experience and Election in which all three aspects are present in varying degrees of intensity. The Three Times are actually the three aspects of an experience whose goal is God's Will for the exercitant. This Will of God makes itself felt at different levels in the exercitant's being. God's immediate, direct action constitutes the core of this experience; this action, however, is explicitly experienced at different levels in the exercitant's being. When the exercitant experiences God's immediate action predominantly in the core of his being, this is the First Time. If this core experience dissipates itself into consolations and desolations not experienced predominantly in the inner core, then this is the Second Time. And finally, when this core experience manifests itself predominantly as a tranquillity which allows the exercitant the calm and peaceful use of his own abilities, this is the Third Time.

Some commentators have noted that without a direct and immediate experience of God in some way, no Election is possible.[30] This means that elements of the First Time actually constitute the Second and Third Times. The First Time can be found in some way in the Second and Third Times. The CSCP can be found to some extent in all three Times. During the First Time, the CSCP contains as a moment of its realization an explicit, God-guaranteed communication which is thematic and conceptual. During the Second Time, the CSCP acts as the touchstone experience, the consolation which measures and judges all other motions. During the Third Time, the

[29] M. Giuliani, "Se décider sous la motion divine," *Chr* 4(1957), p186.
[30] A. Gagliardi, p93; P. Penning de Vries, p65; J. Bökmann, p124.

CSCP is experienced primarily as "tranquillity" in Christ our Lord and as "the love which moves me and causes me to make this choice should come from above" (*Ex* 180, 184). The Second and Third Times are echoes of the First Time heard at different levels in the exercitant's being, but echoes whose source must in some way be found. The Second and Third Times contain the mystagogical, God-initiated experience of the First Time. They are a deficient mode of the First Time.

The First Time, however, also contains elements of the Second and Third Times. We have already seen that the CSCP relates itself dialectically to the "time that follows" and to CCCP. To discern the CSCP from "the time that follows" or from CCCP requires great skill, experience and understanding. This can be said of the First Time. The First Time *tends* to dissipate itself into a Time when "the soul makes various plans and resolutions which are not inspired directly by God our Lord." There comes a time when even the most powerful God-initiated experience must be discerned and distinguished from the human echoes it produces. St. Paul himself went up to Jerusalem and "laid before them the Gospel which I preached . . . lest somehow I should be running or had run in vain" (*Gal.* 2.1ff). Was St. Matthew's First Time experience powerful enough to override his doubts about Jesus even after the Resurrection (*Acts* 1.6ff)? Admittedly, Ignatius never seemed to have doubted his Cardoner experience. At the request of his confessor, however, he did examine the meat vision. "But he, examine it as he would, could never have any doubt about it." Although Ignatius had had experiential certitude about many God-initiated experiences, he also demanded reflexive certitude, a certainty drawn from the realization that even the First Time contains a time-after, "during which time the soul continues in fervor and feels the divine favor and the aftereffects of the consolation," necessitating that "they be very carefully examined."

The First Time contains elements of the Second Time, therefore, insofar as the First Time tends to shatter into consolations and desolations requiring discernment. The First Time contains elements of the Third Time, because only during a period of tranquillity can the First Time be discerned from the time afterwards.

Elements of the Third Time can also be found in the First Time because of the ecclesial and service characteristics of Ignatian mysticism. As H. Rahner (pp214-38) has shown, Ignatius' ecclesial, Roman and papal spirituality meant an incarnational yardstick for even the most profoundly theocentric experiences. A First Time Election must conform to the Rules for Thinking with the Church (*Ex* 352-70), for "there is but one spirit, which governs and directs us . . . [and] our Holy Mother Church" (*Ex* 365). A First Time Election most likely prompted Ignatius to Jerusalem. Because the Franciscan Provincial had papal authority to order Ignatius away under pain of excommunication, Ignatius knew "it was not our Lord's will that he remain there in those holy places."[31] The service dimension of Ignatius' mysticism meant that the practical success of his apostolate and the course of events and not only the inner experience of God grounded his discernment. The practical course of events led Ignatius to study for the apostolate and to find his Jerusalem in Rome.[32] Ignatius' service orientation prompted him to study, to reject consolations in favor of sleep, to reject the gift of tears because he was going blind, etc. Ignatius wanted to be with Christ to serve in His Church. The experience of God at the core of his being, the experience of what was necessary to promote the growth of the visible, hierarchical Church and the experience of the practical success in the apostolate formed a dialectical unity in practically all of Ignatius' decisions.

Elements of the Third Time also belong to the Second Time. During the Third Time one reasons and then is moved and attracted by the love from above. During the Second Time, however, one is moved and attracted and must reason why. Reasoning, understanding and discernment definitely belong to the Second Time. Moreover, as A. Dulles says:

> A prudent decision presupposes accurate information about what the decision involves in the actual order . . . the technique of discernment, in its affective aspects, reveals only the harmony between my personal religious orientations and my idea of the object under consideration.[33]

The Second Time can also be the basis of the First and Third Times. The christocentric meditations of the Exercises produce consolations and desolations in such a way that a First Time may arise out of the Second Time. We saw in chapter II that the CSCP often arises out of the CCCP. In like manner, the First Time may arise out of the Second Time. The christocentric basis of the First Time during the Exercises cannot be missed. On the other hand, the christocentric consolations of the Second Time may give rise to that "tranquillity,"

---

[31] *Autobiography*, pp32-4.

[32] T. Baumann, "Compagnie de Jésus: la confirmation de ce nom," *RAM* 38(1962), pp61ff. See also: J. Sudbrack, pp206-25.

[33] A. Dulles, "Finding God's Will," *WL* 94(1965), p151.

"peace and quiet in Christ our Lord," or feeling of what is "more for the glory and praise of God our Lord" (*Ex* 179, 184). The interpenetration of the Three Times seems evident.

The Ignatian Mystical Horizon

The interpenetration of the Three Times of Election clearly manifests the Ignatian mystical horizon. The Three Times of Election illustrate three aspects of a single experience which is anthropocentric, christocentric and mystagogical. We have shown throughout this work the anthropocentric, christocentric and mystagogical aspects of the Ignatian mystical horizon, for the Exercises plunge the exercitant into the Mystery, Revelation and Love of the triune God in Christ through a series of christocentric meditations which also plunges the exercitant into his own deepest mystery as man.

All three Times contain and reveal the mystagogical quality of Ignatius' mystical horizon. All three Times depend upon an immediate, God-initiated, core experience which makes itself felt with varying degrees of intensity and at various levels in the exercitant's being. The First Time in itself, the Second Time as CSCP and the Third Time as the "love from above" plunge the exercitant into a God who gives Himself as Mystery, Revelation and Love.

All three Times contain and reveal the christocentric aspect of Ignatius' mystical horizon, for they all result from the consolations and desolations flowing from the meditations on the life, death and resurrection of Jesus Christ. The christocentric nature of the CSCP with its God-guaranteed, explicit and thematic specification is the First Time. The Second Time results from the discernment of christocentric consolations and desolations evoked by the christocentric meditations. The christocentric aspect of the Third Time is found in that tranquillity in Christ our Lord which constitutes this Time.

All three Times contain and reveal the anthropocentric aspect of Ignatius' mystical horizon, for their goal centers upon God's *individual* Will for the exercitant. The First Time presupposes the exercitant's perfect self-identity and self-surrender to God's irresistible action. The First and Second Times as CSCP totally unify the exercitant and initiate perfect self-identity, for he is to be *wholly* drawn into God's Mystery, Revelation and Love. The Second Time requires his experimentation with his deepest mystery as man, his core religious orientation, and with the object to be elected. The harmony or disharmony of the object elected with his deepest identity, who he is, is the index of God's Will for him. The Third Time focuses upon a tranquillity which allows him to be who he really is in depth, to use his natural powers freely and calmly and to experience himself as another, at the moment of death and at the day of judgment.

Thus, the Three Times of Election as well as the Ignatian mystical horizon are manifestly anthropocentric, christocentric and mystagogical.

⚜ Epilogue

We have examined Ignatius' mystical horizon by focusing upon how he translated it into the Exercises as a *method*. We unfolded this basic mystical horizon by explicating the anthropocentric, christocentric and mystagogical moments of the Exercises. We saw that in and through their implicit and explicit theology and Christology, the exercitant is profoundly "returned" to his own deepest mystery as man, comes to know, love and serve Christ intimately in His personal and cosmic aspects, and is plunged into the triune God whom he experiences as Mystery, Revelation and Love-Given.

What is especially important, however, is that the exercitant experiences all of this as various aspects or phases of his one, primal, core dynamism as man. The Exercises are the successful translation of a mystical horizon into a method which awakens, deepens, strengthens and explicates what the human person is and experiences in the deepest recesses of his being. The Exercises incarnate the anthropocentric-christocentric Mystagogy of Ignatius' mystical horizon. They find their basis in the exercitant, insofar as every person is a mystery referred to Mystery and tastes in Jesus Christ his fulfillment as man and the way to the Mystery which gives itself as Revelation and Love.

Every person experiences in his core the Mystery which enlightens and loves, the Mystery which has given itself absolutely and definitively in the person of Jesus Christ. In short, the Exercises are a method of setting the exercitant's christic and trinitarian existentials into motion, so that he becomes more explicitly aware of what and who he is in the light of the Mystery of God in Jesus Christ.

Although the Exercises speak to something absolutely fundamental in every person, it can be asked, however, if they still have the power they once had as a practical, pastoral method. Much can be said against the Exercises as a pastoral method for today's world. Their strength during Ignatius' day sprang from his ingenious skill in channeling his culture's spontaneous dreams, ideals and ambitions into a method which could fulfill them.

Even a cursory reading of the Exercises reveals that they do not deal with the spontaneous dreams, ideals and ambitions of our age. This is their specific weakness. This shows itself especially in the Ignatian depiction of Christ in terms of his day's courtly, knightly and military traditions. Our age, on the other hand, seems more spontaneously drawn to Christ as the man-for-others, the man of love and peace who gave up his life to free others for full human life. The sixteenth century cultural accretions found in several key Ignatian meditations often strike today's exercitant as foreign and repulsive.

What image do the Exercises have today? This image, as with any image, may be without much foundation, but it does establish the emotional stance with which they will be made or rejected. Many still look upon them as a form of will asceticism which arbitrarily suppresses the emotions. Many see in them an entanglement of minute instructions aimed at destroying all spontaneity. Jesuit prayer, moreover, is frequently understood as Roothaan-prayer, as very detailed application of the intellect, will, memory, imagination to foster practical resolutions.

Their language and manual format are also not helpful. They are often associated with the Jesuits, the Pope's "commandos," who emphasize "Romanitas," blind obedience, discipline and the "jesuitical." Who would not be taken aback to read: "I will believe that the white that I see is black, if the hierarchical Church so defines it" (*Ex* 365)? In addition, because the Exercises belong to institutionalized Christianity and are stamped with a distinctly western face, they will be rejected for more eastern ways of attaining transcendence and religious meaning. Then, too, who has not been shocked by the dubious theology expressed in *Ex* 47 for "considering my soul imprisoned in its corruptible body? " Furthermore, if "no oath, no law, no promise, no indebtedness holds people together when the feeling is gone" [C. Reich, *The Greening of America* (New York, 1970), p228], how many will accept the Exercises as a method for making a life-decision? How many can accept their admonition to lead a good life in the *false*, but *immutable* choice one may have made (*Ex* 172)?

Others reject the Exercises as a "me-Jesus" form of spirituality. Instead of silent prayer and solitude, they prefer communitarian liturgy, Pentecostal prayer, or the experience of God through love of one's neighbor in explicit social action. On the other hand, because the Exercises demand a careful exegesis of Scripture and some theological finesse, albeit on the retreat director's part, they will be rejected by the increasing number of "Jesus people" and Pentecostals who are often extremely fundamentalistic in their biblical interpretation.

The Exercises, on the other hand, possess a number of qualities which make them a highly suitable, contemporary, pastoral method. Perhaps their strongest contemporary quality is the seriousness with which they take the exercitant's *individuality*. They manifest an admirable flexibility in dealing with various exercitants (*Ex* 9, 17, 18, 19). One of their most important dynamics is their intertwining of an objective text with the retreat director's and exercitant's subjectivity. The results, therefore, are as varied as the number of exercitants. Furthermore, because the exercitant's decision must flow from his experienced connaturality or disharmony with the particular object of choice, this respect for individuality is obvious.

The early history of the Exercises indicates that they were especially successful with those who were in some way dissatisfied with their lives. Ignatius himself indirectly, but successfully, healed certain types of affective instability, neuroses and psychic disturbances through the Exercises. We have already mentioned commentators who emphasize the psychotherapeutic usefulness of the Exercises. If it is true that much of the contemporary Jesus movement, Pentecostalism and fascination with eastern meditation techniques is partially rooted in a desire to escape from affective pain, contemporary frustrations and self-disgust, the Exercises have here an excellent starting point.

The Exercises can be used as a contemporary, pastoral method because they emphasize subjective experience and wisdom. Contemporary man does not want to be indoctrinated; he desires personal verification for his life and seeks an overview. The Exercises provide an architechtonic view of life and its meaning. They awaken the exercitant to the deepest depths of the radical meaning of his existence which he often overlooks or suppresses. They help him to integrate his profoundest experiences so that they become more expressly dynamic in his daily living.

The growing number of American subcultures which value contemplation and meditation often reject the values of a technological society which attempts to offer a world view without transcendence. They have experienced that questions about transcendence and man's meaning are inseparable. Some of these subcultures also see meditation and contemplation as a means to demythologize technological man.

The Exercises offer the contemporary exercitant an excellent opportunity to demythologize himself and his values in the light of the Mystery of God in Jesus Christ. They also teach deep prayer and speak directly to today's search for transcendence. Has the Christian tradition, for example, really made its own Ignatius' Application of the Senses or his Third Method of Prayer which utilizes the exercitant's natural breathing rhythm? Is not the polydimensionality of Ignatian prayer, its more mystical aspects, its inclusion and integration of every dimension of the human person, its deeply incarnational dimension a powerful corrective to the contemporary emphasis upon the apophatic way of negation and darkness?

The Exercises have contemporary appeal, because they blend mysticism with humanism. This results in a mysticism of pragmatic service, rooted in discrete love. This blending of mysticism, service and discrete love may not appeal to the more emotional, enthusiastic elements in today's religious subcultures, but we believe that most people's search for transcendence does not really wish to cut itself off from social involvement, pragmatic concerns and reason.

The secret of the Exercises, however, transcends the written text. The retreat director, for Ignatius, was the key to the Exercises. He strove to form disciples who would live the Exercises, be the living directories for them, and for that reason, excel in giving them. Ignatius was ready day and night to answer any questions pertaining to the Exercises that his men might have. The importance of the retreat director remains true today. We have experienced first hand and seen the results of the Exercises today when given by a competent retreat director.

When all is said and done, the Exercises are being given today with great success. We are witnessing a revival of the original form of the Exercises, i.e., one exercitant under the personal guidance of a competent retreat director. There is considerable interest in the discernment of spirits, in communitarian discernment, and in the Exercises and their relationship to liberation theology. The number of books, dissertations and articles being written on Ignatius and the Exercises continues to increase. This in itself is a sign of their current popularity. Although it cannot be denied that Ignatius' sixteenth-century text has lost some of its power and relevance, it also seems true to say that there is much in the Exercises with which the Church as a whole has not yet caught up. The Ignatian mystical horizon and the Exercises as an anthropocentric-christocentric Mystagogy remain amazingly contemporary and fruitful because they give the exercitant to himself in radical freedom by plunging him into the Mystery of God in Jesus Christ.

 **Abbreviations**

used in footnotes

NOTE: Individual abbreviations are also given in footnotes in parentheses following a book's title.

A specific author's name, followed by page numbers in parentheses in my main text or without parentheses in my footnotes, always refers to that specific author's already cited single work or to his most important work for my consideration. This I indicate in the footnotes.

AHSJ *Archivum Historicum Societas Jesu* (Rome).

CBE *Collection de la Bibliothèque des Exercices* (Enghein).

Chr *Christus* (Paris)

Chron *Chronicon Societas Jesu auctore Joanne de Polanco*, 6 vols., Madrid 1894-8 (history of the Society's beginnings).

CTom *Ciencia Tomista* (Madrid).

CyF *Ciencia y Fe* (Buenos Aires).

DSAM *Dictionnaire de Spiritualité ascétique et mystique* (Paris).

DThC *Dictionnaire de théologie catholique* (Paris).

DV *Dieu Vivant* (Paris).

EstEc *Estudios Ecclesiásticos* (Madrid).

FN *Fontes Narrativi de Sancto Ignatio*, 3 vols., Rome, 1943, 1951, 1960 (new and augmented critical edition of contemporary sources on Ignatius).

GuL *Geist und Leben* (Würzburg).

HPTh *Handbuch der Pastoraltheologie* (Freiburg-Wien-Basel, [2]1970ff).

LThK *Lexikon für Theologie und Kirche*. Second edition (Freiburg i.B., 1957ff).

Manr *Manresa* (Madrid).

MI *Monumenta Ignatiana*, in the four following series:

    MI I *Epistolae et Instructiones S. Ignatii*, 12 vols., (Madrid, 1903-11).

    MI II *Exercitia spiritualia S. Ignatii eorumque Directoria*, 3 vols., (Madrid and Rome, 1919, 1955, 1969).

    MI III *Sancti Ignatii Constitutiones Societatis Jesu*, 4 vols., (Rome, 1934-8, 1948).

    MI IV *Scripta de Sancto Ignatio*, 2 vol., (Madrid, 1904 and 1918).

MiCo *Miscelánea Comillas* (Comillas).

M.Nad *Monumenta Nadalis*, 5 vols., (Madrid and Rome, 1898-1905, 1962).

MS *Mysterium Salutis. Grundriß Heilsgeschichtlicher Dogmatik* 5 vols., (Einsiedeln, 1965ff).

MyTh *Jahrbuch für Mystische Theologie* (Klosternburg).

NRTh   *Nouvelle Revue Théologique* (Tournai-Louvain-Paris).

Orient   *Orientierung* (Zürich).

RAM   *Revue d'ascétique et de mystique* (Toulouse).

ScE   *Sciences Ecclésiastiques* (Montréal)

SM   *Sacramentum Mundi. An Encyclopedia of Theology*, 6 vols., (New York, 1968).

StdZ   *Stimmen der Zeit* (Freiburg i.B.).

STh   St. Thomas Aquinas, *Summa Theologiae*, ed. Piana Commission, 5 vols., (Ottawa, 1953).

TD   *Theological Dictionary*, K. Rahner and H. Vorgrimler. Ed. by C. Ernst. Trans. by R. Strachan (Herder and Herder: New York, 1965).

ThGl   *Theologie und Glaube* (Paderborn).

TI   *Theological Investigations*, K. Rahner, 13 vols., (Helicon-Herder and Herder-Seabury: Baltimore, New York, 1961-75).

TS   *Theological Studies* (Woodstock-Washington, DC).

TThZ   *Trierer Theologische Zeitschrift* (Trier).

VSS   *La Vie Spirituelle, Supplément* (Paris).

WL   *Woodstock Letters* (Woodstock).

WW   *Wort und Wahrheit* (Vienna).

ZAM   *Zeitschrift für Aszese und Mystik* (since 1947 *GuL*) (Innsbruck-München-Wurzburg).

ZKTh   *Zeitschrift für Katholische Theologie* (Innsbruck).

⚜ Bibliography

(Three very detailed Ignatian Bibliographies are: E. Lamalle and L. Polgár, *Bibliographia de historia, S.J., AHSJ* from 1933ff; J.F. Gilmont & P. Daman, *Bibliographie Ignatienne* (1894-1957) (Paris-Louvain, 1958); I. Iparraguirre, *Orientaciones bibliográficas sobre San Ignacio de Loyola* (Rome, Inst. Hist. SJ 1957 and 1965). The periodic Ignatian Bibliographies found in *Manr, Chr* and *GuL* should also be consulted.)

Note: Abbreviated Form of Work used found in parentheses.

ALVAREZ DE PAZ, J: *De Inquisitione pacis sive studio orationis*, 6 vols., Paris, 1876.
AMBRUZZI, A.: *The Spiritual Exercises of Saint Ignatius*. With a commentary. Bangalore, ³1939.
ASTRAIN, A.: *Historia de la Companïa de Jesús en la Asistencia de Espana* I. Madrid, 1902.
AYERRA, J.: "Función electiva de la consolación en el segundo tiempo," *MiCo* 26(1956) 91-103.
AYESTARAN, J.: *La experiencia de la divina consolación. Un estudio filosófico-teológico de las Anotaciones sobre los Ejercicios de los Hermanos Pedro y Francisco Ortiz*. Rome Dissert. ad Lauream, PUG, 1964.
BAKKER, J.: *Freiheit und Erfahrung*. Würzburg 1970.
BALTHASAR, H. Urs von: "Exerzitien und Theologie," *Orient* 12(1948) 229-32.
— "Théologie et Sainteté," *DV* 12(1948) 15-32.
— *Herrlichkeit. Eine Theologische Asthetik*. 5 vols., Einsiedeln, 1961-9.
BARTHES, R.: "Comment parler à Dieu? ," *Tel Quel* 38(1969) 32-54.
BAUMANN, T.: "Die Berichte über die Vision des heiligen Ignatius bei La Storta," *AHSJ* 27(1958) 181-208.
— "Compagnie de Jésus. Origine et Sens Primitif de ce Nom," *RAM* 37(1961) 46-60.
— "Compagnie de Jésus: la confirmation de ce nom," *RAM* 38(1962) 52-63.
BEIRNAERT, L.: "Sens de Dieu et sens du péché. Besoins contemporains et spiritualité ignatienne," *RAM* 26(1950) 18-30.
— *Expérience chrétienne et psychologie*. Paris, 1964.
BELLECIUS, A.: *Medulla asceseos seu exercitia S.P. Ignatii accuratiori modo explanata*. Augsburg, 1757.
BERG, J.H.T. van den: *De onderscheiding der geesten in de correspondentie van Sint Ignatius van Loyola*. Canisianum, Maastricht, 1958.
BERGER, P.: *A Rumor of Angels*. New York, 1970.
BERNARD, C.: "Signification des Exercices de saint Ignace," *RAM* 45(1969) 241-61.
BETRAMS, W.: "Die Gleichzeitigkeit des betenden Christen mit den Geheimnissen des Lebens Jesu," *GuL* 24(1951) 414-9.

BÖHMER, H : *Studien zur Geschichte der Gesellschaft Jesu.* vol. I. Bonn, 1914.
RÖHMANN, J.: *Aufgaben und Methoden der Moralpsychologie im geschichtlichen Ursprung der Unterscheidung der Geister.* Köln, 1964.
BOROS, L.: "Dialektik der Freiheit. Gaston Fessards Erhellung der ignatianischen 'Exerzitien' durch Hegel," *WW* (1962) 181-201.
BREMOND, H.: "Saint Ignace et les Exercices," *VSS* (1929) 1-47; 73-111; 147-90.
—— *La Métaphysique des saints. Histoire du sentiment réligieux en France.* Vols. 7 & 8. Paris, 1928.
BRUNNER, A.: "Die Erkenntnis des Willens Gottes nach den geistlichen Übungen des heiligen Ignatius," *GuL* 30(1957) 199-212.
—— "Philosophisches zur Tiefenpsychologie und psychotherapie," *StdZ* 144(1949) 91-102.
CALVERAS, J.: "Es lícito querer saber la voluntad de Dios por via directa? ," *Manr* 14(1942) 247-69.
—— "Tecnicismos explanados," *Manr* 1(1925) 118-28; 307-20.
CANTWELL, L.: *The Theology of the Trinity.* Theology Today Series. Notre Dame, Ind., 1969.
CANTIN, R.: "L'illumination du Cardoner," *ScE* 7(1955) 23-56.
—— "Le troisième degré d'humilité et la gloire de Dieu selon saint Ignace de Loyola," *ScE* 8(1958) 237-66.
CARMODY, J.: "Rahner's Spiritual Theology," *America* Oct. 31, 1970. 345-48.
CARRIER, H.: "La 'caritas discreta' et les exercices spirituels," *ScE* 8(1956) 171-203.
CHOLLET, A.: "Discernement des Esprits," *DThC* IV 1375-1415.
CLAβEN, L.: "Die 'Übung mit den drei Seelenkräften' im Ganzen der Exerzitien," *Loyola-Gestalt.* Hrsg. von F. Wulf. 263-301.
CLÉMENCE, J.: "Le Discernement des esprits dans les Exercices spirituels de saint Ignace de Loyola," *RAM* 27(1951) 347-75; 28(1952) 64-81.
COATHALEM, H.: *Commentaire du livre des Exercices.* Paris, 1965.
CONWELL, J.: *Contemplation in Action. A Study in Ignatian Prayer.* Gonzaga U., Spokane, 1957.
CORETH, E.: "In actione contemplativus," *ZKTh* 76(1954) 55-82.
CROWE, F.: "Complacency and Concern," *Cross and Crown* 11(1959) 180-90.
CUSSON, G.: *Pédagogie de l'expérience spirituelle personnelle* (*=Pédagogie*) Paris, 1968.
—— *Conduis moi sur le chemin d'éternité.* Montreal, 1973.
—— "S. Ignace de Loyola. Les Exercices Spirituels," (="Exercices"), *DSAM* VII 1306-18.
DANIÉLOU, J.: "La vision ignatienne du monde et de l'homme," *RAM* 26(1950) 5-17.
DEDEK, J.F.: *Experimental Knowledge of the Indwelling Trinity. Historical Study of the Doctrine of St. Thomas.* Mundelein, Illinois, 1958.
DENIS, A.: *Commentarii in Exercitia Spiritualia.* 4 volumes. Malines, 1891.
DIERTINS, I.: *Exercitia Spiritualia S.P. Ignatii Loyolae cum sensu eorumdem explanato.* Augustae Tauinorum ex Typographaeo Hyacinthi Marietti, 1836.
DIRKS, G.: "Le 'De Regno Christi' et la Personne du Christ," *RAM* 29(1953) 317-26.
DUDON, P.: *Saint Ignace de Loyola.* Paris, 1934.
DULLES, A.: "The Ignatian Experience as reflected in the Spiritual Theology of Karl Rahner," *Philippine Studies* (1965) 471-91.

—— "Finding God's Will," *WL* 94(1965) 139-52.

DUMEIGE, G.: "Ignace de Loyola. Expérience et doctrine spirituelle," *DSAM* VII 1277-1306.

DUPONT, L.: *Méditations sur les mystères de notre sainte foi avec la pratique de l'oraison mentale.* Traduits sur le texte espagnol de Valladolid (1605). 6 volumes. Paris, 1933.

FERRUSOLAE, P.: *Commentaria in librum Exercitiorum B.P. Ignatii Loiolaei.* Trans. by J. Nonell. Barcinone, 1885.

FESSARD, G.: *La dialectique des Exercices spirituels de saint Ignace de Loyola.* 2 volumes. Paris, 1956 and 1966.

FIORITO, M.A.: "Cristocentrismo del 'Principio y Fundamento' de San Ignacio," *CyF* 17(1961) 3-42.

FRAIGNEAU-JULIEN, B.: "Réflexion sur la signification religieuse du mystère de la St. Trinité," *NRTh* 7(1965) 673-87.

FUTRELL, J.: *Making an Apostolic Community of Love: The Role of the Superior according to St. Ignatius Loyola.* Institute of Jesuit Sources, St. Louis, 1971.

—— "Ignatian Discernment," *Studies in the Spirituality of Jesuits* 2(1970) 47-88.

GAGLIARDI, A.: *Commentarii seu Explanationes in Exercitia spiritualia.* Brugge, 1882.

GAUDIER, A.: *Introductio ad solidam Perfectionem per Manuductionem ad S.P.N. Ignatii Exercitia Spiritualia.* Avenione, 1829.

GIL, D.: *La Consolación sin causa precedente. Estudio hermenéutico-teológico sobre los nn. 330, 331 y 336 del libro de los Ejercicios de San Ignacio.* (=C) Dissertatio ad Lauream, Pontificia Universitas Gregoriana, 1969-70.

—— "Algunas reflexiones sobre la consolación sin causa," (=R) *Manr* 41(1969) 39-64; 121-40.

GIULIANI, M.: "Les motions de l'esprit," *Chr* 4(1954) 62-76.

—— "Trouver Dieu en toutes choses," *Chr* 6(1955) 172-94.

—— "Se décider sous la motion divine," *Chr* 4(1957) 165-86.

—— "Dieu notre Créateur et Rédempteur," *Chr* 6(1959) 329-44.

—— "Une nouvelle traduction des 'Exercices'," (="Traduction") *Chr* 27(1960) 401-15.

GOICOECHEA, A.: *La Santa Misa en la espiritualidad de San Ignacio.* Madrid, 1950.

GÓMEZ NOGALEZ, S.: "Cristocentrismo en la teologiá de los Ejercicios," *Manr* 24(1952) 33-52.

GONZÁLEZ DE MENDOZA, R.: *Stimmung und Transzendenz. Die Antizipation der existentialanalytischen Stimmungsproblematik bei Ignatius von Loyola.* Berlin, 1970.

GONZALES HERNANDEZ, L.: *El primer tiempo de elección según San Ignacio.* Madrid, 1956.

GÖRRES, A.: "Ein existenzielles Experiment zur Psychologie der Exerzitien des Ignatius von Loyola," *Guardini Festschrift. Interpretation der Welt.* Hrsg. von H. Kuhn, H. Kahlefeld, and K. Foster. Würzburg, 1967.

GRANERO, J.M.: "San Ignacio de Loyola, ai servicio de la Iglesia," *CTom* 260(1956) 529-72.

GREELEY, A.: "The New American Religions," *The Concrete Christian Life,* ed. C. Duquoc. *Concilium* 69. NY, 1971 111-23.

GUIBERT, J. de: "L'election dans les Exercices," *Les Grandes Directives de la*

Retraite Fermée Paris, 1930. 172-94.

—— "Mystique ignatienne," *RAM* 19(1938) 3-22; 113-40.

—— "Discernement des esprits," *DSAM* III 1247-91, 1311-91.

—— *The Jesuits. Their Spiritual Doctrine and Practice (=Jesuits)* trans. by W. Young (The Institute of Jesuit Sources: Chicago, 1964).

—— *S. Ignace mystique d'après son Journal Spirituel* (Toulouse, 1938).

—— *The Theology of the Spiritual Life.* trans. by P. Barrett. New York, 1953.

GUY, J.: "Henri Bremond et son commentaire des Exercices de saint Ignace," *RAM* 45(1969) 191-223.

HAAS, A.: *Ignatius von Loyola. Geistliche Übungen.* (=GÜ) Übertragung aus dem spanischen Urtext. Erklarung der 20 Anweisungen. Freiburg i.B., 1967.

—— and KNAUER, P.: *Ignatius von Loyola. Das geistliche Tagebuch (=Tagebuch).* Freiburg i.B., 1961.

HAUSHERR, I.: "Direction spirituelle en Orient," *DSAM* III 1008-60.

HETTINGER, F.: *Die Idee der geistlichen Übungen nach dem Plane des heiligen Ignatius von Loyola.* Regensburg, [2]1908.

HUBY, V.: *Les écrits spirituels du P. Vincent Huby.* 2 volumes Réédites d'après les textes originaux par J.V. Bainvel. Paris, [2]1931.

—— *Oeuvres Spirituelles,* Rouen, 1786.

HUMMELAUER, F. de: *Meditationum et Contemplationum S. Ignatii de Loyola.* Freiburg i.B., 1896.

IPARRAGUIRRE, I.: *Historia de la práctica de los Ejercicios Espirituales de San Ignacio de Loyola.* (=Historia) 2 volumes. Roma, 1946 & 1955.

—— "Ignace de Loyola. Vie et oeuvres," *DSAM* VII 1266-77.

—— "Spirituality," *SM* VI 162-3.

ISERLOH, E.: "Gott finden in allen Dingen," *TThZ* 66(1957) 67-79.

JUDDE, C.: *Retraite spirituelle, appelée grande retraite de trente jours.* 2 volumes. Lyon, 1865.

KOCH, L.: "Alumbrados," *Jesuiten-Lexikon.* Paderborn, 1934. 51-3.

LAPALMA, L. de: *Via Spiritualis. Qualem in Libro Exercitiorum Spiritualium monstrat B.P. Ignatius Loiolaeus.* 2 volumes. trans. from Spanish by I. Nonell. Barcinone, 1887.

LAPLACE, J.: "L'expérience du discernement dans les Exercices spirituels de Saint Ignace," *Chr* 4(1954) 28-49.

LAWLOR, F.X.: "The Doctrine of Grace in the Spiritual Exercises," *TS* 3(1942) 513-32.

LETURIA, P de: "Sentido verdadero en la Iglesia militante," *Estudios Ignacianos* II. 149-86.

LLORCA, B.: *Die spanische Inquisition und die Alumbrados.* Berlin-Bonn, 1934.

—— "Sobre el espíritu de los alumbrados Francisco Hernández y fray Francisco Ortiz," *EstEc* 12(1933) 383-404.

—— *San Ignacio y su relación con los alumbrados, en San Ignacio de Loyola ayer y hoy.* Barcelona, 1958.

LONERGAN, B.: *Insight.* New York, 1958.

LORTZ, J.: *Die Reformation in Deutschland II.* Freiburg, i.B., [3]1949.

LOTZ, J.B.: "Die ignatianische Betrachtungsmethode im Lichte einer gesunden Wertlehre," *ZAM* 10(1935) 1-16, 112-23.

LYONNET, S.: "La méditation des Deux Étendards et son fondement scriptuaire," *Chr* 12(1956) 435-57.

MARÉCHAL, J.: "Note sur la methode d'application des sens dans les Exercices de S. Ignace." *CBE* 61-2(1920) 50-64.

—— *Studies in the Psychology of the Mystics.* Trans. by A. Thorold. New York, 1927.

MARXER, F.: *Die inneren geistlichen Sinne.* Freiburg, i.B., 1963.

MATIGNON, A.: *Exercices spirituels de saint Ignace; commentaire suivi d'une retraite de 30 jours.* St. Germaine, 1920.

MEISSNER, W.: "Psychological Notes on the Spiritual Exercises," *WL* 92(1963) 349-66 & 93(1964) 31-58, 165-99.

MENDIZÁBAL, L.: "El 'hecho eclesiástico' de la obedience ignaciana," *Manr* 36(1964) 403-20.

—— "Sentido intimo de la obediencia ignaciana," *Manr* 37(1965) 53-76.

MERCIER, V.: *Manuel des Exercices de saint Ignace.* Poitiers, 1894.

MERK, A.: "Gottesliebe und Gottesdienst in den Exerzitien des heiligen Ignatius," *ZAM* 7(1932) 117-34.

MESCHLER, M.: *Das Exerzitienbuch des heiligen Ignatius von Loyola.* 3 volumes. Hrsg. von W. Sierp. Freiburg, i.B., [2]1928.

METZ, J.B.: Christliche Anthropozentrik. München 1962.

—— "Religious Act," *SM* V 287-290.

MOLLAT, D.: "Le Christ dans l'expérience spirituelle de saint Ignace," *Chr* 1(1954) 23-47.

NADAL, J.: "Defense of the Exercises," *M.Nad.* IV 820-73 & *Chron* III 525-76.

NAVATEL, I.I.: "La dévotion sensible, les larmes et les Exercices de saint Ignace," *CBE* 64(1920) 1-19.

NEVADO, J.: "El segundo tiempo de elección en los Ejercicios," *Manr* 39(1967) 41-54.

NIERMANN, E.: "Spirituality, Spiritual Exercises," *SM* VI. 164-5.

NONELL, J.: "Étude sur le texte des Exercices de saint Ignace. Traduit du P. E. Thibaut. *CBE* 73-4(1922) 1-225.

PEETERS, L.: *Vers l'union divine par les Exercices de saint Ignace.* Louvain, [2]1931.

PEGON, J.: "Discernement des esprits. Période moderne," *DSAM* III 1266-1281.

PENNING DE VRIES, P.: *Discernimiento. Dinamica existencial de la doctrine y del espritu de San Ignacio de Loyola.* Versión espanola de Horacio Bojorge e I. Iparraguirre. Bilbao, 1967.

PETERS, W.: *The Spiritual Exercises of St. Ignatius — Exposition and Interpretation.* Program to Adapt the Spiritual Exercises, New Jersey, 1968.

PETITDIDIER, P.J.: *Exercitia Spiritualia.* Paris, [9]1880.

PINAMONTI, J.P.: *Esercizi spirituali di S. Ignazio.* Padova, 1711.

PINARD DE LA BOULLAYE, H.: "Jésus dans les Exercices," (="Jésus") *RAM* 18(1937) 217-42.

—— "Expérience religieuse," *DThC* II 1786-1868.

—— *Les étapes de rédaction des Exercices de saint Ignace.* (=*Étapes*) Paris, 1945.

—— *Exercices spirituels selon la méthode de saint Ignace* 4 volumes. Paris, [7]1950.

—— "Sentir, sentimiento y sentido, dans le style de saint Ignace," (="Sentir") *AHSJ* 25(1956) 416-30.

PONLEVOY, A. de: Commentaire sur les Exercices spirituels de saint Ignace. Eureux, [2]1889.

POULLIER, L.: "Les règles du discernement des esprits," *Les grandes directives de la retraite fermée.* Paris, 1930. 198-217.

PRZYWARA, E.: *Deus semper maior. Theologie der Exerzitien.* (=*Deus*) 3

volumes. Freiburg i.B., 1938-9.
— *Ignatianisch.* Frankfurt a.M., 1956.
— *Majestas divina. Ignatianische Frömmigkeit.* Augsburg, 1925.
RAHNER, H.: *Ignatius The Theologian* (=*Ignatius*) Trans. by M. Barry. Herder & Herder; N.Y.; 1968.
RAHNER, H.: Review of Fessard's *La Dialectique. AHSJ* 27(1958) 137-42.
— "Notes on the Spiritual Exercises," (="Notes") *WL* (1956) 281-336.
— "Die Liebe in den Exerzitien," *Orient* 12(1948) 129-31.
— *Ignatius von Loyola und das geschichtliche Werden seiner Frömmigkeit.* (=*Werden*) Salsburg, 1947.
— "Die Vision des heiligen Ignatius in der Kapelle von La Storta," (="La Storta") *ZAM* 10(1935) 17-35; 124-39; 202-20; 265-82.
— "Exerzitien," *LThK* III 1297-1300.
— "Exerzitien," *Lexikon der Pädagogik* I. Freiburg i.B., 1952, 1105-8.
RAHNER, K.: *The Dynamic Element in the Church* (=*Dynamic*). Trans. by W.J. O'Hara. New York, 1964.
— *Theological Investigations* (=*TI*). 13 volumes. Baltimore and New York, 1961ff.
— *On the Theology of Death.* Revised by W.J. O'Hara. New York, 1967.
— *Grace in Freedom.* Trans. & adapted by H. Graef. New York, 1969.
— *Spiritual Exercises.* Trans. by K. Baker. New York, 1965.
— "Mystik," *LThK* VII 743-5.
RAITZ VON FRENTZ, E. (hrsg.) & FEDER, A. (übersetz.): *Geistliche Übungen Ignatius von Loyola.* Freiburg i.B., 1951.
RAITZ VON FRENTZ, E.: "Ludolphe le Chartreux et les Exercices de S. Ignatius de Loyola," *RAM* 25(1949) 386-88.
RAMBALDI, G.: "Cristus heri et hodie-temas cristologicos en el pensamiento ignaciano," *Manr* 28(1956) 105-20.
REICH, C.: *The Greening of America.* New York, 1970.
RICHARD, R.: "Deux traits de l'expérience mystique de saint Ignace," *AHSJ* 25(1956) 431-6.
RICOEUR, P.: *The Conflict of Interpretations · Essays on Hermeneutics.* Northwestern U.: Evanston, 1974.
ROI, J.: "L'élection d'après saint Ignace," *RAM* 38(1962) 305-23.
ROOTHAAN, J.: *Exercices spirituels de saint Ignace de Loyola.* Annotés par le R.P. Roothaan et traduit par le P.P. Jennesseaux. Paris, 1891.
ROUQUETTE, R.: "Le Directoire des Exercices: histoire du texte," *RAM* 14(1933) 395-408.
— "Essai critique sur les sources relatant la vision de saint Ignace de Loyola à La Storta," *RAM* 33(1957) 34-61; 150-70.
ROUSTANG, F.: "Dialektik der Exerzitien," *Orient* 24(1960) 244-6.
— *Growth in the Spirit.* Trans. by N. Pond. New York, 1966.
ROY, L.: "Faut-il chercher la consolation dans la vie spirituelle? Saint Ignace et saint Jean de la Croix," *ScE* 8(1956) 109-70.
ROYON, E.: "Anthropologia cristocéntria del Principio," *Manr* 39(1967) 349-54.
SAILER, J.: *Übungen des Geistes zur Gründung und Förderung eines heiligen Sinnes und Lebens.* Mannheim, 1804.
SBANDI, P.: *Eine Untersuchung zur zweiten Wahlzeit in den geistlichen Übungen.* Dissert., Innsbruck, 1966.

SCARAMELLI, J.B.: *Le discernement des esprits.* Tras. par A. Brasseur Paris, 1893.

SCHEUER, P.: *An Interior Metaphysics.* Ed. by D. Shine. Weston College Press, 1966.

SCHLINGEN, H.: "Die Bedeutung der Betrachtung über die Liebe in den Exerzitien des heiligen Ignatius," *ZAM* 8(1933) 329-35.

SCHNEIDER, B.: "Die Kirchlichkeit des heiligen Ignatius von Loyola," *Sentire Ecclesiam.* Hrsg. von J. Daniélou und H. Vorgrimler. Freiburg i.B., 1961. 268-300.

SCHWAGER, R.: *Das dramatische Kirchenverständnis bei Ignatius von Loyola.* Zürich-Einsiedeln-Koln, 1970.

SIERP, W.: "Das Christusbild der ersten ignatianischen Exerzitienwoche," *ThGl* 20(1928) 812-30.

SIERP, W.: *Hochschule der Gottesliebe.* (*=Hochschule*) 4 volumes. Warendorf, 1935-39.

— "Recte sentire in Ecclesia," *ZAM* 16(1941) 31-6.

SILOS, R.. "Cardoner in the Life of St. Ignatius of Loyola," *AHSJ* 33(1964) 3-43.

SOLANO, J.: "Jesucristo bajo las denominaciones divinas de San Ignacio," *EstEc* 118(1956) 325-42.

— "Jesucristo en la Primera Semana de Ejercicios," *MiCo* 26(1056) 165-76.

STEGER, A.: "Der Primat der göttlichen Gnadenführung im geistlichen Leben nach dem heiligen Ignatius von Loyola," *GuL* 21(1948) 94-108.

— "La place de la grâce dans la spiritualité de saint Ignace," *NRTh* (1948) 561-75.

STIERLI, J.: "Das ignatianische Gebet: 'Gott suchen in allen Dingen' ", *Loyola-Gestalt.* Hrsg. von F. Wulf. 151-83.

STRASSER, S.: *The Soul in a Metaphysical and Empirical Psychology.* Duquesne: Pittsburg, 1967.

SUAREZ, F.: *Tractatus de Religione Societatis Jesu.* Bruxellis-Parisiis, 1857.

SUDBRACK, J.: "Fragestellung und Infragestellung der ignatianischen Exerzitien," *GuL* (1970) 206-25.

TONQUEDEC, J. de: "De la certitude dans les états mystiques. A propos d'une règle ignatienne du discernement des esprits," *NRTh* 75(1953) 399-404.

TRUHLAR, K.: "La découverte de Dieu chez saint Ignace pendant les dernières années de sa vie," *RAM* 24(1948) 313-37.

VERCRUYSSE, O.: "Our Creator and Lord," *Ignatiana* (1956) 244-9.

VERNY, L.: "In actione contemplativus," *RAM* 26(1950) 60-78.

VILLER, M.: "Le XVIIᵉ siécle et l'origine des retraites spirituelles," *RAM* 19(1928) 139-62; 359-84.

VINCKE, J.: "Alumbrados," *LThK* I 407.

VOGT, P.: *Exercitia Spiritualia Sancti Ignatii. Sententiis Sanctorum Patrum Illustrata.* 3 volumes. Bilbao, 1923.

WULF, F. (hrsg.): *Ignatius von Loyola. Seine geistliche Gestalt und sein Vermächtnis.* (*=Loyola-Gestalt*) Wurzburg, 1956.

YOUNG, W. (trans.): *Letters of St. Ignatius of Loyola.* (*=Letters*) Chicago, 1959.

— (trans.): *St. Ignatius own Story as told to Luis Gonzalez de Camara.* (*=Autobiography*) Chicago, 1956.

—— *The Spiritual Journal of St. Ignatius* (=*SJ*, followed by date). *WL* 87(1958). 195-267.

ZEIGER, I.: "Gefolgschaft des Herrn, ein rechtsgeschichtlicher Beitrag zu den Exerzitien des Ignatius von Loyola," *ZAM* 17(1942) 1-16.

Index
of Names

**Index
of Marginal Numbers in
the Spiritual Exercises**